MIXED METHODS RESEARCH
and CULTURE-SPECIFIC INTERVENTIONS

SAGE Mixed Methods Research Series

Vicki L. Plano Clark and Nataliya V. Ivankova,
Series Editors

MIXED METHODS RESEARCH

and CULTURE-SPECIFIC INTERVENTIONS

Program Design and Evaluation

Bonnie K. Nastasi
Tulane University

John H. Hitchcock
Indiana University

Los Angeles | London | New Delhi
Singapore | Washington DC | Boston

Los Angeles | London | New Delhi
Singapore | Washington DC | Boston

FOR INFORMATION:

SAGE Publications, Inc.
2455 Teller Road
Thousand Oaks, California 91320
E-mail: order@sagepub.com

SAGE Publications Ltd.
1 Oliver's Yard
55 City Road
London, EC1Y 1SP
United Kingdom

SAGE Publications India Pvt. Ltd.
B 1/I 1 Mohan Cooperative Industrial Area
Mathura Road, New Delhi 110 044
India

SAGE Publications Asia-Pacific Pte. Ltd.
3 Church Street
#10-04 Samsung Hub
Singapore 049483

Acquisitions Editor: Vicki Knight
Editorial Assistant: Yvonne McDuffee
eLearning Editor: Katie Bierach
Production Editor: Kelly DeRosa
Copy Editor: QuADS Prepress (P) Ltd.
Typesetter: Hurix Systems Pvt. Ltd.
Proofreader: Alison Syring
Indexer: Maria Sosnowski
Cover Designer: Michelle Kenny
Marketing Manager: Nicole Elliott

Copyright © 2016 by SAGE Publications, Inc.

Printed in the United States of America.

Library of Congress Cataloging-in-Publication Data

Nastasi, Bonnie K.

Mixed methods research and culture-specific interventions : program design and evaluation / Bonnie K. Nastasi, Tulane University, John H. Hitchcock.

pages cm. — (SAGE mixed methods research series ; 2)

Includes bibliographical references and index.

ISBN 978-1-4833-3382-3 (pbk. : alk. paper)

1. Research—Methodology. 2. Social sciences—Research—Methodology. I. Hitchcock, John H. (Educational psychologist) II. Title.

H62.N2694 2016

001.4'2—dc23   2015012491

This book is printed on acid-free paper.

15 16 17 18 19 10 9 8 7 6 5 4 3 2 1

BRIEF CONTENTS

DETAILED CONTENTS

We dedicate this book to interventionists who build on the strengths of those they endeavor to help and continuously learn from the diverse global population.

EDITORS' INTRODUCTION

The global expansion of mixed methods research makes it a viable approach for addressing complex problems in diverse cultural settings. Moreover, mixed methods research can transcend the boundaries of existing methodological frameworks, such as program evaluation, and enhance its application for reaching programmatic goals in unique cultural contexts. By integrating quantitative outcome-based oriented methods with culturally tailored qualitative approaches, mixed methods can provide a rigorous methodological foundation for developing and evaluating effective culture-specific interventions.

While the need for cultural specificity is growing in program development and evaluation, the demand for practical guidance about how to address this need is becoming more evident. In this book, Bonnie Nastasi and John Hitchcock provide a strong response to this call by addressing the complexity of applying mixed methods in developing, testing, and refining culturally relevant interventions. We initiated the SAGE Mixed Methods Research Series to provide researchers, reviewers, and consumers with practice-focused books that aim to help scholars navigate the field of mixed methods and develop an understanding of its contemporary issues and debates in a practical, applied way. We believe this book is an important addition to the Series because the authors effectively unravel the multiple influences of cultural, political, interpersonal, and programmatic contexts on the mixed methods research process that is involved in the design and implementation of interventions meeting diverse needs.

There are several features of this book that merit highlighting. The authors provide a framework for the use of mixed methods in culture-specific intervention development and offer a step-by-step process of how to design, implement, adapt, and evaluate programs that address unique cultural needs from multiple stakeholder perspectives. Their approach capitalizes on the existing literature about conducting mixed methods and evaluation research, which the authors effectively synthesize to guide the readers through the process of culture-specific intervention development. The book abounds in practical advice from the authors' personal experiences of designing and conducting mixed methods program evaluation. A particular asset of the book is the inclusion of the full example of applying mixed methods research to inform development, implementation, adaptation, and evaluation of culture-specific interventions based on the multi-year and multi-stage program for promoting psychological well-being of school-aged populations in Sri Lanka.

We envision this book will be a valuable practical resource for those who are involved in program development and evaluation and consider applying mixed methods to help enhance and better tailor programmatic goals to specific cultural contexts. Besides advancing the science related to development of effective interventions, the book offers implications for translational research and implementation science and may compel all researchers using mixed methods to more thoughtfully consider the role of culture in the context of their research. We welcome this book as the second volume in the Series and believe this book makes a contribution in helping to effectively navigate through the messiness of mixed methods research!

Nataliya V. Ivankova and Vicki L. Plano Clark
Editors, *SAGE Mixed Methods Research Series*

PREFACE

Accounting for culture and context when engaged in intervention and evaluation work has long been recognized by ethnographers to be a required element of strong social science research. It is also the case that a broader but related idea, engaging in ecologically informed inquiry, has been of interest to researchers for decades. These topics in fact receive a reasonable amount of attention in a number of undergraduate and graduate training programs. After all, most introductory texts on research dedicate at least some discussion to ethnographic work, and ideas from ecological systems theory are found in most introductory texts in areas such as education and psychology. Furthermore, many contemporary researchers have explicitly called for more careful handling of context when providing intervention services. Yet it appears that accounting for culture and context when developing interventions, or when evaluating the outcome of interventions, has too many times been glossed over or even ignored. This claim is based on accounts lamenting well-meaning but arguably invasive attempts to address mental health needs in international settings and the exporting of Western (i.e., European and North American) ideas about social services. These accounts can be found in professional and scientific journals, popular press books, newspapers, and so on.

Further complicating matters is the idea that accounting for cultural differences is not a concern that should be reserved only when crossing international borders. Few nations, if any, are sufficiently homogeneous that cultural awareness is not warranted. We, the authors, rely on professional literature to support these arguments within the book. But for now, we expect that almost anyone who would bother to turn to this page will have enough of a social science background to intuit that there are groups of people who have values, behavioral norms, and ways of thinking that might be different from their own. Furthermore, most readers can quickly appreciate that such differences can make any efforts to educate, counsel, or otherwise help a complex task.

A running theme throughout this book is to not only be aware of such differences but also be conscious of a common human condition to see one's own culture as normal and, by implication, others as being somehow not "normal." We are aware of this because there is a tradition in psychology that focuses on the phenomena where members of a majority group can have difficulty recognizing the influence of their own culture. We also have spent time and conducted professional work in cultures very different from our own. Still, we find that it can be difficult to keep cultural nuances and factors in the forefront of our own thinking. This is a challenge that was recognized by the ancient Greeks and remains fully relevant today. But if you need a concrete example of what we mean, you are probably a member of a majority culture wherever you live. If so, then to get a sense of this, next time you're in a group setting, ask others if you have an accent (if you teach, a great place for this exercise is a classroom). If you are indeed a member of the majority culture, and by definition spend a considerable amount of time with similar people, you will almost always be told that you do not have an accent. But of course you have one, in whatever language you speak, except for the most unusual of settings. And if you're told otherwise, you're just being informed that you sound like a person who comes from the very place in which you are working. This observation is not meant to offer political commentary, or cause any sense of discomfort. Rather, we're just making a point that it can be hard for members of a majority to be cognizant of cultural influences because there is typically little reason to think about such issues. Furthermore, this is no personal failing but rather a long-standing human trait. But this human trait can create complexities in the social sciences because, sooner or later, people in this business will have the responsibility of providing some sort of service in cross-cultural settings.

We therefore hope that this book provides not only an awareness of cultural influences but also a methodological basis for handling them when engaged in intervention and/or evaluation work. The literature provides details on how to develop culturally specific programs and engage in subsequent evaluation, but it is also complex and dispersed widely across disciplines such as ethnography, program evaluation, education research, and so on. We have written this book with practicing social scientists and graduate students in mind. Its purpose is to provide a discussion of concepts and methodological guidelines for researchers and practitioners who wish to be able to think through culture when doing intervention and evaluation work. The book can be a stand-alone text for those who have a basic understanding of research methods, evaluation work, and intervention programming. For those who have minimal background in the arenas of intervention and evaluation, we recommend using this book as a supplemental text.

There are eight chapters in the book. The first focuses on convincing readers to attend to culture and context and provides several key definitions of terms and background concepts. From there, the book reviews models we have developed through our own work and provides considerable detail about how mixed methods research can be used to address a number of cultural and contextual nuances. Mixed methods research approaches have been indispensable in our efforts and permeate so much of our thinking that their use is in our very nature as researchers. The use of qualitative inquiry to explore and interpret research participants' perceptions combined with quantitative approaches, such as surveying samples to understand populations or determine if interventions yield intended impacts, are fundamental to our efforts. We have been mixing methods for more than 20 years, and we have used many types of mixed methods designs. We've also gone beyond thinking about single mixed methods studies to mixed methods programmatic research. We have benefited greatly from leaders in this arena as they have generated strategies that we have tried, gave names to techniques we were essentially using already, and provided outlets to talk about our efforts. Over time, we've developed some mixed methods ideas to which we aspire, but have yet to achieve, when doing culturally specific work. All of these points are summarized in Chapters 2 through 6. In Chapter 7, we review a number of challenges we have encountered when using mixed methods to engage in culturally informed work and discuss some strategies to handle each of them. In Chapter 8, we offer some ideas about future directions.

Some of this may sound complex, but we're confident that we have developed models that are accessible and well articulated by graphs and figures. We have found that these figures in turn offer quick references when making plans. We also developed a set of learning objectives for each chapter and continuously define key terms throughout the book. Judging from editorial feedback and external review, we're confident that these descriptions can give readers, who want to think through cultural issues and more generally adopt mixed methods research techniques, a great head start. We hope that you'll agree after reading the book.

SAGE was founded in 1965 by Sara Miller McCune to support the dissemination of usable knowledge by publishing innovative and high-quality research and teaching content. Today, we publish more than 750 journals, including those of more than 300 learned societies, more than 800 new books per year, and a growing range of library products including archives, data, case studies, reports, conference highlights, and video. SAGE remains majority-owned by our founder, and after Sara's lifetime will become owned by a charitable trust that secures our continued independence.

Los Angeles | London | New Delhi | Singapore | Washington DC | Boston

ACKNOWLEDGMENTS

We express our gratitude to the series editors and reviewers of this book for their thoughtful, constructive feedback that contributed to the overall quality of the final product. We also recognize those who have contributed to our research over the past two decades—participants, community stakeholders, coinvestigators, colleagues, and graduate and undergraduate students. And finally, we would like to thank those who reviewed this book at its different stages:

Jeral R. Kirwan, Ashford University

Marc K. Fudge, California State University San Bernardino

Sebastian Galindo, University of Florida

Muhammad Mizanur Rashid Shuvra, International Center for Diarrheal Disease

Elizabeth Anne Roumell, North Dakota State University

C. Todd White, Rochester Institute of Technology

Amy Orange, George Mason University

Stacey A. Britton, The University of Mississippi

Janet de Merode, The Chicago School of Professional Psychology

Anna M. Ortiz, California State University, Long Beach

Jeffrey J. Bulanda, Aurora University

Emmanuel Tetteh, Capella University

ABOUT THE AUTHORS

Bonnie Kaul Nastasi, PhD (Kent State University, 1986, School Psychology & Early Childhood Education), is a professor in the Department of Psychology, School of Science and Engineering, at Tulane University, New Orleans, Louisiana, the United States. She codirects a trauma specialization in the School Psychology PhD Program at Tulane. Her research focuses on the use of mixed methods designs to develop and evaluate culturally appropriate assessment and intervention approaches for promoting mental health and reducing health risks such as sexually transmitted infections (STIs) and HIV, both within the United States and internationally. She has worked in Sri Lanka since 1995 on development of school-based programs to promote psychological well-being and directed a multicountry study of psychological well-being of children and adolescents with research partners in 12 countries from 2008 to 2013. She was one of the principal investigators of an interdisciplinary public health research program to prevent STIs among married men and women living in the slums of Mumbai, India, from 2002 to 2013. Most recently, she has been engaged in development of culturally and contextually relevant school-based mental health services in New Orleans as part of the redevelopment of public education following the 2005 Hurricane Katrina, working with community stakeholders and a team of Tulane University students. She is active in promotion of child rights and social justice within the profession of school psychology and has directed the development of a curriculum for training school psychologists internationally on child rights, a joint effort of International School Psychology Association (ISPA), International Institute of Child Rights and Development, Division 16 of the American Psychological Association (APA), and Tulane University's School Psychology Program. Dr. Nastasi is a past president of APA's Division 16 past cochair of APA's Committee on International Relations in Psychology, and President-elect of ISPA.

John H. Hitchcock, PhD (University at Albany, State University of New York, 2003, Educational Psychology), is an associate professor of instructional systems technology within Indiana University's School of Education, Bloomington, Indiana, the United States. He is also the Director of the Center for

Evaluation & Education Policy. His research focus is on the use of mixed methods and other types of designs to evaluate interventions and policies that focus on helping students with specialized learning needs. He has served as a principal investigator, methodological lead, and content expert for the What Works Clearinghouse (WWC) at the Institute of Education Sciences at the U.S. Department of Education to complete a systematic review of interventions designed for children with emotional–behavioral disorders. He also served on a panel that drafted standards for assessing the causal validity of single-case design studies for the WWC. He has served as a coprincipal investigator of two large-scale randomized controlled trials to assess the impact of reading and math curricula. He has contributed to efforts to develop programs that promote psychological well-being in Sri Lanka since 1998, and he is a past Associate Editor for *School Psychology Review*.

✄ ONE ✄

INTRODUCTION

The Role of Culture and Context in Developing Intervention and Prevention Programs

Learning Objectives

The key objectives of this chapter are for readers to understand the following:

- That culture and context impact service delivery
- That culture and context are critical considerations when engaged in program design (selection), implementation (service delivery), and evaluation
- Why explicit attention to culture and context is not more widely embraced

INTRODUCTION

This chapter introduces key terminology, provides the rationale for attending to culture and context in the development and evaluation of intervention and prevention programming, discusses implementation science and translational research, describes limitations of standard approaches, and discusses the potential role **mixed methods research (MMR)** has for addressing such limitations. The chapter concludes with a description of the content and structure of the book.

WHY SHOULD WE ATTEND
TO CULTURE AND CONTEXT?

This book is predicated on what we believe to be a common proposition: *Context and culture matter when one attempts to influence, or assess, the behavior, thought patterns, and perceptions of others*. We begin with definitions of key constructs—context and culture.

Context refers to the specific setting or set of circumstances within which an intervention is designed, delivered, and evaluated. We conceive of context from a developmental–ecological perspective drawing on the work of Bronfenbrenner (1998, 1999[1]). Context, in Bronfenbrenner's parlance, is the *microsystem* (immediate context) in which the interventionists and participants directly interact, in this case during the delivery of the intervention. This microsystem, however, is influenced by surrounding systems as conceived in Bronfenbrenner's (1989, 1999) ecological systems theory (EST): *exosystem*, those that embody the microsystem; *mesosystem*, those that embody the relationship between ecological systems; *macrosystem*, those that embody the larger society or community and the inherent values, beliefs, norms; and *chronosystem*, those that embody historical or developmental influences. For example, delivering an intervention within a classroom requires attention to the immediate context (classroom or microsystem), the system in which the classroom is embedded (school or exosystem), other systems that have indirect influence on the interactions of teachers and students in the classroom (also exosystems, e.g., peer group, family, neighborhood), the interactions among these systems (mesosystem, e.g., school–family relationships), the larger society (macrosystem), and the historical factors (chronosystem, e.g., history of education in the community). The importance of context in intervention development and delivery has been recognized by contemporary researchers and practitioners (e.g., Burns, 2011; Ringeisen, Henderson, & Hoagwood, 2003).

Culture is defined as "shared language, ideas, beliefs, values, and behavioral norms" (Nastasi, Moore, & Varjas, 2004) or "common heritage or set of beliefs, norms and values" (U.S. Department of Health and Human Services [DHHS], 2001, p. 9) relevant to the particular context or group. We use the term **culture specific** to refer to the embodiment of "an individual's real-life

---

[1] A full description of Bronfenbrenner's developmental-ecological systems theory (EST) is beyond the scope of this chapter. For more information, consult the cited references.

experiences within a given cultural context (e.g., neighborhood) and his or her understanding of those experiences" (Nastasi, Varjas, Bernstein, & Jayasena, 2000, p. 403). With regard to guiding behavior change (i.e., intervention), culture refers to "a dynamic system of meanings, knowledge and actions that provides actors collectively, interpersonally, and individually with community-legitimized strategies to construct, reflect upon, and reconstruct their world and experience, and guide behaviour" (Nastasi et al., 2015, p. 96; see also Bibeau & Corin, 1995).

We think of culture as a ubiquitous construct that can influence intervention and prevention **program** design, implementation, and evaluation, thus necessitating a need for consideration of culture throughout the process of program development (Hitchcock & Nastasi, 2011). We use the term **cultural (co-)construction** to refer to the cultural process that occurs during an intervention. Cultural co-construction has been defined as

> the process of dialogue among equal partners across class, ethnic/ racial, disciplinary, cultural, and other boundaries that integrates knowledge, values, perspectives, and methods derived from all parties, resulting in shared innovation. The co-construction of cultural and other forms of knowledge is an ongoing process that reflects the nature of participatory research and intervention development, and the more dynamic nature of the social construction. (Nastasi et al., 2015, p. 94)

Within the intervention context, co-construction refers to the interaction or dialogic process that occurs between the interventionists (health providers, therapists, teachers/educators, etc.) and the recipients (patients, clients, students, etc.). Thus, when talking of the *cultural process* within intervention development and evaluation, we prefer the term *cultural co-construction* to "more static contemporary concepts for addressing culture in practice, such as culturally sensitive, culturally appropriate, culturally specific, culturally competent, or culturally relevant" (Nastasi et al., 2015, p. 94). The latter set of terms is more appropriately applied to the *products* of the co-construction process, for example, the culturally specific intervention program that resulted from a dialogic development process.

As we will explicate throughout this text, the delivery of interventions requires attention to the cultural experiences and interpretations of participants within the given context. We contend that attention to culture and context in the design, implementation, and evaluation of an intervention is likely to enhance the acceptability (i.e., the degree of stakeholder buy-in pertaining to a program), social and ecological validity (i.e., the degree to which the program goals and outcomes are relevant to the real-life experiences of participants), integrity (the degree to which a particular program is implemented as intended), outcomes, and sustainability (see also Alkin, 2013; Nastasi et al., 2004; Ringeisen et al., 2003; Whaley & Davis, 2007). Culture is not only about the shared norms, values, beliefs, and knowledge but also about how the individuals interpret the shared aspects of culture. When we consider culture while providing intervention or prevention services, we must take into account the experiences of not only all key players (at a minimum the client and the service provider) but also those who influence these dyadic relationships (e.g., parents of child clients, teachers, administrators, society, and interactions among them)—that is, all aspects of the ecological system, or context, that encompasses the provider and the client.

To demonstrate the point that culture and context matter, consider trying to help a group of students learn algebra. A review of the National Council of Teachers of Mathematics (NCTM) position on algebra makes clear that the topic is critical (e.g., NCTM, 2008), and some have even characterized learning it to be a civil rights concern (Dubinsky & Moses, 2011). With the understanding that this is not a trivial endeavor, consider working with a group of children who have been reared in a culture that emphasizes rote memorization of arithmetic facts over other aspects of learning, to a point that these children would judge any test items that were not explicitly covered in curricula and emphasized for memorization purposes to be unfair. For example, the item "$2(x) = 8$, therefore, $x =$___" would be construed as fair if it were covered in class, whereas "$10(x) = 80$, therefore, $x =$___" would not be, even if the point of the item was to see if basic skills can be applied to novel problems. Most readers of this book would be hard pressed to think of an example where stakeholders might think such an item to be unfair. But this is not unheard of; according to Cole (1996), the Kpelle tribe of Liberia did indeed at one point focus on teaching math in this manner. For various reasons, such memorization was valued and expected to be of use in later work life. We argue then that if one is working with a group that historically placed such emphasis on memorization, the cultural backgrounds of participants would influence how curricula are delivered given algebra's focus on symbolism and abstraction. That is, a mathematics teacher in this context would be well served by attempts to explicitly address this expectation before getting into the teaching of algebra.

As we address further in Chapter 2, the cultural experiences of a teacher in the preceding example also matter, and the teaching–learning process might be conceived as a process of co-constructing meaning based on shared and unique cultural experiences of both teacher and students. Moreover, the context of the classroom is situated within a school, a community, and a society and is influenced by the cultural expectations, values, and norms of these surrounding contexts. We contend that the development of effective and sustainable programs requires attention to the broad array of cultural factors that influence the ecological system in which the intervention is embedded. For example, consider the experiences of one of the book's authors when introducing a new mathematics education program that emphasized higher order thinking (e.g., problem solving, critical thinking) (Young, Nastasi, & Braunhardt, 1996). The researchers worked with the school administration and teachers prior to program initiation to ensure acceptability and during program implementation to ensure continued acceptability, integrity, projected impact, and sustainability. The program yielded evidence of improved higher order thinking, but the school board was concerned that the basic mathematical skills (e.g., computational skills) were not neglected, as the new program replaced the traditional drill and practice. To promote program continuation and address concerns of the school board, the researchers examined effects on both basic and higher order math skills and reported the documented improvements in both to the school board. This experience illustrates the importance of understanding the context of an intervention from an ecological perspective (in this case, at micro-, exo-, and macrosystem levels).

To generalize the point that culture and context matter, consider these questions that exemplify real-life professional dilemmas:

- What are the implications of providing mental health services to an adolescent girl who appears to be independent but hails from a culture that demands compliance and adherence to tradition?
- What if one were involved with diagnosing and treating mental health disorders but encountered a member of the Old Order Amish who was struggling with bipolar disorder?
- How should a practitioner construe clients who claim that they regularly talk to God but then learns that these clients are members of a fundamentalist religious order?
- Should practitioners consider ethnic backgrounds when delivering a program designed to prevent or treat eating disorders?

- Does it make sense to use behavior rating scales normed in the United States in a country like India?
- Would you consider the cultural background of families when providing marital therapy?
- If you were trying to understand if a school environment were generally accepting of lesbian, gay, bisexual, and transgender youth, would it make sense to understand the community the school serves?
- Can a reading program designed to help Cuban Americans in Miami with word comprehension be applied to Mexican Americans in a Texas city bordering Mexico?
- How can a disaster preparedness program take advantage of familial connections that are emphasized by a marginalized group residing in a specific region?
- Would a bullying prevention program designed to be used in high socioeconomic status schools work well in schools that serve large numbers of children who live in poverty?

When pondering these questions, one might think that they represent some unusual scenarios. But we suspect that most readers can easily conjure examples from their own lives that will support the basic proposition we make for this book, which again is—*culture and context matter*. Indeed, some readers may have such an easy time coming up with their own examples that they may wonder why we would bother to point any of this out. Who would not consider culture and context when engaged in professional practice? By extension, why should one bother to read a book that purports to offer ideas on developing and evaluating interventions that account for culture and context?

We offer a two-point response to these questions. One point is that much of Western[2] training in the social sciences (education, psychology, etc.) and in medicine emphasizes the notion of standardization. Standardization is assumed by social scientists to promote the uniform conduct of assessment

---

[2] We use the term *Western* to refer to theories, research, interventions, and so on, developed in what are considered Western cultures such as those in the United States and Western Europe. Arnett (2008), for example, criticizes American psychology research (specifically, research published in APA journals) for neglecting 95% of the world's population, resulting in an "understanding of psychology that is incomplete and does not adequately represent humanity" (p. 602). We will return to this discussion in Chapter 7.

and intervention efforts, a practice that may be at odds with the need for practitioners to make adaptations based on culture and context. But standardization
is not a bad thing; indeed, it is often necessary. Anyone trained in assessment
will understand the critical role of standardized procedures and its role in valid
measurement; variation in assessment procedures makes it harder to assess if
a score has been influenced by the behavior of the tester or variables that are
ideally external to the purpose of measurement. Standardization also applies
to policy work. Much of the general dialogue in the U.S. education industry
focuses on achievement, and this dialogue is predicated on notions of standardized assessment and even movement toward standardized outcomes of
teaching (consider the United States' federal agenda to convince states to
adopt Common Core curricula; Common Core Standards Initiative, 2015).
Whereas the aforementioned bulleted questions depicting dilemmas in practice are designed to make the need for flexibility and adaption self-evident,
readers should appreciate that this creates a tension with a fundamental element of much of how the social sciences and policy operate. Furthermore, this
tension does not exist solely in education settings. There is an ongoing belief
by many that psychological and psychiatric disorders have biological mechanisms common to all human beings and, therefore, are not bound by contextual and cultural influences. For example, there is a growing body of evidence
that the activation of the sympathetic nervous system (and release of norepi-
nephrine and epinephrine) and hypothalamic–pituitary–adrenal axis
(and release of cortisol) associated with responses to acute stress also may be
associated with mood disorders and behavioral adjustment (Vigil, Geary,
Granger, & Flinn, 2010). Such evidence and related beliefs are likely to promote the assumption that many psychological/psychiatric interventions can be
carried out in a uniform manner, which in turn can influence critical policy
around mental health treatment (e.g., the number of clients a single psychia-
trist can take on, the types of treatment insurance will cover). Yet such unifor-
mity may not help service providers think through concerns such as the
acceptability of medication, willingness to follow dosage directions, and so
on. Furthermore, in some of our own work, we have found the very notion of
stress itself to be culturally specific, meaning that which is stressful in one
culture may be less stressful in another. In sum, we believe that standardization is widely regarded as something that describes good assessment,
intervention, and policy, and this informs practice in areas such as education,
mental health, public health, and medicine. Indeed, our read is that many think

that evidence-based interventions (EBIs)[3] should be routinely informed by evidence that supports a standard way of treating people. But this creates a tension with the need to adapt to cultural and contextual variations when attempting to apply research evidence. Part of the goal of this book is to impart ideas that can help readers strike a balance between standardization and adaptation and think about evidence in local settings.

The second point we raise when responding to professional dilemmas such as those raised earlier (see bulleted list above) is that while it is easy to call for flexibility and adaption, understanding how to do this, or even the need for it, is not always obvious. Consider that researchers such as Sue, Bingham, Porche-Burke, and Vasquez (1999) and organizations such as the DHHS (2001) have expressed concerns that members of a majority culture can have limited self-awareness about their own norms, values, and so on. Obtaining advanced training in the social sciences appears to offer little protection from this concern. Indeed, Cole (1996) asks, "Why do psychologists find it so difficult to keep culture in mind?" (p. 1). We suspect that standardization, norms, and a desire to estimate population parameters can make it easy to miss culturally laden nuances, and this can even lead one to construe cultural differences as pathology and dysfunction (see also Castillo, 1997; Hitchcock & Nastasi, 2011; Sue et al., 1999). To help address this concern in our own work, we draw from qualitative research traditions that focus on the importance of being reflexive (i.e., examining one's assumptions and engaging in critical self-reflection) when engaged in inquiry. Germane to this discussion is the idea of *implicit assumptions* (or tacit theories; see LeCompte, 2000). Implicit assumptions are ones that can be so basic as to escape notice without some discipline but must be examined if one is to engage in credible research design, analysis, and interpretation of data. An implicit assumption (e.g., standardization is a good thing) is not necessarily problematic but, if left unchecked, can cause concerns (e.g., standardization is *necessary* or standardization requires "X activity" to be done *only* in one way).[4]

A particularly pernicious outcome of unchecked implicit assumptions is that highly educated, powerful, and well-meaning interventionists may, at best, be less than optimally effective when helping others, and at worst offer

---

[3] We return to the discussion of EBIs in the next section.
[4] We will return to the topic of implicit assumptions in later chapters as we address the cultural competence of program developers, implementers, and evaluators.

interventions that are invasive, iatrogenic, or both. This is not a trivial point. Consider the book *Crazy Like Us: The Globalization of the American Psyche* (Watters, 2010; although published in popular press, the author relies on peer-reviewed literature). Watters (2010) helps demonstrate our concern about interventionists operating from potentially unchecked assumptions. One example that the book offers describes efforts by outside interventionists to help Sri Lankans after the 2004 tsunami (readers will learn later that this is close to our own work). How could these efforts be problematic? It is important to keep in mind that there is a message, perhaps borne out of an unexamined assumption, that indigenous members of a culture are unable to handle tragedies on their own. Such a message can convey a sense of inadequacy and the expectation that survivors need to be rescued. Yet one concern that should be ever present is whether interventionists capitalize on the existing strengths and values of a culture. For example, what aspects of Sri Lankan culture can be used to help a country that has lost thousands of people and suffered extensive economic damage recover as best as possible from such a tragedy? Did Western intervention routinely utilize adaptive characteristics of Sri Lankans (e.g., promotion of community, family, citizenry, and religion) to enhance their efforts? Surely some have, but the Watters account suggests that this was not the norm. Rather, assumptions like Sri Lankans need to be diagnosed and treated for posttraumatic stress disorder appeared to inform most thinking of how to help. The approach was in its way standard, and whether this was best was, apparently, unexamined by many who were trying to help.

On the point of using cultural strengths, Watters (2010) makes a compelling case about how people who struggle with schizophrenia in the so-called developing world may be better off compared with those in countries like the United States, perhaps because a modern biomedical perspective can promote isolation via treatment and stigma by perpetuating an idea that something about a person, in this case a mental health disorder, is innate and static (see also Castillo, 1997). By contrast, people who suffer from schizophrenia can, in some cultures, experience an influx of family and community support informed by a belief that efforts can and will solve a fixable problem. Even if the terminology and thinking expressed in some countries seem mystical by Western standards (e.g., our cousin is plagued by demons), intervention can nevertheless entail a focus on well-being carried out by extended family. Cultural norms in different settings often do not tolerate withdrawal behaviors of a sick person, nor is there an expectation that only a small number of people (e.g., mental health professionals and support staff) should be tasked with leading supportive care. The result of these differences would be that patients are not isolated, but instead, they are cared for by a wide network of people who believe that improvement is to be expected. Such behaviors would seem to represent a cultural strength and can be contrasted with a widespread belief in Western settings that schizophrenia is a lifelong condition and that treatment generally entails some form of isolation (e.g., private therapy at best or hiding someone from others at worst). This suggests that there is value in understanding the practices of existing cultures so as to capitalize on their strengths when intervening.

Another (perhaps implicit) assumption worth noting here is a widespread belief among practitioners in various mental health fields that Western approaches are superior (Cole, 1996; Trimble, Scharrón-del-Río, & Hill, 2012; Watters, 2010). This can lead to troubling scenarios. A particularly worrisome intervention is the selling of antidepressants medication in Japan and pathologizing culturally accepted norms of sadness (Watters, 2010). The charge made in Watters's (2010) book is that a pharmaceutical company purposefully worked toward shifting cultural norms with an eye toward selling medication. Allow an assumption that this effort to change the status quo in Japan was borne out of a sense of altruism; there was first and foremost a desire to help, and any profit motives were secondary. This assumption may be reasonable; after all, according to the World Health Organization (WHO), suicide rates have risen globally by 60% over the past 45 years (WHO, n.d.), and Japan ranks second to Hungary among Organisation for Economic Co-operation and Development (OECD) nations in terms of suicide rates per 100,000 (Amano, 2005). On the other hand, it is also reasonable to question if a higher rate of antidepressant use is optimal, or even good, for Japanese citizens. Is it better to rely on medication than promoting some of the country's existing traditions that focus on finding meaning and value in sadness? With the exception of those who are at high risk of committing suicide, is it preferable to teach coping skills rather than relying on psychopharmacological intervention? Does Japanese culture have some already existing functions (e.g., social obligations to others, harmony) that can be promoted when treating those with clinical depression? Alternatively, are there cultural and contextual factors that might be contributing to increasing rates of depression and suicide? If so, might we intervene to change the social–cultural context rather than focusing solely on the affected individuals? These are complex questions and ones that deserve full attention. For now, we wish only to point out that such concerns can be informed by the careful examination of implicit assumptions that intervening and changing things will help improve matters, as opposed to making a situation worse.

Before moving on, an important caveat must be clarified. Much of our work has focused on accounting for culture in program design and evaluation. As rewarding an experience as this has been, we do not advocate that readers always assume that a new intervention has to be developed when thinking about culturally informed evaluation. A contrasting approach is to use what we think of as EBIs, many of which have prepackaged elements and strategies, and some prior evidence that supports the adoption of the scheme. Adopting such programs should always be informed by existing evidence and theory, and if there is ample reason to believe that a program can work, then by all means use it (some of the key trade-offs here are described in Chapter 2). But otherwise, we assume that readers have exhausted this option and are thinking about developing an intervention approach because their knowledge of context dictates that doing so is the best way to proceed. In such cases, program development may involve creating a new intervention or adapting an existing one for cultural and contextual fit. In these cases, program design is still informed by the best evidence available but is shaped to meet the needs of the target population. Furthermore, doing so requires systematic evaluation of the program's effectiveness.

IMPLEMENTATION SCIENCE AND TRANSLATIONAL RESEARCH

Evidence-based practice (EBP) in psychology refers to "the integration of the best available research with clinical expertise in the context of patient characteristics, culture, and preference" (American Psychological Association [APA] Presidential Task Force on Evidence-Based Practice, 2006, p. 273). This definition is consistent with the definition developed by the Institute of Medicine (2001) that focuses on the combination of research, clinician expertise, and client values. The key elements of EBP are (a) existing research evidence on treatment, intervention, prevention, and so on; (b) the expertise and experience of the clinician or therapist (i.e., professional competence and judgment); and (c) consideration of culture as reflected in the client's beliefs, values, and behaviors (i.e., client interpretation of culture). EBP involves the application of EBIs, that is, those interventions supported by research evidence, typically through the use of experimental designs (randomized controlled trials [RCTs]) or quasi-experimental designs. The primary distinction is that EBP involves the use of clinical judgment informed by cultural and contextual considerations. (We return to discussion of related issues in later chapters of the book.)

Implementation science is a widely used term that encompasses the development of a knowledge base for understanding and applying effective treatments and interventions (i.e., for applying EBIs and engaging in EBP). Implementation science is used in multiple disciplines, including medicine, psychology, education, and public health. Applied to health services, Eccles and Mittman (2006) defined it as

> the scientific study of methods to promote the systematic uptake of research findings and other evidence-based practices into routine practice, and, hence, to improve the quality and effectiveness of health services. It includes the study of influences on healthcare professional and organisational behavior. (p. 1)

See also Helfrich et al. (2010), Rabin and Brownson (2012), Raghavan, Bright, and Shadoin, (2008). The APA's Division 16 (School Psychology Division) Working Group on Translating Science to Practice extended this definition to "understanding the processes and factors related to successful integration" (Foman et al., 2013, p. 80) of EBIs in school settings, with particular attention to core components, adaptations to the local context, and attention to culture and climate of the school or community (see also Capella, Reinke, & Hoagwood, 2011; Glover & DiPerna, 2007; Kratochwill et al., 2012).

Consistent with implementation science, **translational research** also deals with the application and adaptation of empirically validated (i.e., evidence-based) interventions across cultural and contextual variations. The primary concern in translational research is whether we can effectively translate research to practice. It recognizes the importance of, and answers questions related to, program acceptability (i.e., the degree of stakeholder buy-in pertaining to a program), social or ecological validity (i.e., the degree to which the program goals and outcomes are relevant to the real-life experiences of participants), integrity (the degree to which a particular program is implemented as intended), effectiveness, and necessary adaptations across cultural and contextual variations (see also Alkin, 2013; Nastasi et al., 2004; Ringeisen et al., 2003; Whaley & Davis, 2007). We include both implementation science and translational research in our discussion, as they are both focused on facilitating effective application of EBIs. The important aspect of both areas of study is that we see a natural fit for consideration of culture and context as we consider the conditions needed for effective implementation (implementation science) and answer questions about the translation of research to practice (translational research). We return to these questions throughout the book.

LIMITATIONS OF STANDARD RESEARCH APPROACHES AND POTENTIAL CONTRIBUTIONS OF MMR

Whether one wishes to adopt an existing program or develop one (we hope in either case, this entails program evaluation), a key set of challenges should be identified and then overcome. An initial basic concern is properly identifying a problem or need. Consulting literature (e.g., Erchul & Sheridan, 2008) points out that incorrect problem conceptualization will undermine subsequent efforts to address it. Efforts to intervene or prevent must be informed by the systematic understanding of context so that proper conceptualization occurs. This can be a vexing problem because interventionists will not always know what to ask at the outset, and even if this were not so, it can be difficult to assess the quality of information. Fortunately, there are powerful methods that can help address these concerns. These are generally conceptualized as qualitative research (Denzin & Lincoln, 2000; Patton, 2014) but can also entail the use of rapid reconnaissance methods (e.g., Chen, 2005; Patton, 2014) that may or may not use qualitative inquiry. Such inquiry is characterized as being emergent (i.e., more knowledge of context is needed before the design or even the questions can be fully conceptualized), exploratory, interpretive, and flexible. Qualitative work can be done with a series of credibility techniques that can be used to promote rigor and some assurance that investigators are drawing defensible conclusions when answering needed questions (details in Chapter 3). In sum, these techniques can be well suited for understanding context. A fundamental problem with most qualitative applications, however, is that they tend to trade breadth for depth. One can do only so many interviews and observations or review so many extant documents before resources are exhausted. Researchers may want to have a sense of how well findings generalize to some wider population of interest. It is also typical that evaluators want to have causal evidence about program effects. We believe that qualitative inquiry can provide a basis for causal arguments, but they are generally not able to yield evidence that is as clear as that emanating from approaches that many classify as quantitative in orientation (e.g., randomized experiments; see Shadish, Cook, & Campbell, 2002).

Researchers and other stakeholders often need to show that they have a grasp of context, they need to have a strong rationale for why they ask questions a certain way before including related items on a survey, they need to know that an intervention sufficiently targets needs before determining if there is evidence that it does in fact meet those needs, and so on. But they also often need to show that their findings can generalize beyond the immediate context in which data were collected. Such needs place great demands on any research design. But there are answers from the MMR field. MMR has been defined in several ways. Loosely speaking, it is research that systematically combines qualitative and quantitative inquiry. As a class of methods, it has garnered considerable attention in multiple fields. At a research paradigm level, which can be thought of as a set of common beliefs, assumptions, values, and even a culture shared by a group of researchers (Johnson, Onwuegbuzie, & Turner, 2007), MMR has been defined as

> an intellectual and practical synthesis based on qualitative and quantitative research. . . . It recognizes the importance of traditional quantitative and qualitative research but also offers a powerful third paradigm choice that often will provide the most informative, complete, balanced, and useful research results. Mixed methods research . . . (a) partners with the philosophy of pragmatism in one of its forms (left, right, middle); (b) follows the logic of mixed methods research (including the logic of the fundamental principle and any other useful logics imported from qualitative or quantitative research that are helpful for producing defensible and usable research findings); (c) relies on qualitative and quantitative viewpoints, data collection, analysis, and inference techniques combined according to the logic of mixed methods research to address one's research

question(s); and (d) is cognizant, appreciative, and inclusive of local and broader sociopolitical realities, resources, and needs. (Johnson et al., 2007, p. 129)

Consider the idea that MMR can provide the most *informative, complete, balanced, and useful research results.* We have experienced this in our own work when developing and evaluating culturally informed interventions. By way of example, Hitchcock et al. (2005) report on a mixed methods survey development effort. The approach balanced qualitative and quantitative inquiry so as to draw on the strengths of one approach to compensate for the weaknesses of the other. The survey was designed to understand what students viewed to be culturally relevant competencies and stressors. In terms of item writing, we found that prior qualitative inquiry yielded critical ideas on not only what to ask about but also how to go about asking questions in a survey format. Had we assumed that we knew about competencies and stressors, we could have just written a number of items without the benefit of prior inquiry. But we learned from interviews, focus groups, observations, and archival analyses of a number of stressors and competencies that we might not have initially imagined. As an aside, we also obtained information on where to place items within the survey and engage in some subtle vocabulary choices to best tap the constructs of interest. Although qualitative inquiry was critical for understanding the context and culture of our work, it was not feasible to apply these methods across a very large sample. Follow-up inquiry using more quantitatively oriented survey procedures made this possible. These two aspects (qualitative exploration followed by quantitative work with a larger sample) alone demonstrate the power of mixed methods, but triangulating (for now, this means comparing and contrasting findings from each mode of inquiry) results yielded some insights about certain aspects of the culture that would have been difficult to identify given a mono-method investigation. As an example, recall the first question from the bulleted list presented earlier in this chapter: What are the implications of providing mental health services to an adolescent girl who appears to be independent but hails from a culture that demands compliance and adherence to tradition? This question was rooted in one of our findings that girls in Sri Lanka who are assertive and "act like boys" (i.e., act, speak, or/and dress like boys) are viewed as having adjustment difficulties. As products of U.S. culture, the authors might be inclined to interpret such behavior as indicating a sense of emancipation from gender norms and development of self-identity and further to support individualization in an intervention. However, in broader Sri Lankan culture, at the macrosystem level, this behavior is considered "unsuitable" for adolescent girls and would likely have negative social consequences (e.g., disfavor or rejection by others, disciplinary responses by school staff). Understanding the cultural context might change the focus of interventions with the individual (e.g., exploring the consequences of individual choice) as well as extend the intervention to include relevant ecological contexts (e.g., working with family, school, peer group) (see Hitchcock & Nastasi, 2011, for a longer discussion). Our point here is that the balancing of qualitative and quantitative inquiry, along with comparing and contrasting findings from the different approaches, can yield the complete, balanced, and useful research results described in the MMR definition.

Describing the application of MMR to developing and evaluating culturally (and sometimes contextually) informed interventions is the key purpose of this book. Existing literature provides details on how to do this sort of work, but it is complex and dispersed widely across disciplines such as ethnography, program evaluation, and education research. This book is meant to offer an accessible discussion for readers who are new to this arena, and it adopts a practical focus by using illustrative examples to explain abstract ideas. The intended audience for the book spans graduate students to experienced researchers who seek guidance on how to apply MMR to develop culturally specific programs and conduct subsequent evaluations. Specific types of professionals who should be interested include psychologists, particularly school and community psychologists; social workers; educational interventionists; and program evaluators.

OVERVIEW OF THE BOOK'S CONTENT AND STRUCTURE

The remainder of this book includes seven more chapters. Chapter 2 introduces a conceptual model for how to use MMR to develop and evaluate culturally specific interventions and contrasts this approach with using evidence-based programs. Chapter 3 focuses on using MMR to systematically study context and use this information to guide program design. Chapter 4 deals with how MMR can be used to guide intervention implementation and adaptation. The chapter provides information about (a) monitoring program acceptability, integrity or fidelity, and social or ecological validity; (b) guiding program adaptations to address cultural and contextual variations; (c) evaluating skill development of program implementers; and (d) conducting formative and summative evaluation of program impact or outcomes. Chapter 5 presents validity issues relevant to program evaluation. Chapter 6 illustrates the application of MMR to program development and evaluation in a community setting, drawing from experiences of the authors. Chapter 7 describes common challenges in conducting mixed methods program evaluation and provides strategies for addressing these challenges. Chapter 8 closes by discussing future directions related to evolving methods for MMR program evaluation and potential applications to a range of settings.

CONCLUSION

Recall that the key learning objectives of this chapter were to introduce the idea that context and culture affect service delivery and to help readers understand why this is a critical point when engaged in intervention development, service delivery, and program evaluation. Furthermore, we hope that the chapter helped readers more fully appreciate why explicit accounting for context and culture is not more widely embraced. We provide two concluding exercises to help you reflect on the content of the chapter. We expect the exercises may raise more questions than answers. We hope the remainder of the book will help provide answers to inform your work in intervention development and evaluation.

Key Terms

- **Context:** Refers to the specific setting or set of circumstances within which an intervention is designed, delivered, and evaluated. We conceive of context from a developmental–ecological perspective drawing on the work of Bronfenbrenner (1989, 1999). Context, in Bronfenbrenner parlance, is the *microsystem* (immediate context) in which the interventionists and participants directly interact, in this case during the delivery of the intervention. This microsystem, however, is influenced by surrounding systems as conceived in Bronfenbrenner's EST (1998, 1999):

exosystem, those that embody the microsystem; *mesosystem*, those that embody the relationship between ecological systems; *macrosystem*, those that embody the larger society or community and the inherent values, beliefs, norms; and *chronosystem*, those that embody the historical or developmental influences.

- **Culture:** Has been defined as "shared language, ideas, beliefs, values, and behavioral norms" (Nastasi et al., 2004) and "a common heritage or set of beliefs, norms and values" (DHHS, 2001, p. 9). With regard to guiding behavior change (i.e., intervention), culture refers to "a dynamic system of meanings, knowledge and actions that provides actors collectively, interpersonally, and individually with community-legitimized strategies to construct, reflect upon, and reconstruct their world and experience, and guide behaviour" (Nastasi et al., 2015, p. 96). Culture is viewed as a ubiquitous construct that can influence intervention and prevention program design, implementation, and evaluation, thus necessitating a need for the consideration of culture in program development and evaluation.

- **Cultural (co-)construction:** Refers to the dialogic process among individuals that leads to development of shared beliefs, values, and norms reflecting the integration of thinking from all parties. Within the intervention context, cultural co-construction refers to the dynamic dialogic *process* that occurs between interventionists (health providers, therapists, teachers/educators, etc.) and recipients (patients, clients, students, etc.); whereas terms such as culturally sensitive or relevant apply to the *products* of the co-construction process. (For further discussion and illustration, see Nastasi et al., 2015.)

- **Culture specific:** Refers to the embodiment of "an individual's real-life experiences within a given cultural context (e.g., neighborhood) and his or her understanding of those experiences" (Nastasi et al., 2000, p. 403).

- **Evidence-based practice (EBP):** In psychology refers to "the integration of the best available research with clinical expertise in the context of patient characteristics, culture, and preference" (APA Presidential Task Force on Evidence-Based Practice, 2006, p. 273). This definition is consistent with the definition developed by the Institute of Medicine (2001) that also focuses on the combination of research, clinician expertise, and client values. EBP thus involves the application of EBIs with due consideration to clinical judgment and cultural and contextual factors.

- **Implementation science:**

  The scientific study of methods to promote the systematic uptake of research findings and other evidence-based practices into routine practice, and, hence, to improve the quality and effectiveness of health [mental health, educational] services. It includes the study of influences on healthcare [mental health, educational] professional and organisational behavior. (Eccles & Mittman, 2006, p. 1)

- **Mixed methods research (MMR):** Research that systematically combines qualitative and quantitative inquiry. MMR "relies on qualitative and quantitative viewpoints, data collection, analysis, and inference techniques combined according to the logic of MMR to address one's research question(s); and is cognizant, appreciative, and inclusive of local and broader sociopolitical realities, resources, and needs" (Johnson et al., 2007, p. 129).

- **Program:** Refers to an organized and purposeful effort to promote development, learning, or well-being; or intervene to prevent the occurrence of problems or mitigate existing problems. Programs can occur at individual, provider (therapist, teacher), system (organizations, communities), or multiple (individual, provider, system) levels (Nastasi & Hitchcock, 2009). Programming encompasses screening, identification, diagnosis, planning and design, implementation, monitoring and oversight, evaluation, staffing and staff training. *Program services*, delivered directly or indirectly, can entail promotion, prevention, intervention, treatment/remediation, and maintenance (Hess, Short, & Hazel, 2012). *Program evaluation* entails the systematic and empirical investigation of the merit, worth, and value of a program (Scriven, 1991). A comprehensive evaluation of the program involves data collection from multiple sources to assess program acceptability, social or ecological validity, implementation (integrity or fidelity), outcomes, sustainability, and institutionalization (Nastasi et al., 2004; Nastasi & Hitchcock, 2009).

- **Translational research:** A complex topic that deals with the application and adaptation of empirically validated (i.e., evidence-based) interventions across cultural and contextual variations. It answers questions related to program acceptability (i.e., the degree of stakeholder buy-in pertaining to a program), social or ecological validity (i.e., the degree to which the program goals and outcomes are relevant to the real-life experiences of participants), integrity (the degree to which a particular program is implemented as intended), effectiveness, and necessary adaptations across cultural and contextual variations (see also Alkin, 2013; Nastasi et al., 2004; Ringeisen et al., 2003; Whaley & Davis, 2007).

Reflective Questions and Exercises

1. As a concluding exercise, consider revisiting the bulleted list of questions provided earlier in the chapter. Then, think of a story you've recently heard of, or know from your own life circumstances, where some sort of intervention might benefit a group of people, but it is critical to have an intervention that accounted for local context and culture. At a minimum, address the following questions:
   a. What was the problem/reason for intervening? Who are the primary and secondary intended beneficiaries of your services?
   b. What would you have done to address the need? Were there prior attempts to help, and if so, for what reason do you think your approach might lead to better outcomes for the people you wish to help?
   c. Based on your knowledge of the situation, what special circumstances do you think would need to be addressed to make your services as effective as possible?
   d. How would you evaluate your efforts?

2. Identify an EBI or manualized treatment in your area of interest. Describe and critique the program, using the following questions to guide the critique:
   a. Does the program have sufficient evidence to warrant its use in an applied setting (e.g., school, community, hospital)?
   b. In what contexts and with what populations has the program been empirically tested?
   c. What modifications might be necessary to adapt the program to your intended context or population (i.e., with whom you are currently working or intend to work)?
   d. Would you use this program? Why or why not?

References

Alkin, M. C. (2013). *Evaluation roots: A wider perspective of theorists' views and influences* (2nd ed.). Thousand Oaks, CA: Sage.

Amano, K. (2005). *An international comparison and analysis of Japan's high suicide rate* (NLI Research). Retrieved from http://www.nli-research.co.jp/english/socioeconomics/2005/li050906.pdf

American Psychological Association Presidential Task Force on Evidence-Based Practice. (2006). Evidence-based practice in psychology. *American Psychologist, 61*(4), 271–285. doi:10.1037/0003-066X.61.4.271

Arnett, J. J. (2008). The neglected 95%: Why American psychology needs to become less American. *American Psychologist, 63*(7), 602–614. doi:10.1037/0003-066X.63.7.602

Bibeau, G., & Corin, E. (1995). From submission to the text to interpretative violence. In G. Bibeau & E. Corin (Eds.), *Beyond textuality: Asceticism and violence in anthropological interpretation* (Approaches to semiotics series, pp. 3–54). Berlin, Germany: Mouton de Gruyter.

Bronfenbrenner, U. (1989). Ecological systems theory. In R. Vasta (Ed.), *Annals of child development* (Vol. 6, pp. 187–249). Greenwich, CT: JAI Press.

Bronfenbrenner, U. (1999). Environments in developmental perspective: Theoretical and operational models. In S. L. Friedman & T. D. Wachs (Eds.), *Measuring environment across the life span: Emerging methods and concepts* (pp. 3–28). Washington, DC: American Psychological Association.

Burns, M. K. (2011). School psychology research: Combining ecological theory and prevention science. *School Psychology Review, 40,* 132–139.

Capella, E., Reinke, W. M., & Hoagwood, K. E. (2011). Advancing intervention research in school psychology: Finding the balance between process and outcome for social and behavioral interventions. *School Psychology Review, 40*(4), 455–464.

Castillo, R. J. (1997). *Culture and mental illness: A client-centered approach.* Pacific Grove, CA: Brooks-Cole.

Chen, H. (2005). *Practical program evaluation: Assessing and improving planning, implementation and effectiveness.* Thousand Oaks, CA: Sage.

Cole, M. (1996). *Cultural psychology: A once and future discipline.* Cambridge, MA: Harvard University Press.

Common Core Standards Initiative. (2015). *Preparing America's students for success.* Retrieved from http://www.corestandards.org/

Denzin, N. K., & Lincoln, Y. S. (Eds.). (2000). *Handbook of qualitative research* (2nd ed.). Thousand Oaks, CA: Sage.

Dubinsky, E., & Moses, R. P. (2011). Philosophy, math research, math education research, K–16 education, and the civil rights movement: A synthesis. *Notices of the American Mathematical Society, 58*(3), 401–409.

Eccles, M. P., & Mittman, B. S. (2006). Welcome to implementation science [Editorial]. *Implementation Science, 1*(1), 1–3. doi:10.1186/1748-5908-1-1

Erchul, W. P., & Sheridan, S. M. (Eds.). (2008). *Handbook of research in school consultation.* New York, NY: Lawrence Erlbaum.

Foman, S. G., Shapiro, E. S., Codding, R. S., Gonzales, J. E., Reddy, L. A., Rosenfield, S. A., . . . Stoiber, K. C. (2013). Implementation science and school psychology. *School Psychology Quarterly, 28*(2), 77–100. doi:10.1037/spq0000019

Glover, T. A., & DiPerna, J. C. (2007). Service delivery for response to intervention: Core components and directions for future resaerch. *School Psychology Research, 36*(4), 526–540.

Helfrich, C. D., Damschroder, L. J., Hagedorn, H. J., Daggett, G. S., Sahay, A., Richie, M., . . . Stetler, C. B. (2010). A critical synthesis of literature on the promotion action on research implementation in health services (PARIHS) framework. *Implementation Science, 5*(82). doi:10.1186/1748-5908-5-82

Hess, R. S., Short, R. J., & Hazel, C. E. (2012). *Comprehensive children's mental health services in schools and communities: A public health problem-solving model.* New York, NY: Routledge.

Hitchcock, J. H., & Nastasi, B. K. (2011). Mixed methods for construct validation. In P. Vogt & M. Williams (Eds.), *Handbook of methodological innovation* (pp. 249–268). Thousand Oaks, CA: Sage.

Hitchcock, J. H., Nastasi, B. K., Dai, D., Newman, J., Jayasena, A., Bernstein-Moore, R., . . . Varjas, K. (2005). Illustrating a mixed-method approach for validating culturally specific constructs. *Journal of School Psychology, 43,* 259–278. doi:10.1016/j.jsp.2005.04.007

Institute of Medicine. (2001). *Crossing the quality chasm: A new health system for the 21st century.* Washington, DC: National Academies Press.

Johnson, R. B., Onwuegbuzie, A. J., & Turner, L. A. (2007). Toward a definition of mixed methods research. *Journal of Mixed Methods Research, 1,* 112–133. doi:10.1177/1558689806298224

Kratochwill, T. R., Hoagwood, K. E., Kazak, A. E., Weisz, J. R., Hood, K., Vargas, L. A., & Banez, G. A. (2012). Practice-based evidence for children and adolescents: Advancing the research agenda in schools. *School Psychology Review, 41*(2), 215–235.

LeCompte, M. D. (2000). Analyzing qualitative data. *Theory Into Practice, 39*(3), 146–154.

Nastasi, B. K., & Hitchcock, J. (2009). Challenges of evaluating multi-level interventions. *American Journal of Community Psychology, 43,* 360–376. doi:10.1007/s10464-009-9239-7

Nastasi, B. K., Moore, R. B., & Varjas, K. M. (2004). *School-based mental health services: Creating comprehensive and culturally specific programs.* Washington, DC: American Psychological Association.

Nastasi, B. K., Schensul, J. J., Schensul, S. L., Mekki-Berrada, A., Pelto, B., Maitra, S., . . . Saggurti, N. (2015). A model for translating ethnography and theory into culturally constructed clinical practice. *Culture, Medicine and Psychiatry, 39,* 92–109. doi:10.1007/s11013-014-9404-9

Nastasi, B. K., Varjas, K., Bernstein, R., & Jayasena, A. (2000). Conducting participatory culture-specific consultation: A global perspective on multicultural consultation. *School Psychology Review, 29*(3), 401–413.

National Council of Teachers of Mathematics. (2008, September). *Algebra: What, when, and for whom: A position of the National Council of Teachers of Mathematics.* Retrieved from https://board.madison.k12.wi.us/files/boe/NCTM%20Algebra%20 Position%20Paper_0.pdf

Patton, M. Q. (2014). *Qualitative research and evaluation methods: Integrating theory and practice* (4th ed.). Thousand Oaks, CA: Sage.

Rabin, B. A., & Brownson, R. C. (2012). Developing the terminology for dissemination and implementation research. In R. C. Brownson, G. A. Colditz, & E. K. Proctor (Eds.), *Dissemination and implementation research in health* (pp. 23–51). New York, NY: Oxford University Press.

Raghavan, R., Bright, C. L., & Shadoin, A. L. (2008). Toward a policy ecology of implementation of evidence-based practices in public mental health settings. *Implementation Science, 3*(26), 1–9. doi:10.1186/1748-5908-3-26

Ringeisen, H., Henderson, K., & Hoagwood, K. (2003). Context matters: Schools and the "research to practice gap" in children's mental health. *School Psychology Review, 32*(2), 153–168.

Scriven, M. (1991). *Evaluation thesaurus* (4th ed.). Newbury Park, CA: Sage.

Shadish, W. R., Cook, T. D., & Campbell, D. T. (2002). *Experimental and quasi-experimental designs for generalized causal inference.* Boston, MA: Houghton Mifflin.

Sue, D. W., Bingham, R. P., Porche-Burke, L., & Vasquez, M. (1999). The diversification of psychology: A multicultural revolution. *American Psychologist, 54,* 1061–1069.

Trimble, J. E., Scharrón-del-Río, M. R., & Hill, J. S. (2012). Ethical considerations in the application of cultural adaptation models with ethnocultural populations. In G. Bernal & M. M. Domenech Rodríguez (Eds.), *Cultural adaptations: Tools for evidence-based practice with diverse populations* (pp. 45–67). Washington, DC: American Psychological Association. doi:10.1037/13752-003

U.S. Department of Health and Human Services. (2001). *Mental health: Culture, race and ethnicity a supplement to mental health: A report of the surgeon general.* Rockville, MD: Department of Health and Human Services, Substance Abuse and Mental Health Services Administration, Center for Mental Health Services, National Institutes of Health, National Institutes of Mental Health.

Vigil, J. M., Geary, D. C., Granger, D. A., & Flinn, M. V. (2010). Sex differences in salivary cortisol, alpha-amylase, and psychological functioning following Hurricane Katrina. *Child Development, 81*(4), 1228–1240. doi:10.1111/j.1467-8624.2010.01464.x

Watters, E. (2010). *Crazy like us: The globalization of the American psyche.* New York, NY: Free Press.

Whaley, A. L., & Davis, K. E. (2007). Cultural competence and evidence-based practice in mental health services: A complementary perspective. *American Psychologist, 62*(6), 563–574. doi:10.1037/0003-066X.62.6.563

World Health Organization. (n.d.). *Suicide data.* Retrieved from http://www.who.int/ mental_health/prevention/suicide/suicideprevent/en/

Young, M. F., Nastasi, B. K., & Braunhardt, L. (1996). Implementing Jasper immersion: A case of conceptual change. In B. Wilson (Ed.), *Constructivist learning environments: Case studies in instructional design* (pp. 121–134). Englewood Cliffs, NJ: Educational Technology.

☙ TWO ❧

CONCEPTUAL MODELS FOR MIXED METHODS AND CULTURE-SPECIFIC INTERVENTION DEVELOPMENT

Learning Objectives

The key objectives of this chapter are for readers to understand the following:

- Models for designing culture-specific interventions
- Conceptual foundations for applying MMR to culture-specific program development and evaluation
- Issues related to adopting existing EBIs, developing new culture-specific programming, or adapting EBIs to match culture and context

INTRODUCTION

As discussed in Chapter 1, translating research to practice has been at the center of discussions in intervention and prevention literature across multiple disciplines (psychology, education, public health, and medicine). In particular, at the center of these discussions have been questions about how to facilitate the translation of EBIs to applied settings; how to ensure effective implementation of EBIs given the multiple factors that affect feasibility, fidelity, and sustainability; and, most important to our discussion, how to promote cultural and contextual match. As we contended in Chapter 1, attention to context and culture is essential to effective application of EBIs. Moreover, we contend that the use of MMR is essential to answering questions about translation of research to practice in order to address the complexity inherent in applied settings.

We begin the chapter with an exploration of models for conceptualizing intervention programs, drawing from research across multiple disciplines. We then explore models for the application of MMR to program development. We conclude with an MMR design framework to guide subsequent discussion of development of culture-specific intervention programs.

CONCEPTUAL MODELS FOR INTERVENTION DEVELOPMENT

We propose a categorization of conceptual models for intervention development based on the primary focus of research: (a) establishing the evidence base for intervention effectiveness, (b) facilitating interventions within a systems framework, (c) facilitating effective implementation, (d) adapting programs to local culture and context, (e) ensuring **cultural competence** of stakeholders in program development, and (f) adding participatory models. These models reflect the current thinking in the field of implementation science and the progression from establishing EBIs to addressing the challenges in the application of EBIs to real-life settings. As we describe each model, we attend to the extent to which the model addresses several key factors: (a) cultural specificity or cultural (co-)construction, (b) **program adaptation** (i.e., the modification of program to local culture and context), (c) the application or applicability of MMR, and (d) partnership/collaboration with key stakeholders.

Establishing Evidence of Intervention Effectiveness

The first conceptual model addresses questions related to establishing empirical support for specific interventions and reflects a progression from basic research, or the study of key construct and relationships, to EBP, or the translation of empirically validated interventions (under highly controlled conditions) to applications in real-life settings (see Forman et al., 2013; Kratochwill & Stoiber, 2002; Ringeisen, Henderson, & Hoagwood, 2003; Saul et al., 2008; Wandersman et al., 2008). Although there are variations across specific depictions of the process, generally the progression reflects the following sequence: (a) **basic (formative) research** to establish understanding of the phenomenon and develop theory to guide interventions; (b) **efficacy (small-scale) trials** to test theory-driven interventions, typically under highly controlled conditions (using experimental designs, i.e., RCTs); (c) **effectiveness (small-scale) trials** to test the interventions in naturalistic settings (using experimental or quasi-experimental designs); (d) **dissemination (large-scale) trials** ("scaling up") to test the interventions across multiple naturalistic settings (e.g., using quasi-experimental designs or RCTs); and (e) **implementation (large-scale)**, with evaluation research to establish effectiveness and identify variables that influence program success (e.g., systemic factors, implementer expertise, and population variables).

Effectiveness research has traditionally relied on quantitative research methods; for example, in basic research, testing relationships among variables or establishing individual differences based on developmental and sociodemographic variables; using experimental designs (typically RCTs) to establish intervention efficacy; or using quasi-experimental design to establish effectiveness across multiple settings and populations. However, large-scale dissemination and implementation efforts are more likely to rely on MMR through the inclusion of qualitative research to explore contextual and cultural factors that influence the success of implementation. At this level, programmers also are more likely to consider issues related to cultural specificity, program adaptation, and involvement of key stakeholders in decision making.

The progression from basic to implementation research reflects chronological influences in the field of **intervention research** across multiple disciplines (e.g., psychology, public health), characterized by a growing concern about failures in research-to-practice efforts and recognition of the influence of systemic (e.g., organizational, community, policy) factors, the complexity of human behavior and its relationship to ecological factors including culture, the roles of multiple stakeholders (decision makers, implementers, recipients), and the dynamic nature of program implementation. We address responses to these concerns as we explore the remaining models.

Interventions Within a Systems Framework

Bronfenbrenner's (1989, 1999) EST has been a major influence in psychology and related disciplines in terms of underscoring the importance of social ecology for understanding human behavior and development. We have used EST as the major systems framework to guide our own research and intervention development work (e.g., Nastasi, Moore, & Varjas, 2004) and employ the theory to structure discussions about culture and context and application of MMR in this book. Figure 2.1 depicts the ecological system of the child in all of its complexity. According to EST, the individual (child) functions within an unlimited number of *microsystems*—that is, immediate social contexts that define the person's social ecology (e.g., school, family, neighborhood, peer group) and in which critical social interactions occur (e.g., parent–child, child–sibling). Each microsystem is embedded within an *exosystem* (e.g., larger family unit of parents and siblings and extended family), which indirectly influences interactions in the microsystem (e.g., parent–parent relationship can influence each parent's interaction with the child). Interactions across system boundaries (depicted by arrows in Figure 2.1) are referred to as the *mesosystem* and can occur within respective ecosystems (family) or across systems (family–peer group). The broadest level of the ecology is the *macrosystem*, which includes the social, cultural, economic, and political factors that have indirect influence on the child's interactions within specific microsystems. For example, the beliefs, values, and norms within the society or within a particular cultural group influence expected behaviors for the individual and the interactions between individuals. Similarly, the federal and state laws influence public educational practices at the school district, building, and classroom level. Also critical to EST is the *chronosystem*, the developmental and historical background for the individuals and systems (e.g., child's early developmental experiences, history of racial segregation in schools). There is a reciprocal nature of interactions within any given ecosystem; that is, the child is not only influenced by the social environment but also has influence over it. Thus, the child (individual) is viewed as an active agent in the social ecology. Furthermore, one's interpretations of experiences also affect the nature of interactions. The interactions across systems (mesosystemic) are also bidirectional (as indicated by arrows in Figure 2.1). The bidirectionality of interactions across the elements of the ecological system contributes to the dynamic and complex nature of the social ecology. As we explore throughout this book, EST provides a structure for exploring the complexity and ever-changing nature of the cultural and contextual factors that influence design, implementation, and evaluation of interventions.

Figure 2.1 Child's Ecological System

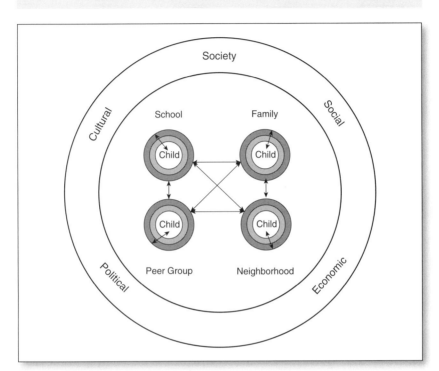

SOURCE: From Nastasi, Moore, and Varjas (2004, p. 40). Copyright 2004 by the American Psychological Association. Adapted with permission. The use of APA information does not imply endorsement by APA.

NOTE: Depiction of the social ecology of the child is based on Bronfenbrenner's EST (1989, 1999). The *microsystem* (white inner circle) is the immediate context in which the *child* is interacting with key social agents, for example, with teachers and classmates in school. The *exosystem* (outer grey circles) refers to the systems that encompass the microsystem and have indirect influence on the child and the interactions within the microsystem (e.g., school [light grey], school district [darker grey]). The *mesosystem* refers to the connections or interactions between systems (e.g., between school and family, or between micro- and exosystems within the school, indicated by arrows) that have an indirect influence on the child and the interactions within the microsystem. The *macrosystem* refers to the societal or global level, specifically, the social, cultural, political, and economic factors that influence the systems in which the child functions (e.g., cultural values influence expectations within the school district, school, and classroom and the interactions of the child with the teacher and classmates). Note that interactions are bidirectional, including the child's direct interactions within the microsystem. The bidirectionality of interactions across the ecological system contributes to the dynamic and complex nature of the social ecology.

Several systems models have been proposed to guide intervention dissemination and implementation—that is, to bridge the research-to-practice gap. These models generally focus on identifying and understanding the systemic factors that influence the application and sustainability of EBIs. In particular, researchers using systemic approaches call attention to factors such as institutional and community context (including resources, mission, etc.); role of stakeholders, training, and expertise of implementers; and match of the EBI to cultural and population factors.

The APA Task Force on Evidence-Based Practice for Children and Adolescents (Kazak et al., 2010; Kratochwill et al., 2012) proposed a *meta-systems social–ecological framework*, consistent with EST. The task force identified key elements of the child's "metasystem" as follows (note the match to components of the EST):

> The various contexts and environments that surround and influence a child's adaptations and development. The core contexts that typically exert the most direct influence on children include their family; the cultural norms and values of their heritage; their peers; social institutions created to inculcate certain societal values (such as churches or schools); and for children with emotional or behavioral needs, the various systems that society creates to provide services to address these problems. (Kazak et al., 2010, p. 86)

This group acknowledged the importance of contextual and cultural factors related to organizational and population diversity. While citing the current body of research evidence to guide EBP, the task force members called attention to the lack of research on implementation and dissemination.

Wandersman et al. (2008) proposed the *interactive systems framework (ISF)* to guide both researchers and practitioners in the dissemination and implementation of EBIs. The ISF calls attention to three systems that interact to influence dissemination and implementation: (1) the synthesis and translation system—that is, those responsible for the synthesis and translation of existing research evidence (making EBI knowledge available); (2) the delivery system—that is, the site of delivery and its capacity to support the interventions; and (3) the support system that provides technical assistance and consultation to enhance the capacity for successful implementation and sustainability. Influencing these three systems are factors such as the body of existing research and theory, organizational climate, funding and other resources, and macrolevel policies. Though not explicitly addressed by Wandersman et al., MMR could facilitate the articulation of the myriad factors in the ISF to inform our understanding of dissemination and implementation. Moreover, the multisystemic focus requires the consideration of collaboration across stakeholders. Finally, Gregory et al. (2012) have proposed incorporating a cultural component into ISF, through attention to organizational culture and cultural competence of partners (i.e., researcher, program developers, and implementers). (We return to the topic of cultural competence in a later section of this chapter.)

Program Implementation

Although models to facilitate the dissemination of research are important and can inform program selection and adoption, the "translation" of EBIs to practice has taken center stage within the field of implementation science, an interdisciplinary field applied to health sciences, psychology, and other social sciences. In this section, we explore conceptual models and research frameworks within this emerging field (Fixsen, Naoom, Blase, Friedman, & Wallace, 2005; Forman et al., 2013; May, 2013; Weisz, Sandler, Durlak, & Anton, 2005).

Fixsen et al. (2005), building on a comprehensive review of existing implementation research, proposed a conceptual model for guiding future implementation research and practice. For the purposes of discussion, Fixsen et al. defined *implementation* as "a specific set of activities [intervention activities and implementation activities] designed to put into practice an activity or program of known dimensions" (p. 5). Furthermore, two sets of program activities warrant attention in practice and research: (1) *intervention* activities (what is delivered to participants, e.g., an EBI) and (2) *implementation* activities (those related to the efforts of practitioners and other organizational or community stakeholders). The importance of both intervention and implementation cannot be overstated and is reinforced as we subsequently discuss issues related to adaptation, cultural specificity, cultural competence, and partnerships.

With regard to implementation, Fixsen et al. (2005) propose a model of *multilevel influences on successful implementation*, represented as a set of three concentric circles: (1) core components (at center, e.g., staff training and coaching), (2) organizational components (e.g., administration), and (3) macrosystemic factors (e.g., social, economic, or political). The model is intended to emphasize the complexity of implementation and to guide program developers from the outset of program design (e.g., assessing all levels prior to program initiation). At the center are a set of integrated and compensatory core components: (a) staff selection (implementers, evaluators, etc.), (b) staff training, (c) staff consultation and coaching, (d) formative evaluation of staff (e.g., fidelity and competence), (e) program evaluation (fidelity and effectiveness), and (f) administrative support. The inclusion of staff competence, training, and support as core components reflects the perceived importance of staff for successful program implementation: "In human services, *practitioners are the intervention*" (Fixsen et al., 2005, p. 45). In guiding future research on implementation, Fixsen et al. (2005) recommend MMR (in recognition of the complexity of program implementation), partnerships between interventionists and researchers, site-specific communities of practice, and dissemination across sites.

Forman et al. (2013) examined implementation science in the context of school psychology, and thus the implementation of EBIs in the context of schools with psychologists as agents of implementation. They propose four common elements of implementation: (1) the innovation (e.g., an EBI), (2) a communication process (e.g., about the innovation), (3) a social system (context for implementation such as a school), and (4) the change agents (those attempting to bring the innovation to the system). They adopted the definition of implementation science proposed by Eccles and Mittman (2006), "The scientific study of methods to promote the systematic uptake of research findings and other evidence-based practices into routine practice, and, hence, to improve the quality and effectiveness" (p. 1) of service delivery. Moreover, they identified the purpose of implementation science in school psychology as understanding the factors and processes that influence successful integration of EBIs into schools, including enhancing organizational readiness (e.g., organizational culture), translation of EBIs to practice, adaptation of program components to local context, and evaluation of program acceptability and engagement, fidelity, and outcomes (see also Odom, 2009; Rabin & Brownson, 2012). With regard to future research directions, they recommend attention to examining core components of EBIs; effectiveness of EBIs across diverse contexts and populations (including necessary adaptation); effective methods for engaging stakeholders, training and supporting implementers, and ensuring fidelity; and conditions that influence the success (or failure) of implementation as well as sustainability and capacity building. Furthermore, Forman et al. (2013) encourage researcher–practitioner collaboration. Although not directly addressing the use of MMR, these authors commented on the limitations of and ongoing debates about the use of traditional research designs focused on establishing causal relationships (e.g., RCTs, single-case designs) given the complexity of program implementation.

May (2013) proposed an interdisciplinary *general theory of implementation* to depict and elucidate the implementation process. In recognition of the complexity and multiplicity of interrelated components of any intervention, he characterizes the focus of implementation science as "complex interventions" and describes the implementation processes as

> interactions between "emergent expressions of agency" (i.e., the things that people do to make something happen, and the ways that they work with different components of a complex intervention to do so); and as "dynamic elements of context" (the social-structural and social-cognitive resources that people draw on to realize that agency). (p. 1)

The core components of May's (2013) model include (a) *capability*, the likelihood that the agents (those responsible for implementation) can operationalize the intervention based on feasibility and contextual fit; (b) *capacity*, the social–structural resources available to implementation agents (i.e., social norms, roles, material, and cognitive resources within the system) and the agents' capacity to interact with these resources; (c) *potentials*, social–cognitive resources (beliefs and values) available to implementation agents and the agents' capacity to link social–cognitive and social–structural resources to bring about collective action (i.e., the intervention); and (d) *contributions*, what the agents (individually and collectively) do to implement the intervention, both cognitively (e.g., sense making, reflexive monitoring) and behaviorally (e.g., collective action). Thus, May acknowledges the importance of individual and collective action within the dynamic organizational context. Though not explicitly addressed, May's general theory of implementation could be applied to the study of cultural specificity, program adaptation, and participatory processes. The complexity of the implementation process also warrants the application of MMR.

Finally, Weisz et al. (2005) propose an *integrated model* for linking prevention and treatment for youth mental health that necessitates consideration of service delivery within a public health model (ranging from health promotion to treatment to continuing care) and an ecological systems approach (e.g., viewing youth as embedded in family, community, and culture). Based on a review of existing research, these authors recommended research directions consistent with the focus of this text and with the current efforts within implementation science: (a) Identifying core elements of interventions, including change processes that account for outcomes; (b) addressing mismatch between research-based interventions and clinical practices that influences translation of research to practice; (c) understanding the contexts in which and populations for whom interventions work (i.e., limits of translation to practice); and (d) addressing the cultural appropriateness of existing interventions across diverse populations. The recommendations of Weisz et al. call into question the application of manualized treatments/interventions (detailed in the manual for standardized application) without attention to contextual and population/cultural variables. In the next section, we examine models for program adaptation as a response to such concerns.

Program Adaptations

Drawing on the ISF proposed by Wandersman et al. (2008), Lee, Altschul, and Mowbray (2008) proposed a model of *planned adaptation* to guide practitioners in adapting EBIs to address population needs (e.g., cultural and contextual variations) while maintaining core program components (i.e., those elements that account for outcomes and are determined by theoretical or conceptual foundations of the intervention). Successful adaptations require that researchers identify and articulate the core components for dissemination (e.g., in program manuals) and possibly provide technical assistance to practitioners in making adaptations. Furthermore, documenting adaptations and outcomes can facilitate further dissemination.

Planned adaptation involves a four-step process for the practitioner (Lee et al., 2008): (1) examine the theory of change for the selected EBI (i.e., understanding the causal and moderating mechanisms that account for outcomes); (2) identify population differences (i.e., between original and intended population) and determine the extent to which these differences are likely to affect the core program elements; (3) systematically adapt program content based on population differences; and (4) adapt the evaluation to examine outcomes given the changes. This type of adaptation is referred to as *designer adaptation* (i.e., by the program developer) and is distinguished from *implementer adaptation* (i.e., by the practitioners engaged in implementation) (see Colby et al., 2013).

One limitation of planned adaptation is that population differences (Step 2) are identified based on practitioner experiences with the population and existing research that suggests that these differences may moderate outcomes, and they typically focus on the most apparent differences (e.g., race and ethnicity). We propose, and discuss in a later section, a stage of formative research conducted by program developers to systematically examine the potential cultural and contextual factors and use these data to guide adaptations. Thus, adaptations are based on an inductively derived understanding of cultural narratives that reflect population beliefs, values, and norms relevant to the intervention—what we refer to as *cultural construction* (cf. cultural grounding, Colby et al., 2013; Hecht & Krieger, 2006)—which in turn drives "evidence-based cultural adaptation" of EBIs (Barrera, Castro, & Steiker, 2011; Colby et al., 2013).

Colby et al. (2013) articulate the process of *cultural grounding* as an approach to designer adaptation to ensure cultural sensitivity in program design (i.e., evidence-based cultural adaptation). Critical to this discussion is the distinction between surface and deep structure intervention components: *Surface structure* components refer to more superficial elements in "'packaging' the programs to give the appearance of cultural appropriateness" (e.g., images, language; Colby et al., 2013, p. 192). *Deep structure* components refer to the more fundamental elements such as cultural values, beliefs, and practices, which are more likely to influence program messages, narratives, and potentially core elements.

As suggested by the work of Colby et al. (2013) and others (Cappella, Jackson, Bilal, Hamre, & Soule, 2011; Cappella, Reinke, & Hoagwood, 2011; Goldstein, Kemp, Leff, & Lochman, 2013; Nastasi et al., 2004; Nastasi, Hitchcock, Varjas, et al., 2010), achieving **evidence-based cultural grounding** is best facilitated by an iterative, reflexive, and participatory research process that relies on qualitative methods (e.g., observations, focus groups, interviews; see Chapter 3) to facilitate understanding of the culture (beliefs, values, norms) of the target group and engages stakeholders as partners in the process of program development and/or adaptation. This process is potentially transferable across intervention sites to promote cultural and contextual fit, as an alternative or complement to manualized EBIs. We will return to the discussion of methodology in a later section of this chapter.

Cultural Competence for Programming

Culture has become an important part of the discussion about EBP, with a particular focus on questions about cultural relevance, cultural specificity, and/or cultural grounding of interventions. In addition to ethical concerns about the development and implementation of interventions that address the needs of particular cultural groups (e.g., racial and ethnic groups; Fisher et al., 2002; Trimble, Scharrón-del-Río, & Hill, 2012), concerns about the external validity of EBIs have been raised (e.g., generalizability across diverse populations; Whaley & Davis, 2007). The concerns focus on the extent to which we can confidently use EBIs that were validated on restricted segments of the population (e.g., White, middle-class, suburban, U.S.) without adaptation to culture and context (e.g., African American, poor, urban; populations in Asia or Africa). The responses to such concerns have focused on the design or adaptation of interventions to be culturally and contextually specific (e.g., evidence-based cultural grounding), as well as the cultural competence of the program designers, implementers, and evaluators. In this section, we explore *cultural competence models*.

Different definitions of *cultural competence* have been proposed in the literature.[1] We adopt a dynamic, and process-oriented, definition of cultural competence consistent with the notion of cultural co-construction (see Chapter 1) and with the definition adopted by Whaley and Davis (2007):

> Cultural competence [is] as a set of *problem-solving* skills that includes (a) the *ability to recognize and understand* the dynamic interplay between the heritage and adaptation dimensions of culture in shaping human behavior; (b) the *ability to use the knowledge* acquired about an individual's heritage and adaptational challenges to maximize the effectiveness of assessment, diagnosis, and treatment;

---

[1] A full discussion of the varied definitions in the literature is beyond the scope of this chapter. For readers interested in more in-depth discussion, see D'Augelli (2003), Fisher et al. (2002), Gregory et al. (2012), Serpell, Clauss-Ehlers, and Weist (2013), Whaley and Davis (2007).

and (c) *internalization* (i.e., incorporation into one's clinical problem-solving repertoire) of this process of recognition, acquisition, and use of cultural dynamics so that it can be routinely applied to diverse groups. . . . It should also be noted that the internalization stage of cultural competence proposed here is akin to Lopez's (1997; Lopez et al., 2002) notion of *shifting cultural lenses* in his model of cultural competence. (p. 565)

Particularly noteworthy for our discussions of applying MMR to intervention development is the assumption that cultural competence is critical for all intervention agents (developers, implementers, evaluators). In addition, cultural competence is a way of thinking and acting that enables intervention agents to engage in a dynamic process of considering cultural and contextual variables throughout the process of program development, implementation, and evaluation. This process requires perspective taking and communication skills that facilitate the negotiation of perspectives to reach a shared understanding that in turn guides collective action (see Friedman & Antal, 2005; Kapadia, Mehrota, Nastasi, & Rodriquez, in press.) Furthermore, the consideration of culture is not restricted to the individual but encompasses the social ecology (e.g., at micro-, exo-, meso-, and macrosystem levels; see also Bronfenbrenner's [1989, 1999] EST), thus necessitating consideration of organizational culture (Gregory et al., 2012). The dynamic nature of both culture and program implementation requires continual attention to cultural and contextual factors.

As D'Augelli (2003) suggests, culturally competent intervention research necessitates a *culturally sensitive methodology*, which he characterizes as a mixed qualitative–quantitative approach:

Developing a culturally sensitive methodology is no easy task. . . . As is common among analysts arguing for a strong cultural analysis, Zea et al. [2003] stress the importance of qualitative methodologies to map the nature of relevant cultural meanings. These methodologies must be complemented by quantitative methods so that ideographic and nomothetic perspectives can be integrated. The challenge is one faced by any cultural analyst: the systematic deconstruction of embedded meanings must be followed by a reconstruction of some kind. There are, unfortunately, no scripts for the reconstruction process except for the requirement of the use of multiple sources of data gathered in diverse ways as well as methods to determine the correspondence of interpreted meanings by different observers. (p. 348)

In a subsequent section of this chapter on MMR models, we discuss the importance of participatory, synergistic approaches for facilitating the process of reconstruction of a shared narrative—that is, the cultural (co-)construction of interventions. Essential to our discussion of negotiated meaning is consideration of collaborative or participatory models of intervention research.

Participatory Models

Participatory approaches to intervention development are grounded in the work of applied anthropology and international development, and in recent years, they have been adopted in educational, social, and health sciences to facilitate EBP. **Participatory action research (PAR)**, with roots in applied anthropology (Greenwood, Whyte, & Harkavy, 1993; Schensul, 1998; Schensul & Schensul, 1992), stems from efforts to create social change by involving stakeholders (those with vested interests and/or resources) in a recursive integration of theory, research, and action (action research [AR] or praxis, i.e., theory → research → practice or policy; Partridge, 1985). Intervention researchers have adopted PAR to achieve cultural grounding and/or to facilitate program acceptability, social validity (i.e., relevance to daily life), ownership, and sustainability (Cappella, Jackson, et al., 2011; Leff et al., 2009; Nastasi et al., 2004).

Before we move forward, we would like to clarify terminology. First, our choice of the term *participatory*, rather than collaborative, is based on the distinction made by Serrano-Garcia (1990): "*Collaboration* . . . denotes engaging the researched in executing the research; whereas *participation* entails their full involvement both [*sic*] in planning, decision making, and execution of tasks in the research process" (p. 174). Second, we use the term *participatory action research* although other intervention researchers use the terms *community-based participatory research* (CBPR; e.g., Jacquez, Vaughn, & Wagner, 2013; Lindamer et al., 2009) or *community-based participatory action research* (CBPAR; e.g., Maiter, Simich, Jacobson, & Wise, 2008) to denote the involvement of community members as partners in the research process. We prefer PAR because of its origins in AR *or praxis* (see Partridge,

1985) that denotes the application of research to bring about social and cultural change. Finally, the notion of praxis is consistent with science-based or reflective practice that characterizes current approaches in professional psychology, health care, and education. That is, service providers in these professions are expected to engage in EBP that relies on the recursive and reflective integration of theory, research, and practice. Indeed, concerns about translation of research to practice have their origins in the world of practice, as service providers have struggled with the mismatch between EBIs and the needs of individual clients.

Also important to our discussion is the purpose for which intervention researchers/developers have adopted participatory approaches. As noted in the previous section, participatory approaches have been recommended as critical for facilitating cultural grounding or the development of programs that address cultural and contextual diversity (e.g., Cappella, Jackson, et al., 2011; Colby et al., 2013; Gregory et al., 2012; Leff et al., 2009; Nastasi et al., 2004). Participatory approaches also have been applied for the purpose of facilitating capacity building and sustainability (Gregory et al., 2012; Ozer et al., 2008).

Furthermore, the responsibilities of intervention researchers engaged in partnerships with community members warrant attention. For example, Maiter et al. (2008) suggest that reciprocity, "[the] ongoing process of exchange with the aim of establishing and maintaining equality between parties" (p. 305), guides our relationships with community partners. Jacquez et al. (2013) propose that we examine the potential impact of research partnerships on the community members, such as the extent to which engagement of children and adolescents as partners in CBPR contributes to their own development.

In the remainder of this book, we draw examples from our own work based on the **Participatory Culture-Specific Intervention Model (PCSIM**; Nastasi et al., 2004; see also Bell, Summerville, Nastasi, MacFetters, & Earnshaw, 2015; Nastasi, Hitchcock, Varjas, et al., 2010; Varjas et al., 2006). The PCSIM reflects the application of PAR to the design, implementation, evaluation, and institutionalization of culture-specific (i.e., culturally grounded) interventions. The key elements include the involvement of key stakeholders as partners throughout the process (depicted in Figure 2.2); the recursive integration of theory, research, and practice; the primary focus on developing culturally and contextually relevant interventions; the goal of developing organizational capacity to meet the changing contextual and cultural needs; and the use of MMR.

Figure 2.2   Participatory Culture-Specific Intervention Model

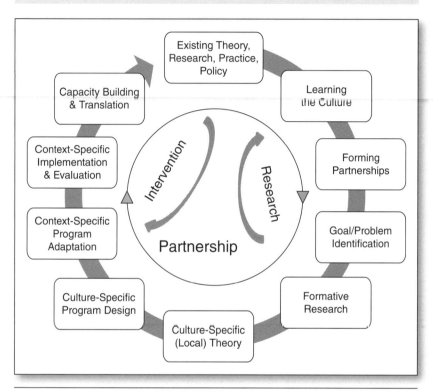

SOURCE: From Nastasi, Moore, and Varjas (2004, p. 54). Copyright 2004 by the American Psychological Association. Adapted with permission. The use of APA information does not imply endorsement by APA.

NOTE: The model includes 10 phases of program development, starting from existing research, theory, practice, and policy and concluding with capacity building and translation. The process as depicted is dynamic and recursive and involves continual reflective application of research to inform program design, implementation, adaptation, and evaluation. The goal of PCSIM is to develop acceptable, sustainable, and culturally grounded (i.e., culturally constructed or culture-specific) interventions in partnership with key stakeholders (e.g., researchers, developers, implementers, recipients, administrators).

MMR MODELS FOR PROGRAM DEVELOPMENT

This section addresses the use of MMR in intervention research to facilitate implementation, adaptation, and cultural grounding within a systems framework. The challenges faced by attempts to implement EBIs, given the myriad cultural and contextual factors that influence effective programming, have led to considerations of alternative research designs. The traditional designs for testing the efficacy of interventions are RCTs or single-case designs. Fabiano, Chafouleas, Weist, Sumi, and Humphrey (2014) identified current alternative designs that address some of the challenges we have explored in this chapter. For example, they describe cluster RCTs (CRCTs), a variation of RCT in which the unit of randomization is the context (e.g., classroom, school, school district) rather than the individual. CRCTs can be helpful in testing the efficacy of interventions delivered to groups defined by context (all students in classroom) and for examining contextual (e.g., at the school organization level) and mediating (e.g., intervention fidelity) factors. Fabiano et al. also describe adaptive treatment designs, which permit examination of the efficacy of adaptations. In these designs, when adaptations are warranted (based on ongoing evaluation), participants in the original design (e.g., RCT) are randomly reassigned to the adapted intervention, which is then tested for efficacy. The adaptive treatment designs are intended to correspond to what happens in actual practice when adaptations to the original intervention are made because there was evidence that the intervention was not effective in this context (e.g., through progress monitoring or formative evaluation). Fabiano et al. also acknowledge the potential contributions of mixed methods designs when quantitative designs are not appropriate or feasible, for example, to examine acceptability or feasibility in pilot studies or to help explain quantitative findings.

Whaley and Davis (2007) also recognize the limitations of efficacy trials; for establishing external validity and especially for addressing issues related to cultural adaptations (i.e., changes to an EBI to incorporate the cultural values, beliefs, norms, and practices of the target group). Although they do not discuss the use of mixed methods, they endorse an expanded definition of "evidence" to include qualitative methodology as a complement to traditional quantitative designs (see also Gergen, Josselson, & Freeman, 2015).

In the remainder of this section, we examine MMR designs that address the issues raised by researchers such as Fabiano et al. (2014) and Whaley and Davis (2007), namely, how to expand our definition of evidence to better examine factors related to implementation, adaptation, and cultural grounding within a systems framework. To do this, we draw from our own examination of MMR design typologies (Nastasi, Hitchcock, & Brown, 2010[2]).

---

[2] The scope of this chapter does not permit a full articulation of all MMR design typologies; for a detailed treatment of the topic, see Nastasi, Hitchcock, and Brown (2010).

First, we clarify some terminology. We use the term *research phase* to refer to the conceptualization–experiential–interferential process inherent in a research study. *Conceptualization* refers to establishing theoretical foundations, identifying purpose, and formulating research questions; e*xperiential* refers to the data collection and analysis process; and *inferential* refers to data interpretation, application, and dissemination (Nastasi, Hitchcock, & Brown, 2010). Complex designs are typically **mixed methods multistrand designs**— that is, the researchers engage in two or more research phases (i.e., iterations of conceptualization–experiential–interferential; Teddlie & Tashakkori, 2009). Multistrand designs are distinguished from *monostrand*, which refer to those with a single conceptualization–experiential–interferential sequence.

Multistrand designs require (a) the mixing of qualitative and quantitative research methods within or across two or more research phases and (b) the integration of qualitative and quantitative data during analysis and inference (see Teddlie & Tashakkori, 2009, for full discussion). Multistrand designs, by definition, go beyond single studies and thus are more likely to be implemented in multiyear research projects. *Iterative multistrand designs* involve the mixing of quantitative and qualitative methods in a dynamic and recursive manner over the course of the research project, with earlier research phases and related findings influencing decisions about later phases. **Synergistic multistrand designs**, the most complex of iterative mulitstrand designs, are those in which the integration of qualitative and quantitative methods occurs at conceptual, experiential, and interpretative stages in each phase/strand of the research. Hall and Howard (2008) propose four core principles that define synergistic MMR designs: (1) *concept of synergy*—that is, the combined effect of mixing is greater than the effect of qualitative or quantitative alone; (2) *position of equal value*—that is, qualitative and quantitative data are equivalent in importance to research; (3) *ideology of difference*—that is, the dialectical process of mixing qualitative and quantitative is critical to synergism; and (4) *reflective stance of the researcher*—that is, the necessity of critical reflection to resolve potentially conflicting qualitative–quantitative perspectives.

This integration of qualitative–quantitative perspectives in a synergistic design is likely to require interactions among multiple researchers (Hall & Howard, 2008). The reliance on partnerships and collaboration also characterizes participatory research approaches (e.g., PAR) discussed in an earlier section, but it extends the notion of partnership to include a range of stakeholders such as developers, implementers, recipients, and administrators (Denscombe, 2008; Mertens, 2007; Nastasi et al., 2007; Shulha & Wilson, 2003). The primary assumption of participatory approaches is that inclusion of other stakeholders can contribute to the development of acceptable and sustainable interventions that meet cultural and contextual needs.

We contend that multistrand (complex) MMR designs, particularly synergistic participatory approaches, are required to address the myriad questions related to implementation, adaptation, cultural grounding, and systemic factors in intervention research. The remainder of this book addresses how those

Figure 2.3 Synergistic Partnership-Based Fully Integrated Mixed Methods Research: Cycle of Research

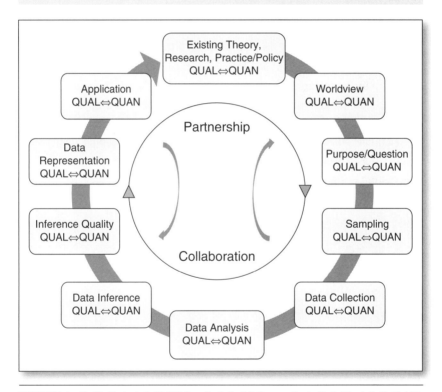

SOURCE: by B. K. Nastasi, J. H. Hitchcock, & L. M. Brown. In A. Tashakkori & C. Teddlie (Eds.), *Handbook of mixed methods in social and behavioral research* (2nd ed.; p. 323), 2010, Thousand Oaks, CA: Sage. Copyright 2010 by Sage. Reprinted with permission

NOTE: This cycle reflects the proposed inclusive framework for MMR designs applied to intervention research. The key features of the cycle are the (a) centrality of partnership with stakeholders and collaboration among researchers; (b) the cyclical nature of research from conceptualization to application; (c) the iterative nature of the cycle, depicted by the central arrows (reflecting the potential return to earlier stages based on outcomes of subsequent stages; e.g., data inference leads back to more data collection); and (d) the ongoing "mixing" and attempts at synthesizing qualitative and quantitative perspectives, methods, and data at each stage in the cycle (depicted as QUAL ⟵⟶ QUAN).

designs can be applied in a recursive research–intervention approach. To frame the subsequent discussion, we use the **synergistic partnership-based fully integrated mixed methods design model**, depicted in Figure 2.3 (Nastasi, Hitchcock, & Brown, 2010). The model is aspirational and meant to guide researchers in developing MMR designs that involve the inclusion and mixing of qualitative and quantitative data at each phase of the research process. Thus, researchers are encouraged to consider, and integrate, qualitative and quantitative perspectives as they (a) examine existing theory and research, (b) consider the worldviews of all partners, (c) formulate research purpose and questions, (d) formulate sampling strategies, (e) identify data collection and analysis methods, (f) engage in data inference, (g) plan for assurances of inference quality (e.g., reliability, validity, trustworthiness), and (h) prepare data for dissemination and application. In addition, intervention researchers are encouraged to engage research partners to maximize the expertise and perspectives necessary for an integration of qualitative and quantitative methods. Furthermore, researchers are advised to engage as community partners the full range of stakeholders who have vested interests and resources and, most important, can facilitate cultural grounding of the intervention. The model depicted in Figure 2.3 is expected to guide considerations of research design as we explore intervention design, implementation, and evaluation in subsequent chapters.

Key Terms[3]

- **Cultural competence:** Refers to a set of skills that lead to the internalization of a process of problem solving by which one recognizes, acquires, and uses information about cultural dynamics to facilitate effective interactions (communication, negotiation, intervention) across culturally diverse individuals and groups (Whaley & Davis, 2007).
- **Evidence-based cultural grounding:** Refers to an approach to adaptation that is based on formative research to systematically examine the cultural factors relevant to the intervention (see Cappella, Jackson, et al.,

---

[3] See also Chapter 1 Key Terms: context (also, ecological systems theory [EST]), culture, culture specific, cultural (co-)construction, evidence-based practice (EBP), implementation science, program (also, program services and program evaluation), translational research, and mixed methods research (MMR).

2011; Cappella, Reinke, et al., 2011; Colby et al., 2013; Nastasi et al., 2004; Nastasi, Hitchcock, Varjas, et al., 2010).

- **Intervention research:** The study of interventions that encompasses formative, efficacy, effectiveness, dissemination, and implementation studies (see Forman et al., 2003; Kratochwill & Stoiber, 2002; Ringeisen et al., 2003; Saul et al., 2008; Wandersman et al., 2008).
  - **Basic (formative) research** focuses on understanding target phenomena and developing theory to guide interventions.
  - **Dissemination (large-scale) trials** ("scaling up") are conducted to test interventions across multiple naturalistic settings (e.g., using quasi-experimental designs).
  - **Efficacy (small-scale) trials** are typically conducted under highly controlled conditions (using experimental designs, i.e., RCTs) to test theory-driven interventions that were developed based on basic (formative) research.
  - **Effectiveness (small-scale) trials** are designed to test the interventions in naturalistic settings (using experimental or quasi-experimental designs), typically following efficacy trials.
  - **Implementation (large-scale) research** is conducted in naturalistic settings to not only establish effectiveness but also to identify variables that influence program success (e.g., systemic factors, implementer expertise, population variables). Implementation research is typically concerned with identifying the conditions under which interventions are effective (see also implementation science defined in Chapter 1).
- **Mixed methods multistrand designs:** A form of complex MMR design in which researchers apply the mixing of qualitative and quantitative methods in two or more iterations of the basic research cycle (i.e., study conceptualization, data collection and analysis, data interpretation and dissemination) and engage in the integration of qualitative and quantitative data during analysis and inference (Teddlie & Tashakkori, 2009).
  - **Synergistic multistrand designs** involve the integration of qualitative and quantitative methods in all phases of the research cycle—that is, in conceptualization, data collection and analysis, and data interpretation (Hall & Howard, 2008).
  - **Synergistic partnership-based fully integrated mixed methods design model** aims to address the myriad questions related to

implementation, adaptation, cultural grounding, and systemic factors in intervention research (Nastasi, Hitchcock, & Brown, 2010). It involves the mixing of qualitative and quantitative methods and engagement of partners (coresearchers and other stakeholders) at every stage of a recursive (iterative) research process, from conceptualization to interpretation and translation. The goal of the model is to facilitate the cultural grounding of interventions that address cultural and contextual factors and promote sustainable interventions through capacity building.

- **Participatory action research (PAR):** Refers to the conduct of research in partnership with key stakeholders (those with vested interests and/or resources) for the purpose of creating social change. PAR typically involves a recursive integration of theory, research, and action (see Greenwood et al., 1993; Nastasi, Varjas, Bernstein, & Jayasena, 2000, 2004; Partridge, 1985; Schensul, 1998; Schensul & Schensul, 1992).

- **Participatory Culture-Specific Intervention Model (PCSIM):** Involves the application of PAR to the design, implementation, evaluation, and institutionalization of culture-specific (i.e., culturally grounded) interventions (Nastasi et al., 2004).

- **Program adaptation:** Refers to making changes in EBIs to accommodate cultural and contextual needs. *Designer adaptations* (by the program developer) have been distinguished from *implementer adaptations* (by the program implementers; Colby et al., 2013). In addition, *surface structure* changes to superficial elements of the program (e.g., language, images) are distinguished from *deep structure* changes to fundamental elements such as cultural values, beliefs, and norms. Adaptations to deep structure elements are more likely to threaten the internal validity of the intervention if they affect core elements (i.e., those components that are theory driven and account for program efficacy or effectiveness).

Reflective Questions and Exercises

1. Conduct a literature review on intervention programs in your area of interest. Critique the research using the following questions:

   a. What is the nature of evidence supporting the program's effectiveness? Have researchers conducted formative research? Efficacy trials? Effectiveness trials? Dissemination trials? Implementation trials?

b. To what extent have researchers considered systemic factors when establishing evidence of program effectiveness?

c. If researchers have conducted implementation trials, what variables have been investigated? Consider factors related to staff competence, organization (e.g., policies), and macrosystem (e.g., social and cultural considerations). Which of these factors were identified through the research as critical (influential) for program implementation?

d. To what extent does the research address cultural competence of stakeholders, particularly program planners, implementers, and evaluators? Describe how cultural competence is addressed.

e. To what extent was the research participatory?

2. Related to your area of interest, identify an example of program adaptation. Describe the approach to adaptation and critique for attention to deep and surface structural elements, cultural grounding, and perspectives of key stakeholders. Based on your critique, make recommendations for how you might address the aforementioned elements.

3. Identify an intervention in your area of study and outline how you would approach adaptation for a particular culture and context. Outline the steps using PCSIM as a guide. Consider how you would use MMR to facilitate adaptation and evaluation. This task may seem daunting but is a good start for thinking about application of PCSIM and MMR to program development and evaluation. Use the outline to further develop your plan as we explore application of MMR and PCSIM in subsequent chapters.

References

Barrera, M., Castro, F. G., & Steiker, H. (2011). A critical analysis of approaches to the development of preventive interventions for subcultural groups. *American Journal of Community Psychology, 48,* 439–454.

Bell, P. B., Summerville, M. A., Nastasi, B. K., MacFetters, J., & Earnshaw, E. (2015). Promoting psychological well-being in an urban school using the Participatory Culture Specific Intervention Model. *Journal of Educational and Psychological Consultation, 25,* 1–18. doi:10.1080/10474412.2014.929955

Bronfenbrenner, U. (1989). Ecological systems theory. In R. Vasta (Ed.), *Annals of child development* (Vol. 6, pp. 187–249). Greenwich, CT: JAI Press.

Bronfenbrenner, U. (1999). Environments in developmental perspective: Theoretical and operational models. In S. L. Friedman & T. D. Wachs (Eds.), *Measuring environment across the life span: Emerging methods and concepts* (pp. 3–28). Washington, DC: American Psychological Association.

Cappella, R., Jackson, D. R., Bilal, C., Hamre, B. K., & Soule, C. (2011). Bridging mental health and education in urban elementary schools: Participatory research to inform intervention development. *School Psychology Review, 40*(4), 486–508.

Cappella, E., Reinke, W. M., & Hoagwood, K. E. (2011). Advancing intervention research in school psychology: Finding the balance between process and outcome for social and behavioral interventions. *School Psychology Review, 40*(4), 455–464.

Colby, M., Hecht, M. L., Miller-Day, M., Krieger, J. L., Syvertsen, A. K., Graham, J. W., & Pettigrew, J. (2013). Adapting school-based substance use prevention curriculum through cultural grounding: A review and exemplar of adaptation processes for rural schools. *American Journal of Community Psychology, 51,* 190–205. doi:10.1007/s10464-012-9524-8

D'Augelli, A. R. (2003). Coming out in community psychology: Personal narrative and disciplinary change. *American Journal of Community Psychology, 31,* 343–354. doi:10.1023/A:1023923123720

Denscombe, M. (2008). Communities of practice: A research paradigm for the mixed methods approach. *Journal of Mixed Methods Research, 2,* 270–283.

Eccles, M. P., & Mittman, B. S. (2006). Welcome to *implementation science. Implementation Science, 1*(1). doi:10.1186/1748-5908-1-1

Fabiano, G. A., Chafouleas, S. M., Weist, M. D., Sumi, W. C., & Humphrey, N. (2014). Methodological considerations in school mental health research. *School Mental Health.* Advanced online publication. doi:10.1007/s12310-013-9117-1

Fisher, C. B., Hoagwood, K., Boyce, C., Duster, T., Frank, D. A., Grisso, T., . . . Zayas, L. H. (2002). Research ethics for mental health science involving ethnic minority children and youths. *American Psychologist, 57*(12), 1024–1040. doi:10.1037//0003-066X.57.12.1024

Fixsen, D. L., Naoom, S. F., Blase, K. A., Friedman, R. M., & Wallace, F. (2005). *Implementation research: A synthesis of the literature* (FMHI Publication No. 231). Tampa: University of South Florida, Louis de la Parte Florida Mental Health Institute, The National Implementation Research Network. Retrieved from http://nirn.fpg.unc.edu/resources/implementation-research-synthesis-literature

Forman, S. G., Shapiro, E. S., Codding, R. S., Gonzales, J. E., Reddy, L. A., Rosenfield, S. A., . . . Stoiber, K. C. (2013). Implementation science and school psychology. *School Psychology Quarterly, 28*(2), 71–100. doi:10.1037/spq0000019

Friedman, V. J., & Antal, A. B. (2005). Negotiating reality: A theory of action approach to intercultural competence. *Management Learning, 36*(1), 69–86. doi:10.1177/1350507605049904

Gergen, K. J., Josselson, R., & Freeman, M. (2015). The promises of qualitative inquiry. *American Psychologist, 70*(1), 1–9. doi:10.1037/a0038597

Goldstein, N. E. S., Kemp, K. A., Leff, S. S., & Lochman, J. E. (2013). Guidelines for adapting manualized interventions to new target populations: A step-wise approach using anger management as a model. *Clinical Psychology Science and Practice, 19*(4), 385–401.

Greenwood, D. J., Whyte, W. F., & Harkavy, I. (1993). Participatory action research as a process and as a goal. *Human Relations, 46,* 175–192.

Gregory, H., Van Orden, O., Jordan, L., Portnoy, G. A., Welsh, E., Betkowski, J., . . . DiClemente, C. C. (2012). New directions in capacity building: Incorporating cultural competence into the interactive systems framework. *American Journal of Community Psychology, 50,* 321–333. doi:10.1007/s10464-012-9508-8

Hall, B., & Howard, K. (2008). A synergistic approach: Conducting mixed methods research with typological and systemic design considerations. *Journal of Mixed Methods Research, 2,* 248–269.

Hecht, M. L., & Krieger, J. K. (2006). The principle of cultural grounding in school-based substance use prevention: The drug resistance strategies project. *Journal of Language and Social Psychology, 25,* 301–319. doi:10.1177/0261927X06289476

Jacquez, F., Vaughn, L. M., & Wagner, E. (2013). Youth as partners, participants or passive recipients: A review of children and adolescents in community-based participatory research (CBPR). *American Journal of Community Psychology, 51,* 176–189. doi:10.1007/s10464-012-9533-7

Kapadia, S., Mehrotra, C., Nastasi, B. K., & Domenech Rodriguez, M. M. (in press). International research: Possibilities and partnerships for psychology and psychologists. In M. Bullock & C. Shealy (Eds.), *Going global: How psychologists and psychology can meet a world of need.* Washington, DC: American Psychological Association.

Kazak, A. E., Hoagwood, K., Weisz, J. R., Hood, K., Kratochwill, T. R., Vargas, L. A., & Banez, G. A. (2010). A meta-systems approach to evidence-based practice for children and adolescents. *American Psychologist, 65*(2), 85–97. doi:10.1037/a0017784

Kratochwill, T. R., Hoagwood, K. E., Kazak, A. E., Weisz, J. R., Hood, K., Vargas, L. A., & Banez, G. A. (2012). Practice-based evidence for children and adolescents: Advancing the research agenda in schools. *School Psychology Review, 41*(2), 215–235.

Kratochwill, T. R., & Stoiber, K. C. (2002). Evidence-based interventions in school psychology: Conceptual foundations of the *Procedural and Coding Manual* of Division 16 and the Society for the Study of School Psychology Task Force. *School Psychology Quarterly, 17*(4), 341–389.

Lee, S. J., Altschul, I., & Mowbray, C. T. (2008). Using planned adaptation to implement evidence-based programs with new populations. *American Journal of Community Psychology, 41,* 290–303. doi:10.1007/s10464-008-9160-5

Leff, S. S., Gullan, R. L., Paskewich, B. S., Abdul-Kabir, S., Jawad, A. F., Grossman, M., Power, T. J. (2009). An initial evaluation of a culturally-adapted social problem solving and relational aggression prevention program for urban African American relationally aggressive girls. *Journal of Prevention & Intervention in the Community, 37*(4), 260–274. doi:10.1080/10852350903196274.

Lindamer, L. A., Lebowitz, B., Hough, R. L., Garcia, P., Aguirre, A., Halpain, M. C., . . . Jeste, D. V. (2009). Establishing an implementation network: Lessons learned from community-based participatory research. *Implementation Science, 4*(17). doi:10.1186/1748-5908-4-17

Maiter, S., Simich, L., Jacobson, N., & Wise, J. (2008). Reciprocity: An ethic for community-based participatory action research. *Action Research, 6*(3), 305–325. doi:10.1177/1476750307083720

May, C. (2013). Towards a general theory of implementation. *Implementation Science, 8*(18). Retrieved from http://www.implementationscience.com/content/8/1/18

Mertens, D. M. (2007). Transformative paradigm: Mixed methods and social justice. *Journal of Mixed Methods Research, 1,* 212–225. doi:10.1177/1558689807302811.

Nastasi, B. K., Hitchcock, J. H., & Brown, L. M. (2010). An inclusive framework for conceptualizing mixed methods design typologies: Moving toward fully integrated synergistic research models. In A. Tashakkori & C. Teddlie (Eds.), *Handbook of mixed methods in social and behavioral research* (2nd ed., pp. 305–338). Thousand Oaks, CA: Sage.

Nastasi, B. K., Hitchcock, J., Sarkar, S., Burkholder, G., Varjas, K., & Jayasena, A. (2007). Mixed methods in intervention research: Theory to adaptation. *Journal of Mixed Methods Research, 1*(2), 164–182. doi:10.1177/1558689806298181

Nastasi, B. K., Hitchcock, J. H., Varjas, K., Jayasena, A., Sarkar, S., Moore, R. B., . . . & Albrecht, L. (2010). School-based stress and coping program for adolescents in Sri Lanka: Using mixed methods to facilitate culture-specific programming. In K. M. T. Collins, A. J. Onwuegbuzie, & Q. G. Jiao (Vol. Eds.), *Research on stress and coping in education: Vol. 5. Toward a broader understanding of stress and coping: Mixed methods approaches* (pp. 305–342). Charlotte, NC: Information Age.

Nastasi, B. K., Moore, R. B., & Varjas, K. M. (2004). *School-based mental health services: Creating comprehensive and culturally specific programs.* Washington, DC: American Psychological Association.

Nastasi, B. K., Varjas, K., Bernstein, R., & Jayasena, A. (2000). Conducting participatory culture-specific consultation: A global perspective on multicultural consultation. *School Psychology Review, 29*(3), 401-413.

Odom, S. L. (2009). The tie that binds: Evidence-based practice, implementation science, and outcomes for children. *Topics in Early Childhood Special Education, 29,* 53–61.

Ozer, E. J., Cantor, J. P., Cruz, G. W., Fox, B., Hubbard, E., & Moret, L. (2008). The diffusion of youth-led participatory research in urban schools: The role of the prevention support system in implementation and sustainability. *American Journal of Community Psychology, 41,* 278–289. doi:10.1007/s10464-008-9173-0

Partridge, W. L. (1985). Toward a theory of practice. *American Behavioral Scientist, 29,* 139–163.

Rabin, B. A., & Brownson, R. C. (2012). Developing the terminology for dissemination and implementation research. In R. C. Brownson, G. A. Colditz, & E. K. Proctor (Eds.), *Dissemination and implementation research in health* (pp. 23–51). New York, NY: Oxford University Press.

Ringeisen, H., Henderson, K., & Hoagwood, K. (2003). Context matters: Schools and the "research to practice gap" in children's mental health. *School Psychology Review, 32*(2), 153–168.

Saul, J., Wandersman, A., Flaspohler, P., Duffy, J., Lubell, K., & Noonan, R. (2008). Research and action for bridging science and practice in prevention. *American Journal of Community Psychology, 41,* 165–170. doi:10.1007/s10464-008-9169-9

Schensul, J. J. (1998). Community-based risk prevention with urban youth. *School Psychology Review, 27,* 233–245.

Schensul, J. J., & Schensul, S. L. (1992). Collaborative research: Methods of inquiry for social change. In M. D. LeCompte, W. L. Millroy, & J. Preissle (Eds.), *The handbook of qualitative research in education* (pp. 161–200). San Diego, CA: Academic Press.

Serpell, Z. N., Clauss-Ehlers, C. S., & Weist, M. D. (2013). Next steps: Advancing culturally competent school mental health. In *Handbook of culturally responsive school mental health: Advancing research, training, practice, and policy* (pp. 251–260). New York, NY: Springer.

Serrano-Garcia, I. (1990). Implementing research: Putting our values to work. In P. Tolan, C. Keys, F. Chertok, & L. Jason (Eds.), *Researching community psychology: Issues of theory and methods* (pp. 171–182). Washington, DC: American Psychological Association.

Shulha, L. M., & Wilson, R. J. (2003). Collaborative mixed methods research. In A. Tashakkori & C. Teddlie (Eds.), *Handbook of mixed methods in social and behavioral research* (pp. 639–670). Thousand Oaks, CA: Sage.

Teddlie, C., & Tashakkori, A. (2009). *Foundations of mixed methods research: Integrating quantitative and qualitative approaches in the social and behavioral sciences.* Thousand Oaks, CA: Sage.

Trimble, J. E., Scharrón-del-Río, M. R., & Hill, J. S. (2012). Ethical considerations in the application of cultural adaptation models with ethnocultural populations. In G. Bernal & M. M. Domenech Rodríguez (Eds.), *Cultural adaptations: Tools for evidence-based practice with diverse populations* (pp. 45–67). Washington, DC: American Psychological Association.

Varjas, K., Meyers, J., Henrich, C. C., Graybill, E. C., Dew, B. J., Marshall, M. L., . . . Avant, M. (2006). Using a Participatory Culture-Specific Intervention Model to develop a peer victimization intervention. *Journal of Applied School Psychology, 22*(2), 35–57. doi:10.1300/J370v22n02_03

Wandersman, A., Duffy, J., Flaspohler, P., Noonan, R., Lubell, K., Stillman, L., . . . Saul, J. (2008). Bridging the gap between prevention research and practice: An interactive systems framework for building capacity to disseminate and implement innovations. *American Journal of Community Psychology, 41*(3–4), 171–181. doi:10.1007/s10464-008-9174-z

Weisz, J. R., Sandler, I. N., Durlak, J. A., & Anton, B. S. (2005). Promoting and protecting youth mental health through evidence-based prevention and treatment. *American Psychologist, 60*(6), 628–648. doi:10.1037/0003-066X.60.6.628

Whaley, A. L., & Davis, K. E. (2007). Competence and evidence-based practice in mental health services: A complementary perspective. *American Psychologist, 62*(6), 563–574. doi:10.1037/0003-066X.62.6.563

❊ THREE ❊

USE OF MMR TO UNDERSTAND CONTEXT AND GUIDE PROGRAM DESIGN

Learning Objectives

The key objectives of this chapter are for readers to understand the following:

- Ethnography and its inherent MMR nature
- Ethnographic research methods and criteria for establishing trustworthiness
- The use of MMR via ethnography to understand context
- The use of MMR via ethnography to guide program development

INTRODUCTION

How does one begin if one is planning to develop and evaluate a set of services in a context that is novel to the interventionist? How does one attend to cultural influences within the target ecological system? There can of course be no single answer or system, which is the driving rationale for this book. There is simply too much variation in terms of cultural nuances as they interact with intervention goals, the experience of people who deliver services, the resources that are brought to bear, and the reasons for intervening. We can, however, offer a series of general ideas that can help program designers and evaluators gather empirical data to inform decisions that make sound program design and evaluation. Put another way, we see the systematic application of research methods as the key for identifying how to conceptualize program design and evaluation, and as the title of this book hints, we see MMR as one of the best means through which to meet these objectives.

A basic stance that we adopt is that any important decision is best made in the context of good information, and systematic MMR procedures offer the key for informed programming. To this end, we hope that this book offers some ideas that are useful to a wide range of professionals who collectively have very different intervention goals, across a wide range of settings. Some of the ideas presented here, by the way, have clear relevance when intervening in a context one does not know well (e.g., responding to a crisis in a country with which one has minimal experience), but they may also be of use when dealing with familiar circumstances. When dealing with familiar cases, it may be that some operating assumptions are efficient, but it might also prevent the expert from perceiving sundry problems and opportunities. In short, we hope that the ideas presented here are applicable whether doing intervention work in a novel culture where one is operating in a country one has just set foot in or when trying an existing approach but with a new cultural group in one's own country.

ETHNOGRAPHY AND ASSOCIATED MMR
PRACTICES FOR CULTURAL STUDY AND PROGRAM DESIGN

Although we see how some ideas presented here can be applied in familiar circumstances, put that aside for a moment. Imagine that you are interested in helping with intervention conceptualization to address some given problem, and imagine that you must admit to yourself that you do not know the context well. This can be intimidating to researchers and practitioners. In our efforts to intervene, we want to make sure that we provide needed services while avoiding any potential harm because of our limited knowledge about the culture. We want to avoid engaging in EBPs that, while empirically validated for some populations, are unproven for the target population. In such situations, making connections with cultural brokers (potential liaisons who are knowledgeable about the culture and can help guide us in navigating the context) and employing ethnographic methods such as those we detail in this chapter are critical.

For those readers who are not immersed in mixed methods work, allow a brief digression about the so-called paradigm wars. Social scientists have likely heard of the idea, or, if not, most readers have probably heard that qualitative work is a weak form of inquiry. It can be described as soft, unsystematic, and inherently biased (see Patton, 2014). There is also some literature that explicitly states that one cannot mix qualitative and quantitative inquiry (e.g., Smith, 1983), and yet others who take issue with the mixing of methods (e.g., Denzin, 2010). At the outset of an MMR presentation, readers should know that we see these paradigm wars as a distraction, and we think the term itself is overwrought (disagreement seems more appropriate than war, see Onwuegbuzie, 2012). It is also hard to draw meaningful distinctions between quantitative and qualitative work, especially if one sees conducting strong research as a primary concern and any paradigm affiliation as being, at most, a secondary worry (Hitchcock & Newman, 2013; Newman & Hitchcock, 2011). There is an interesting history on the topic of paradigmatic methodological arguments (see also Creswell & Plano Clark, 2010; Tashakkori & Teddlie, 1998, 2003, 2010), but in this work, we concentrate on how to best apply a mix of different methods in order to understand a context and culture when planning interventions and evaluations. To that end, we offer the following propositions that we hope will be demonstrated by the time you finish this chapter and the book:

- Qualitative methods can be rigorous, systematic procedures that will allow you to learn critical information that is very hard and, in some cases, arguably impossible to obtain without their use.
- This is equally true of so-called quantitative research, and there is nothing inherently rigorous about a set of methods or tools.
- Rigor is found, or not, in how tools are used. Saying something like "quantitative research is rigorous" is like saying "screwdrivers build good homes." People build homes, and such people need to be proficient with using screwdrivers along with a number of other tools. In this sense, methods do not make strong studies that yield solid findings. Studies are led by people who may or may not be adept at using different methods. Once you know of a tool, worry about how well you handle it.
- Qualitative and quantitative approaches are being mixed all the time (see, e.g., the *Journal of Mixed Methods Research*), and this would seem to undermine any claim that mixing should not be done, hopefully leading any notion of a paradigm war (or argument) to become a historical footnote.

With that, in this chapter, we describe some basic concepts that will help you learn to use MMR to guide and evaluate program design in a way that is attentive to context and culture.

Ethnographic Techniques and Considerations

To say **ethnography** is the study of culture and something that anthropologists do is basically correct, but this is also somewhat like stating that psychology is the study of human behavior; this is because both statements are quite broad. Ethnography comes in many different forms, in part because there is argument surrounding the meaning of the term and how culture should be studied. To add to this, there is considerable overlap in terms of qualitative work and ethnographic methods in that both make use of observations, interviews, archival analyses, and focus groups, and they may use any variant of these techniques. Furthermore, ethnographers utilize surveys and extant data sets, and they may even test hypotheses by manipulating circumstances. *If there is an organizing principle to ethnography, it is the systematic investigation of cultural circumstances, and for this reason, ethnographic approaches are of interest to anyone interested in culturally relevant programming.*

In the pages that follow, we describe a number of data collection and broad analytic procedures that ethnographers and mixed methods researchers use to learn about contexts and the inherent culture (i.e., shared norms, beliefs, and values specific to the context). In this sense, we think of ethnography as a type of lens that focuses on cultural understanding rather than as a distinct set of methods. Furthermore, the approach we describe in many ways is guided by EST (Bronfenbrenner, 1989, 1999), which necessitates thinking more broadly of the ecological system that surrounds the context of interest (see discussion in Chapter 1). As these procedures are described, we offer occasional examples of how they may guide program design. The overall purpose of this chapter is to provide a primer on the more commonly used ethnographic techniques so as to set the stage for the remainder of the book. The data collection procedures we cover are as follows:

- Archival and artifact analyses
- Secondary data analyses
- Interviews
- Focus groups

- Naturalistic observation
- Field notes
- Elicitation techniques
- Surveys

We also discuss the criteria and related techniques for establishing the trust-worthiness of the data and briefly discuss mixing of methods. We conclude the chapter with an example of how we used ethnographic mixed methods in our own work.

Archival and Artifact Analyses

A good way to begin a description of ethnographic techniques is to describe a form of inquiry that is often done at the beginning of an investigation: ***archival and artifact analyses***. A synonymous term is *document analyses*. These kinds of analyses entail the search and review of archives, physical artifacts, and documents (Hodder, 2000). These can be documents like newspaper articles, maps, budgetary statements, poems, diaries, handwritten notes, letters, court records, photographs, advertisements, books, and so on that can help describe a setting as well as the thought processes and behaviors of the people in that setting. The use of the terms *archives* and *artifacts* promotes a slightly broader perspective, compared with the term *document analyses*, since ethnographers can and do study things like works of art (e.g., paintings, sculptures), and contemporary work must account for things like websites, e-mails, Internet postings, films, social media, and videos.

The initial examination of any particular archive can be facilitated with a few simple questions. These include but are not limited to the following:

- What is the archive?
- What information is in the archive?
- Why was it developed?
- Who developed it and when?
- How is it relevant to my questions? (Is it entirely or partially relevant?)
- How did I find it?
- How and when was it developed?
- What does it fail to tell me?
- How do I assess its accuracy and completeness?
- How does it link to other data sources?

To elaborate, suppose you are hoping to understand a highly remote, rural community in the United States. If the hope is to understand the history of the county and to gain a perspective of how people who live in and influence a place (i.e., the microsystem) interact with it as a geographic and political entity (e.g., mesosystems and exosystems), and even construe it when first hearing about the place (i.e., macrosystems), consider the above list of archival sources (meeting minutes, maps, etc.). Sometimes critical conceptualizations can be developed from such efforts. As an example, Roush studied a community in a remote, rural part of Appalachia that was home to a number of Melungeon[1] families (Roush, Hitchcock, & Johnson, 2014). Part of the motivation for this research was rooted in the fact that children from the community were required (and still are as of this writing) to travel approximately 2 hours by bus to get to their assigned district school and 2 hours to return, yet there is a neighboring, and public, school district that is about a 30-minute car ride away. It is believed that part of the reason for this kind of districting occurred because of a decision in the 1960s when people with local power did not want their children to attend school with children who were from the community of interest (in particular those who were non-White). This assertion is based on county school board notes. Fifty years on, this sort of marginalization remains, yielding real consequences, including 4 hours of daily commuting. Roush reviewed more than 60 documents, but the school board notes yielded the sort of critical information that informs overall findings, including why the school district that encompasses the community has such an odd geographic shape and some of the consequences of generational marginalization of a group of people.

Getting back to the archival analysis questions, much can be learned if one can determine if a document/archive was never meant for public viewing (e.g., a diary) or, on the other end of the spectrum, as a marketing material. This connects back to the importance of understanding the purpose of the archive. Did the author/developer of the document mean to provoke some target audience? Was it intended to provide factual information only? If so, understanding its author might yield insights into the completeness and veracity. This of course relates back to evaluation of whether the document is fully or only partially relevant to the current research project.

---

[1] The term *Melungeon* comes with some controversy, but generally, it refers to multiracial people with roots close to the Cumberland Gap area within Appalachia (so close to parts of Eastern Kentucky and Tennessee, Southeast Ohio, Western North Carolina, Southwest Virginia, etc.).

Modern software can simplify the integration of archival analyses with data taken from interviews and observations. There are many types of qualitative data analyses (Leech & Onwuegbuzie, 2007, 2008; Saldaňa, 2012), but many of them entail the basic step of condensing information into themes. Fundamentally, the theme is conceptualized as something that underlies data and can be identified by looking for patterns, natural units, incidents, and constructs that both emerge from and categorize data (Ryan & Bernard, 2003). Most readers will appreciate the experience of multiple interview informants uttering the same concept, and software packages can facilitate the search for individual words and patterns of words. This sort of search can now be expanded to archives that can become digitized. Scanned notes from documents, photographs, video, and so on can be incorporated to both expand on and check the veracity of themes (this gets into data triangulation, which is described further below). If, for example, fishermen stated in interviews that the impact of some policy reduced the incentive to fish, then perhaps this theme can be expanded on and checked by locating prior pictures of, say, a wharf where fishing boats can be seen heading out and more current video showing a lack of activity. The impact of a policy (which is an archive) may be further captured by scanning related documents and searching for wording that describes why fishing may have been reduced.

Secondary Data Analyses

In addition to accessing archives or artifacts specific to the context of interest, one might also make use of existing data sources relevant to the context, culture, or people of interest. Secondary data refers to raw data collected for other purposes, including research or evaluation. For example, communities gather census data, crime statistics, weather data, and the like. When entering a new community, one might want to access local crime statistics in order to understand past and current experiences of violence in the community. It is also commonplace for schools to gather data routinely to monitor enrollment, attendance, discipline referrals, suspensions, expulsions, academic scores, and so on. When planning to work in a school setting to intervene to prevent and reduce behavioral problems, access to discipline records would be of value. Such data could be subject to both qualitative (e.g., coding for types of infractions and related dispositions) and quantitative (frequency of discipline referrals, suspensions, and expulsions by grade level and gender) analyses—**secondary data analyses**. The availability of secondary data sets can provide a historical portrayal as well as streamline the data collection process. The availability of such data can also be beneficial as one designs plans for evaluation, as these routine practices are likely to be sustainable.

Interviews

Of the primary methods of data collection in ethnography is the individual **interview**, the purpose of which is to explore particular issues or questions with individual members of the local culture. Whom one interviews depends on the purpose. To explore the culture and topic of interest in-depth, it is typical to select a sample purposefully (rather than randomly) to gather information that will ensure understanding of the topic from the perspective of the members of the community. So, for example, if one wants to develop an intervention to address teacher stress and burnout within a district, it would be critical to first interview teachers who can help you understand the experiences of the teachers from the district. One would likely select teachers to represent the different sectors, for example, recently hired and veteran teachers, teachers across elementary and secondary levels, male and female teachers, those who teach in low-income communities and those who teach in affluent communities, and so on. One type of individual interview is the *key informant* interview; this term is typically used to denote an individual who can provide general knowledge about the context or community and what you need to consider as you approach potential participants (e.g., the local teacher union representative or popular teacher in a school). This person plays a different role from the cultural broker mentioned earlier. Whereas the cultural broker helps you navigate and interpret the culture (often throughout this initial stage and beyond), the key informant is more likely to serve as an initial contact with specific information. Nevertheless, these two roles could be fulfilled by one person, and the key informant could potentially serve in that role beyond the initial contacts.

There is much written about how to conduct interviews, such as the *Handbook of Interview Research* (e.g., Gubrium & Holstein, 2001), and our read of the qualitative research literature indicates that probably every methods text describes the procedure unless there is some highly specialized focus. This is not surprising as the interview is a fundamental data collection approach, and it is hard to conceive how one might get a sense of cultural influences without the use of the technique, unless perhaps if one were doing historical research. General principles for developing interview protocols and procedures are to start with the research questions and to consider the context at hand (due to space considerations, we do not review procedural issues, in-depth, around protocol construction, such as item wording and placement, interview length, data recording, and so on; see associated resources such as the aforementioned handbook, Patton, 2014). Then interview questions can be cross-checked with the research questions. This exercise can then help researchers consider whether they want to use a fully structured (which typically means standard-ized) protocol, a semistructured approach, or an unstructured procedure. This last option is used for fully exploratory investigations where researchers need full flexibility. But even in these cases, it is not unusual for an *emergent design* element to be invoked that allows the researcher to narrow his or her inquiry down to more precise questioning. By emergent design, we refer to an inherent flexibility in qualitative work, where research procedures and even the research questions themselves become more apparent as the researcher learns more. This does not mean that the researcher is winging it; rather, this idea can be a disciplined recognition that one does not yet know enough about a context or culture to narrow down ideas, and so an initial, exploratory stance is neces-sary. And the purpose and research questions ultimately guide this emergent process. To take two extreme examples, suppose a researcher learns of a highly isolated group that has at best had sporadic contact with other communities and historically shunned communication with others. Or suppose one is inter-ested in some cult that has formed recently and some researcher has a chance to talk with its members. In both cases, it is difficult to imagine that research-ers can rightfully conceptualize all of the key interview questions to ask in advance. But these scenarios are of course rare, and so at least the semistruc-tured approach can be advantageous, where some prior questions can be mixed with exploratory ones (e.g., Is there anything else you'd like to tell me that we've not already discussed?).

Another example of emergent design comes from our ethnographic research in Sri Lanka (Nastasi, Varjas, Sarkar, & Jayasena, 1998), in which we were trying to understand the psychological well-being of children with the intent of potentially developing interventions. Using focus group interviews with children, we initially asked questions that would help us identify common stressors. Once we had developed an exhaustive list of stressors (i.e., reached data saturation), we proceeded to gather information about children's reactions (emotional, cognitive, behavioral) to each type through additional focus group interviews. The data from this second round of interviews informed the development of structured (quantitative) questionnaires to examine reactions to stressors with a larger sample (Nastasi et al., 2007).

When a priori questions are generated, they should be informed by the overall research questions and relevant literature. Once they are developed, they can be systematically connected to analytic plans. This is because most analytic approaches follow some version of developing a coding scheme, which inform themes and then finally larger patterns that should yield answers to research questions. Codes can be distinguished as being a priori (deductive) or emerging (inductive) in nature (e.g., Nastasi, 2008). This is because researchers will have an advanced sense of codes and themes that they will likely identify by virtue of the fact that related questions are being asked. For example, if one asks about a topic like school safety, then there will be school safety codes and themes. Moreover, interviews are likely to yield information that was not part of the a priori conceptual framework, especially when one is exploring an unfamiliar culture or context.

Patton (2014) describes a procedure that can be useful in question development, whereby protocol developers are encouraged to consider (a) if they are interested in behavior, opinions, feelings, and/or knowledge; and (b) if they are interested in exploring past, present, and/or future. For example, it might be helpful to know if service providers are familiar with government policy that directs their practice. This would indicate a knowledge question: Do you know the policy? This also implies inquiry about current policy. This can be contrasted with a question such as "Do you know how policy has changed?" This remains a knowledge question but asks about past and current events. Furthermore, a question may be designed to solicit opinion about a future event, such as "In what ways do you think the policy will change over the next 5 years?" or "In what ways do you think the policy should be changed?"

Maintaining this focus can add precision and purpose in the wording and grouping of questions. When gathering interview data, it can be useful to capture not only the words respondents use but also emotions and behavior during the course of an interview—that is, both verbal and nonverbal data. Is the interviewee confident? Agitated? Bored? Evasive? Do different questions seem to elicit different emotions? When offering responses, are they accompanied with a pause, reversals in thought, and occasional wandering? This might indicate that the respondent has not thought of the topic before. By contrast, full, tight responses that are well articulated might indicate that the interviewee is accustomed to thinking about the issue at hand. Depending on the larger research questions, behavior and emotion might be forms of paradata that are secondary in nature, or they may be of primary interest.

Another consideration to individual informant interviews is that of sampling. There are a number of sampling techniques that fall within an MMR framework (see Onwuegbuzie & Collins, 2007). These can include random sampling where one may wish to make probabilistic generalizations about a population on the basis of what was observed (or learned) in a collected sample. Commonly used variants of the approach include simple random samples, stratified random sampling, and cluster sampling (Groves et al., 2009). There are also more than a dozen purposive sampling techniques. For example, one may wish to use a maximum variation approach, wherein key, relevant characteristics of sample members are identified and respondents are selected so as to ensure that a range of respondents are selected along these dimensions. Suppose a research project focused on teachers and the investigator wanted perspectives from teachers across a range of education and experience levels. In this case, purposive sampling involves searching for and selecting novice to midcareer to highly experienced veteran teachers and subdividing the group by education level. There are a number of considerations that inform which type of sampling technique, or blend of techniques, to apply. Assuming that one wishes to make inferences about some target population, random sampling is ideal, but these procedures require a number of components that may not necessarily be applicable. For instance, there should be a sampling frame, which is a list of population members from which to sample, and in some settings, this can be hard to come by (this is revisited below). Furthermore, sample representation may often not be the primary goal when conducting interviews; rather, researchers need to understand how select respondents view an issue, and there may in fact be a very small population of relevant participants. Indeed, one purposive sampling approach involves critical case sampling where a select target group is sought out to understand phenomena. This can be quite common. If the interventionist wishes, for example, to develop a highly targeted violence prevention program for a school and, in preparation, wanted to identify members of the school community who experienced physical violence while on campus, then there may not be very many people to interview. In this case, sampling takes on a very different meaning in that there is not some large population about which to make inferences. Rather, the goal is to understand how representative a set of responses is of participant experiences and perspectives.

Identifying and gaining access to such a select few can be its own challenge. Informant selection may be contingent on access to gatekeepers (e.g., key informants or cultural brokers), who are cultural members with insider knowledge of and/or influence over local context. People who experienced violence might not be initially willing to discuss their experience with strangers or otherwise be easily located, and an inside advocate can promote access. Within a small group, snowball sampling can be a useful technique. In this approach, one can ask respondents at the end of an interview to get them in contact with others who have useful insights on the topic of interest. One strategy that can help one determine if all relevant participants have been identified is *name saturation*, where repeated mention of the same people who have been interviewed yields evidence that everyone necessary has been located.

Focus Groups

Focus groups have been aligned with qualitative research and are widely viewed as a variant of the interview technique. Like individual interviews, they allow for the exploration of respondent thoughts, feelings, and perceptions, and they can follow structured, semistructured, and exploratory (unstructured) approaches. Researchers will likely be interested in both the actual responses and behavior and emotion that are displayed by respondents. The same general sampling concerns apply as well. Focus groups are, however, distinguished by a group focus that can allow for relatively efficient data collection, in that perspectives are gathered from a group of people at once. Generally, a more paramount issue is whether the researcher has questions about group processes and public concerns. If, for example, one wants to know how a group might vote on a school tax where money will be spent on the purchase of metal detectors, then it might be useful to see if the issue is divisive and if, and how, vocal respondents sway opinion as a group process. This relates to two other sides of the fact: that people are asked to describe their thoughts, feelings, opinions, and behaviors in what is essentially a public setting and that focus groups are unlikely to be applied well to private concerns unless one wants to know how such concerns are viewed by the public.

For example, if a researcher wants to understand how "adultery" (or other culturally relevant term for construct of interest) is viewed in a given culture, then a focus group might be a useful data collection technique. But it probably will not do to ask a person if he or she ever engaged in "adultery" in the presence of others. In most settings, there will be little or no variation in the answer to such a question if asked about it in front of others. On a related point, the focus group procedure probably will not work well when talking with experts. This is because answers to questions will tend to be long and involved and focus groups, relative to individual interviews, generally can cover fewer questions (with more respondents, it takes more time to get through a question). It may also be the case that experts are prone to disagree and may even argue about issues that are relatively minutia in the context of the primary research questions. However, if one is interested in identifying a consensual view from experts, a focus group might be appropriate; this would require that the interviewer has the relevant facilitation skills to manage the consensus-building process.

Although focus groups are typically analyzed to yield qualitative data, Onwuegbuzie, Dickinson, Leech, and Zoran (2010) offer a recent treatment of focus groups that is distinguished by its MMR focus. In this case, one looks for themes from focus group data with an inherent quantitative element in mind. That is, in addition to qualitative analysis for themes, one can conduct microlocuter analysis to capture elements such as respondent word counts and interlocutor analysis to capture dynamic interpersonal elements such as the number of interactions. Of course, these analyses depend on the nature of the data collected, for example, recording data in a way that permits identifying the responses of specific participants as well as the interpersonal interactions.

Naturalistic Observations

Like interviews, **naturalistic observations** can be highly structured, semistructured, or exploratory (unstructured). They can also vary in terms of length, ranging from rapid reconnaissance (observing for brief periods, often during a single session) to prolonged immersion (repeated observation over a period of time that permits understanding of full variation of behaviors), spectator status (from an outsider) to more full-participant status (to gain the insider perspective) and disclosure stance (overt cases where it is clear an observation is being done), to covert scenarios (in the hopes of seeing how participants behave in natural settings). Observation styles can also vary in focus, ranging from specific target behaviors that are of interest (e.g., the number of tantrums exhibited in math classes) to broad, holistic perspectives (Patton, 2014), and thus, it can yield quantitative and/or qualitative data. The point here is that observations can be done for very different reasons, even within one study. Furthermore, the particular observation style can be informed by the degree of focus on obtaining an emic, insider perspective at a particular juncture in a study. An MMR perspective can promote broader applications of data compared with a strictly qualitative or quantitative pursuit (again, strict paradigm allegiance may simply limit opportunity) because there can be not only inherently numeric but also exploratory, emergent, and interpretive elements to observation work. After all, one may wish to count the number of times behavior occurred, correlate its association with other events, and even try to make a qualitative inference for the cause or reason for behavior. Additionally, one may want to understand qualitative variations in the behavior and associated factors that were not predicted in advance. Like any other form of data collection, the reason for adopting one type of observational style over another should be a function of a research question. When adopting an ethnographic lens, it can be useful to try to understand the emic perspective so that the long-term and holistic observation may be of interest, but there is no reason to limit oneself to one style. Again, this should be driven by the research question at hand. Thorough recording of observations, through videotaping or detailed notetaking, can facilitate both qualitative and quantitative analysis and allow researchers to return to the data to address follow-up questions.

Field Notes

Structured observation data are generally captured via a protocol, which can even entail a scoring system. Researchers can otherwise maintain **field notes** pertaining to contacts, timing of critical events, thoughts, impressions, and so on. These can be captured in a journal and juxtaposed against initial assumptions, changes in views, and updated knowledge gained through the research process. As Nastasi and Schensul (2005) point out, field notes themselves need not only be a source of records; they can be a source of data in their own right and thus are subject to thematic analyses. Other options can be word counts, association or correlational analyses (i.e., what words tend to be paired with others), and so on. Above all, the use of field notes can promote memory of events that occurred during the course of a study and help reveal assumptions researchers make, as well as how assumptions have changed over time. Field notes are typically distinguished from naturalistic observations based on the intent of the researcher. Whereas naturalistic observations are planned and thus formalized, field notes depend on more informal and impromptu occurrences (e.g., an unplanned encounter with a teacher that provides data relevant to your research questions about discipline practices).

Elicitation Techniques

A common approach to ethnographic data collection is the use of **elicitation techniques** to explore *cultural domains*—that is, constructs or conceptual categories that reflect shared meanings among members of a cultural group (Borgatti, 1999; Spradley, 1979). For example, one might be interested in understanding the conceptualization of the psychological domain of "stressors" by urban elementary students living in a northeastern U.S. city to create local definitions. The repetition of data collection across multiple sites could provide insight into local (cultural) variations. The most common elicitation techniques are *freelist* (brainstorming) and *pilesort* (categorizing), which yield a list of the elements of a domain and the conceptual groupings within that domain (e.g., the list of stressors with groupings by type—academic, peer, family), respectively. Elicitation techniques are commonly used in the context of interviews or focus groups. A full description of these techniques is beyond the scope of this chapter; for details about data collection and analysis techniques, see Borgatti (1999).

An elicitation technique that we initially used in our work as part of an intervention and subsequently as a mixed methods data collection technique, the *ecomap*, provides information about cultural domains of stressors and supports from the perspective of children and adolescents. The use of drawing and the labeling of one's social network followed by written narration or narrative interviews yields qualitative and quantitative data about types of stressors and supports, social network size, the stress–support balance within one's social network, and feelings, cognitions, and behaviors related to stressful and supportive interactions (see Nastasi et al., 2010). (We return to the ecomap as a tool in the illustration we provide in a subsequent section and provide more detailed information about ecomaps in Chapter 6.)

Surveys

Surveys are used by ethnographers (Schensul, Schensul, & LeCompte, 1999) as they represent an efficient way to gather data from a large group of respondents. They may not be able to yield the same degree of depth as interviews and focus groups, but it is also not feasible to engage with interviews with hundreds of respondents sans considerable resources and a fair amount of standardization. Survey work might be divided into two distinct types of work: (1) instrument development and (2) survey design. The former deals with item writing and placement, whereas the latter deals with sampling an inference. MMR can inform both.

One way to think about how it can do so is to conceptualize the four sources of survey error: (1) sampling, (2) nonresponse, (3) coverage, and (4) measurement error (Dillman, Smyth, & Christian, 2009; Groves et al., 2009). Sampling error deals with the fact that sampling statistics yield imperfect estimates of population parameters—assuming that a random sample has been collected, then there is an inverse relationship between the size of such error and sample size. That is, as samples increase in size, error decreases. Nonresponse error deals with both item-level nonresponse (a person fails to complete all parts of the survey) as well as unit nonresponse (i.e., some people who should be in the sample do not respond to any part of the survey). Coverage error was alluded to in the above description of interview considerations. If a sample is to be drawn, then it should be drawn from a list, or sampling frame. If, for example, one wished to randomly sample teachers from a district, the list of employed teachers in the said district would be the relevant sampling frame. If the sampling frame accurately captured all current teachers, there would be no coverage error. But if the frame were dated, say a year old, then any newly hired teachers could not be in the sample, yielding coverage error. The last type of error—measurement— deals primarily with psychometrics and instrument design (although not entirely so). Any survey developer understands that item writing entails not only the obvious point that one needs to know what questions to ask about a phenomenon in pursuit of basic content validity but also that one needs to remain cognizant of the sort of semantic drift that can occur across contexts (consider different professions, geographies, etc.) that happens even within the same language. Add language differences into the mix, and those who study different cultures will quickly appreciate the relevance of engaging in prior qualitative work to generate targeted item writing.

Cross-language applications can be well served by back translation. This is where a survey developed in one language is translated to the target language, and translated back to the original to see if there are important differences in meaning. Thankachan, Price, and Hitchcock (2012) report a case of a survey that was developed in the United States and then was translated to the Malayalam language in India. One of the purposes of the survey was to assess if teachers thought that the use of technology applications helped motivate students to learn. Several of the items used the word *excited* (i.e., some variant of "Do students in your classroom find technology to be exciting?"). When these items were back translated, it was learned that the word *excited* took on a sexual connotation, so clearly rewriting was warranted. It was also most helpful that the step was taken before full survey administration.

From within the survey literature, there is a clear focus on using cognitive interviews to check on whether items are written in such a way so as to capture relevant information and are written in a way that is sensitive to the target population (Willis, 2005). From the MMR literature, ideas like the exploratory sequential design (Creswell & Plano Clark, 2010), where phenomena are explored using qualitative techniques and followed up with quantitative investigation, have been applied to survey design, specifically to promote improved measurement (Hitchcock et al., 2005; Hitchcock et al., 2006; Nastasi et al., 2007; Onwuegbuzie, Bustamante, & Nelson, 2010). But the advantages of this approach can also apply to nonresponse error. This is because motivation to respond to a survey is generally a social process (Dillman et al., 2009; Groves et al., 2009), and highly motivated respondents will result in decreases in nonresponse error. Careful wording of items that indicate some insider knowledge might incentivize response if those taking the survey think that they may be helping one of their own, or at least they are providing data to a group that has taken time to understand them. It is also the case that highly salient and interesting items can be strategically located within the survey. An item that is interesting might be located at the outset of the survey, for example. But, of course, knowing what is interesting generally requires detailed knowledge of the target group or population of interest, and qualitative work can provide the means to learn what is necessary to reduce nonresponse error.

Sequential MMR approaches to survey development and validation are consistent with an ethnographic focus. In doing such work, researchers can use multiple techniques such as individual interviews, focus groups, and observations to explore the meaning of constructs or variables of interest within a given cultural context. Analysis of the qualitative data is then focused on defining the constructs, identifying terminology (vocabulary), identifying examples of items, and exploring response styles that are specific to the culture of interest. These findings are used to generate survey items, and the survey is validated using quantitative methods (e.g., administration to random sample, factor analysis) and potentially normed for the population of interest. Instruments developed in this manner have been referred to as *ethnographic surveys* or questionnaires (Schensul et al., 1999). Examples of this can be found in our own work in Sri Lanka in which we developed self-report measures of perceived cultural competence and stress and coping (Hitchcock et al, 2005; Hitchcock et al., 2006; Nastasi et al., 2007).

Promoting Trustworthiness

Trustworthiness refers to the veracity or authenticity of data through evidence of credibility, transferability, dependability, and confirmability (Lincoln & Guba, 1985). These four trustworthiness criteria are intended to parallel the constructs of internal validity, external validity, reliability, and objectivity, respectively, in quantitative research. Lincoln and Guba (1985) proposed a set of techniques for establishing trustworthiness when engaging in any type of naturalistic inquiry (in our case, ethnography). These techniques encompass design and data collection, analysis, interpretation, and dissemination. Table 3.1 (Nastasi, Moore, & Varjas, 2004) summarizes Lincoln and Guba's (1985) techniques for establishing trustworthiness and relevance to the four criteria: credibility, transferability, dependability, and confirmability.

Table 3.1 Techniques for Promoting Trustworthiness of Naturalistic Inquiry

Technique	Definition
Prolonged engagement[a]	Investing sufficient time to learn the culture, build trust with stakeholders, understand the scope of target phenomena, and test for misinformation or misinterpretation due to distortion by the researcher or informant
Persistent observation[a]	Continuing process to permit identification and assessment of salient factors and investigation in sufficient detail to separate the relevant (typical) from the irrelevant (atypical)
Triangulation[a]	Data collection, analysis, and interpretation based on multiple sources, methods, investigators, and theories

Technique	Definition
Peer debriefing[a]	Engage in analytic discussions with neutral peer (e.g., colleague not involved in project)
Member checks[a]	Test veracity of the data, analytic categories (e.g., codes), interpretations, and conclusions with members of the stakeholder group to ensure the accurate representation of emic perspective
Thick description[b]	Presentation of procedures, context, and participants in sufficient detail to permit judgment by others of the similarity to potential application sites; specify minimum elements necessary to "re-create" findings
Audit trail[c, d]	Records that include raw data; documentation of all data reduction, analysis, and synthesis process and products; methodological process notes; reflexive notes; and instrument development/piloting techniques
Negative case analysis[a]	Investigate any "disconfirming" instance or outlier; continue investigation until all known cases are accounted for so that data reflect the range of variation (vs. normative portrayal)
Reflexive journal[a, b, c, d]	Researcher's personal notes—that is, documentation of researcher's thinking throughout the research process
Referential adequacy[a]	Archiving of a portion of the raw data for subsequent analysis and interpretation—that is, for verification of initial findings and conclusions

SOURCE: Nastasi, Moore, and Varjas (2004, p. 51). American Psychological Association, Washington, DC. Copyright 2004. Reprinted with permission. The use of APA information does not imply endorsement by APA.

NOTE: See Lincoln and Guba (1985) for detailed discussion of criteria and techniques.

[a.] For promoting credibility (i.e., internal validity).
[b.] For promoting transferability (i.e., external validity).
[c.] For promoting dependability (i.e., reliability).
[d.] For promoting confirmability (i.e., objectivity).

From our experience, no single study is likely to use all techniques or even the majority of them. After all, it may be difficult to engage in member checks if the study entailed working with a group that was hard to access. Or persistent observation may not be feasible given the resources or necessary in cases where rapid reconnaissance or when researchers are interested in somewhat immediate reactions to some form of stimulus. Referential adequacy may not be ideal if data are highly sensitive and agreements have been made that require strict control and exclusive access. However, to establish trustworthiness of the data, techniques that address each of the four criteria proposed by Lincoln and Guba (1985)—credibility, transferability, dependability, confirmability—need to be included in the study design and reported in study dissemination. For example, intervention developers might use triangulation through interviews with multiple sources (e.g., students, parents, and teachers), conduct member checks to confirm veracity of data and interpretations, use an audit trail that includes reflexive notes to document the process of data collection and analy sis, and provide thick description when disseminating findings. When engaged in MMR to study culture and context, it will be typical to at least engage in triangulation in one or several forms. The very nature of mixed methods means that multiple forms of data (e.g., interviews and surveys) will be collected, and this allows for the basic check of whether data yield consistent findings, and if not, why not. Indeed, a basic element of MMR work is to seek and evaluate meta-inferences, which entails both an assessment of how the data fit the research question as well as conclusions drawn from both quantitative and qualitative findings (Teddlie & Tashakkori, 2009). Identifying meta-inferences is consistent with cross-method triangulation. To that end, it is possible that the results of one form of inquiry do not necessarily corroborate findings from the other, any more than triangulation of data taken from different stakeholders necessarily need to match up. When discrepancies occur, the key is to explain them or recognize the limitation at hand if you cannot do so. (In Chapter 7, we return to the discussion of types of inference quality in MMR.)

AN ILLUSTRATION

At this juncture, we provide an illustration of the application of ethnographic MMR approach to data collection and design from our own work. The example comes from a multiyear project conducted in a local school setting for the purpose of informing the design of a comprehensive model for school-based mental health service delivery that would be specific to the culture and context. A full articulation of the process and outcomes can be found in Bell, Summerville, Nastasi, MacFetters, and Earnshaw (2015). For the purpose of illustration, we will summarize the way in which we used MMR during an extended 4-year phase of program development in an elementary charter school, delineating the research process and subsequent decisions about programming. This project follows the PCSIM that was outlined in Chapter 2, in which we used a multiyear MMR approach to inform and evaluate sustainable culture-specific programs in partnership with stakeholders.

To explore the culture-specific (school and local population) domain of mental health (psychological well-being or social, emotional, and behavioral well-being), we used an MMR approach to data collection and analysis (Bell et al., 2015). In the initial (formative) stages (Year 1), we used participant observations (e.g., school, classrooms); focus groups with students, parents, and teachers; interviews with administrators (e.g., principal) and support staff (e.g., the behavioral interventionist); ecomaps (elicitation technique) and accompanying narratives from students; and artifacts (e.g., postings in hallways and classrooms to denote school values; available curricula for social–emotional learning). Initial results of data analysis were shared with the school principal and the behavioral interventionist to make decisions about Year 2 activities. Discussion of results from formative research led to decisions to institute universal screening and initial social–emotional learning groups with students identified by the behavioral interventionist. Data collection in Year 2 consisted of the implementation of standardized, norm-referenced universal mental health screening tools to gain an understanding of the levels of risk for mental health problems within the population of students. The universal screening revealed that 53% of the student population was at elevated risk levels for emotional or behavioral problems; this was not surprising given the level of trauma and violence experienced by the student population within their family and neighborhood networks (e.g., as reflected in ecomap data). These findings, in conjunction with continued analysis of ethnographic data from Year 1 and ongoing interaction with school personnel, led to decisions to (a) begin the process of creating multitiered program of services (promotion/prevention, risk reduction/early intervention, treatment) that required establishing relationships with community-based mental health agencies, (b) hire a full-time mental health provider to begin in Year 3, (c) continue the process of screening on a regular basis to monitor mental health needs, and (d) explore the availability of universal programming (e.g., social–emotional learning) that matched the needs and values of the school population. Year 3 brought a change in school administration and necessitated additional ethnographic data collection and decisions to share findings to date with other stakeholders (teachers, parents). A multisession focus group with parents in turn resulted in a parent-led initiative to address school–family communication and educate teachers about local culture. Year 4 brought the continuation of mental health screening and extension of mental health services to include school-based mental health promotion/prevention, risk reduction/early intervention, and treatment in partnership with local agencies. Programming also was linked to ongoing monitoring and decision making (e.g., for adaptation) through the use of mixed methods research and evaluation (a topic we return to in subsequent chapters).

CONCLUSION

This chapter provided researchers and practitioners with an introduction to ethnography as a set of methods for exploring the culture of the ecological system in which one plans to implement interventions. As depicted in earlier sections of the chapter, ethnography can be characterized as a mixed methods approach that includes a range of qualitative and quantitative data collection and analysis techniques. Ethnography can be applied to program development in the formative stages to facilitate understanding of the culture and context from the perspective of stakeholders and to guide design of program elements (e.g., multitiered mental health program). As we illustrated in the example from our work, the use of multiple qualitative and quantitative methods to explore the culture and context intended for intervention can lead to the development of programming that is culture and context specific and that involves the stakeholders as partners in decision making.

In Chapters 4 and 5, we continue our discussion of MMR applied to programming. Chapter 4 addresses the use of MMR to monitor program implementation, guide program adaptations to meet contextual needs, and examine multiple components of program success. Chapter 5 addresses the broader questions about validity in program evaluation using MMR. We continue to illustrate the link between research and intervention programming in each chapter, drawing from our work across multiple settings. Furthermore, Chapter 6 provides a full illustration of MMR applied to the cycle of program design, implementation, and evaluation.

Key Terms

- **Archival and artifact analyses:** The qualitative and/or quantitative analyses of existing documents or tangible cultural products (e.g., books, artwork, photos, school curriculum, media) for the purpose of understanding the norms, values, beliefs, and practices of a specific cultural group.

- **Elicitation techniques:** Encompass a set of structured activities to explore cultural domains (constructs, conceptual categories) that reflect shared meaning among members of a cultural group (Borgatti, 1999; Spradley, 1979). Typically, they involve brainstorming (e.g., freelist) and categorization (e.g., pilesort) activities with the intent of generating a list of culture-specific elements and typology for a specific domain (e.g., stressors).

- **Ethnography:** The study of culture through disciplined inquiry in naturalistic settings to generate culture-specific portrayals of phenomena of interest (e.g., psychological well-being; Nastasi et al., 2004). In the context of this book, ethnography is conceptualized as a MMR approach to data collection and analysis for the purposes of developing interventions and prevention programs that address specific cultural and contextual needs. Common ethnographic techniques include archival/artifact and secondary data analyses, interviews, focus groups, naturalistic observations, field notes, elicitation techniques, and surveys. When using ethnography, the veracity of the findings can be established using trustworthiness techniques.

- **Field notes:** In contrast to purposeful recording that characterizes naturalistic observations, field notes involve the recording of informal interactions, observations, and interpretations of occurrences within a specific cultural context (e.g., observations as one traverses a neighborhood or meets with school personnel in the hallway or teachers' lounge).

- **Focus groups:** Interviews (typically semistructured) conducted with a small group of informants for the purpose of exploring specific topics, domains, constructs, beliefs, values, or experiences from the perspectives of cultural members. Focus groups can be used to achieve consensus among members of a cultural group.

- **Interview:** Formal or informal dialogue between a researcher and a participant for the purpose of exploring specific topics, domains, constructs, beliefs, values, or experiences from the perspective of a cultural member. The format of interviews ranges from structured to unstructured.

- **Naturalistic observations:** Observations that are conducted in real-life contexts for the purposes of studying culture- and context-specific phenomena (e.g., health care practices in community clinic, drug trade on street corner). Observations range from unstructured (narrative) to highly structured (recording occurrence and/or duration of specific behaviors) formats, and from full participation (observer interacts as agent in the setting, e.g., teacher assistant in classroom) to nonparticipation (spectator, potentially unobtrusive) formats.

- **Secondary data analyses:** The qualitative and/or quantitative analyses of existing data sets—that is, raw data collected for other purposes such as research and evaluation (e.g., school attendance records, community crime statistics).
- **Surveys:** Self-report measures for the purpose of gathering data from a large group of respondents. Within ethnography, the content is derived from formative research data (e.g., observations, interviews) to ensure culture specificity. These are referred to as *ethnographic surveys* (Schensul et al., 1999).
- **Trustworthiness:** Refers to the authenticity or veracity of qualitative data with elements that parallel internal and external validity (i.e., credibility and transferability), reliability (dependability), and objectivity (confirmability) in quantitative research (Lincoln & Guba, 1985). Trustworthiness techniques influence study design and data collection, analysis, interpretation, and dissemination (see Table 3.1).

Reflective Questions and Exercises

1. You are interested in developing intervention programs to address the effects of community violence on the psychological well-being of children living in an urban U.S. community. Thinking back to Chapter 1, why would you consider using ethnography to inform program development? How would you apply it? Describe a plan for data collection from key stakeholders.

2. Select a topic related to your discipline or specialty. Conduct a literature review to identify definitions of key constructs (e.g., stress, gender, health, illness, violence). Determine if these constructs were developed to represent the perspectives of your target audience. Develop a set of data collection activities (e.g., interviews, focus

groups, elicitation techniques) to explore the meaning of the key constructs with the intended audience. Be sure to use a variety of data collection techniques and generate specific questions or activities that you might use.

3. Suppose you were interested in the cultural norms of a target community for which you plan to develop an intervention program to promote more effective communication in social situations. How would you use ethnography to explore the cultural norms related to communication, for example, among same-age child/adolescent peers, among equal or unequal status adults, between children and adults, between friends? How might you use naturalistic observations to understand norms related to such interactions, so that you could be prepared to develop interventions to facilitate effective communication?

References

Bell, P. B., Summerville, M. A., Nastasi, B. K., MacFetters, J., & Earnshaw, E. (2015). Promoting psychological well-being in an urban school using the participatory culture specific intervention model. *Journal of Educational and Psychological Consultation, 25,* 1–18. doi:10.1080/10474412.2014.929955

Borgatti, S. P. (1999). Elicitation techniques for cultural domain analysis. In J. J. Schensul & M. D. LeCompte (Eds.), *Enhanced ethnographic methods: Audiovisual techniques, focused group interviews, and elicitation techniques* (Ethnographer's Toolkit: Book 3, pp. 115–151). Walnut Creek, CA: AltaMira Press.

Bronfenbrenner, U. (1989). Ecological systems theory. In R. Vasta (Ed.), *Annals of child development* (Vol. 6, pp. 187–249). Greenwich, CT: JAI Press.

Bronfenbrenner, U. (1999). Environments in developmental perspective: Theoretical and operational Models. In S. L. Friedman & T. D. Wachs (Eds.), *Measuring environment across the life span: Emerging methods and concepts* (pp. 3–28). Washington, DC: American Psychological Association.

Creswell, J. W., & Plano Clark, V. L. (2010). *Designing and conducting mixed methods research* (2nd ed.). Thousand Oaks, CA: Sage.

Denzin, N. K. (2010). Moments, mixed methods, and paradigm dialogs. *Qualitative Inquiry, 16,* 419–427. doi:10.1177/1077800410364608

Dillman, D. A., Smyth, J. D., & Christian, L. M. (2009). *Internet, mail and mixed-mode surveys: The tailored design method* (3rd ed.). Hoboken, NJ: Wiley.

Groves, R. M., Fowler, F. J., Couper, M. P., Lepkowski, J. M., Singer, E., & Tourangeau, R. (2009). *Survey methodology* (2nd ed.). Hoboken, NJ: Wiley.

Gubrium, J. F., & Holstein, J. A. (2001). *Handbook of interview research*. Thousand Oaks, CA: Sage.

Hitchcock, J. H., Nastasi, B. K., Dai, D., Newman, J., Jayasena, A., Bernstein-Moore, R., . . . Varjas, K. (2005). Illustrating a mixed-method approach for validating culturally specific constructs. *Journal of School Psychology, 43,* 259–278. doi:10.1016/j.jsp.2005.04.007

Hitchcock, J. H., & Newman, I. (2013). Applying an interactive quantitative–qualitative framework: How identifying common intent can enhance inquiry. *Human Resources Development Review, 12*(1), 36–52. doi:10.1177/1534484312462127

Hitchcock, J. H., Sarkar, S., Nastasi, B. K., Burkholder, G., Varjas, K., & Jayasena, A. (2006). Validating culture- and gender-specific constructs: A mixed-method approach to advance assessment procedures in cross-cultural settings. *Journal of Applied School Psychology, 22*(2), 13–33. doi:10.1300/J370v22n02_02

Hodder, I. (2000). The interpretation of documents and material culture. In N. K. Denzin & Y. S. Lincoln (Eds.), *Handbook of qualitative research* (2nd ed., pp. 707–716). Thousand Oaks, CA: Sage.

Leech, N. L., & Onwuegbuzie, A. J. (2007). An array of qualitative data analysis tools: A call for qualitative data analysis triangulation. *School Psychology Quarterly, 22,* 557–584. doi:10.1037/1045-3830.22.4.557

Leech, N. L., & Onwuegbuzie, A. J. (2008). Qualitative data analysis: A compendium of techniques and a framework for selection for school psychology research and beyond. *School Psychology Quarterly, 23,* 587–604. doi:10.1037/1045-3830.23.4.587

Lincoln, Y. S., & Guba, E. G. (1985). *Naturalistic inquiry*. Thousand Oaks, CA: Sage.

Nastasi, B. K. (2008). Advances in qualitative research. In T. Gutkin & C. Reynolds (Eds.), *The handbook of school psychology* (4th ed., pp. 30–53). New York, NY: Wiley.

Nastasi, B. K., Hitchcock, J. H., Burkholder, G., Varjas, K., Sarkar, S., & Jayasena, A. (2007). Assessing adolescents' understanding of and reactions to stress in different cultures: Results of a mixed-methods approach. *School Psychology International, 28*(2), 163–178. doi:10.1177/0143034307078092

Nastasi, B. K., Hitchcock, J. H., Varjas, K., Jayasena, A., Sarkar, S., Moore, R. B., . . . Albrecht, L. (2010). School-based stress and coping program for adolescents in Sri Lanka: Using mixed methods to facilitate culture-specific programming. In K. M. T. Collins, A. J. Onwuegbuzie, & Q. G. Jiao (Vol. Eds.), *Research on stress and coping in education: Vol. 5. Toward a broader understanding of stress and coping: Mixed methods approaches* (pp. 305–342). Charlotte, NC: Information Age.

Nastasi, B. K., Moore, R. B., & Varjas, K. M. (2004). *School-based mental health services: Creating comprehensive and culturally specific programs*. Washington, DC: American Psychological Association.

Nastasi, B. K., & Schensul, S. L. (2005). Contributions of qualitative research to the validity of intervention research. *Journal of School Psychology, 42,* 177–195. doi:10.1016/j.jsp.2005.04.003

Nastasi, B. K., Varjas, K., Sarkar, S., & Jayasena, A. (1998). Participatory model of mental health programming: Lessons learned from work in a developing country. *School Psychology Review, 27*(2), 260–276.

Newman, I., & Hitchcock, J. H. (2011). Underlying agreements between quantitative and qualitative research: The short and tall of it all. *Human Resources Development Review, 10,* 381–398. doi:10.1177/1534484311413867

Onwuegbuzie, A. J. (2012). Introduction: Putting the mixed back into quantitative and qualitative research in educational research and beyond: Moving towards the radical middle. *International Journal of Multiple Research Approaches, 6*(3), 192–219.

Onwuegbuzie, A. J., Bustamante, R. M., & Nelson, J. A. (2010). Mixed research as a tool for developing quantitative instruments. *Journal of Mixed Methods Research, 4,* 56–78. doi:10.1177/1558689809355805

Onwuegbuzie, A. J., & Collins, K. M. T. (2007). A typology of mixed methods sampling designs in social science research. *Qualitative Report, 12,* 281–316.

Onwuegbuzie, A. J., Dickinson, W. B., Leech, N. L., & Zoran, A. G. (2010). Toward more rigor in focus group research in stress and coping and beyond: A new mixed research framework for collecting and analyzing focus group data. In G. S. Gates, W. H. Gmelch, & M. Wolverton (Series Eds.) & K. M. T. Collins, A. J. Onwuegbuzie, & Q. G. Jiao (Vol. Eds.), *Research on stress and coping in education: Vol. 5. Toward a broader understanding of stress and coping: Mixed methods approaches* (pp. 243–285). Charlotte, NC: Information Age.

Patton, M. Q. (2014). *Qualitative research and evaluation methods: Integrating theory and practice* (4th ed.). Thousand Oaks, CA: Sage.

Roush, J. R., Hitchcock, J. H., & Johnson, J. (2014, April). *Educational assets, resources, barriers and social capital in a semi-isolated community of Appalachia.* Paper presented at the annual meeting of the American Education Research Association, Philadelphia, PA.

Ryan, G. R., & Bernard, H. R. (2003). Techniques to identify themes. *Field Methods, 15*(1), 85–109. doi:10.1177/1525822X02239569

Saldaňa, J. (2012). *The coding manual for qualitative researchers* (2nd ed.). Thousand Oaks, CA: Sage.

Schensul, S., Schensul, J., & LeCompte, M. (1999). *Essential ethnographic methods.* Walnut Creek, CA: AltaMira Press.

Smith, J. K. (1983). Quantitative versus qualitative research: An attempt to clarify the issue. *Educational Researcher, 12,* 6–13.

Spradley, J. P. (1979). *The ethnographic interview.* New York, NY: Holt, Rinehart, & Winston.

Tashakkori, A., & Teddlie, C. (1998). *Applied social research methods series: Vol. 46. Mixed methodology: Combining qualitative and quantitative approaches.* Thousand Oaks, CA: Sage.

Tashakkori, A., & Teddlie, C. (2003). *Handbook of mixed methods in social and behavioral research.* Thousand Oaks, CA: Sage.

Tashakkori, A., & Teddlie, C. (Eds.). (2010). *Sage handbook of mixed methods in social and behavioral research* (2nd ed.). Thousand Oaks, CA: Sage.

Teddlie, C., & Tashakkori, A. (2009). *Foundations of mixed methods research: Integrating quantitative and qualitative techniques in the social and behavioral sciences.* Thousand Oaks, CA: Sage.

Thankachan, B., Price, E., & Hitchcock, J. H. (2012, November). *Instrument piloting in a cross-cultural context: Lessons learned.* Paper presented at the 2009 annual meeting of the Mid-Western Educational Research Association (MWERA) in Evanston, IL.

Willis, G. B. (2005). *Cognitive interviewing: A tool for improving questionnaire design.* Thousand Oaks, CA: Sage.

⁑ FOUR ⁑

USE OF MMR TO GUIDE IMPLEMENTATION AND ADAPTATION

Learning Objectives

The key objectives of this chapter are for readers to understand the following:

- The Comprehensive Mixed-Methods Participatory Evaluation (CMMPE) model as the basis for using MMR in program evaluation
- The application of CMMPE for formative evaluation during program implementation
- The application of CMMPE for formative evaluation to guide data-based decision making about program adaptations
- The application of CMMPE for determining program success in summative evaluation

INTRODUCTION

In Chapter 3, we discussed the application of MMR to program design, with a focus on using research, particularly mixed methods ethnography, to understand the culture and context of interest and to examine the meaning of key constructs and phenomena from a culture-specific perspective. In this chapter, we begin at the point where program design decisions have been made based on formative research. We explore the application of MMR for purposes of monitoring, adapting, and evaluating program success. Recall the discussion in Chapter 2 of implementation and adaptation. A major concern of program implementers is whether the program is acceptable to stakeholders (e.g., feasible), socially valid (appropriate for the target population), can be implemented with integrity (preserving core features), and is achieving the desired impact (e.g., targeted changes in cognitions or behaviors). Coupled with these concerns is the recognition that *one size does not fit all* and that program modification is likely to be necessary to meet the needs and resources of the participants and context. Finally, program implementers are concerned with whether those responsible for delivering the intervention have the necessary competencies (knowledge, attitudes, skills, cultural sensitivity, etc.). These concerns are the focus of this chapter as we discuss the use of MMR to guide program implementation and adaptation. We explore here issues and methodology related to (a) **formative evaluation**, (b) program monitoring, (c) **program adaptation**, and (d) **summative evaluation**. Chapter 5 addresses validity issues particularly related to summative program evaluation. Whereas *formative evaluation* is concerned with program monitoring and guiding adaptations, *summative evaluation* is concerned with examining outcomes of interventions and the relationship of program process to outcome. In this chapter, we explore process variables in the context of formative evaluation and program monitoring and adaptation. We conclude with an example from intervention research conducted in the slum communities of Mumbai, India, for the purposes of developing sustainable sexual risk prevention programming for married adults, in partnership with local health providers and community organizations.

CONCEPTUAL AND PROCEDURAL FOUNDATIONS

We begin with a discussion of formative evaluation using **Comprehensive Mixed-Methods Participatory Evaluation** (**CMMPE**; see Figure 4.1), initially proposed by Nastasi, Moore, and Varjas (2004) and further articulated by Nastasi and Hitchcock (2008, 2009). CMMPE is based on several assumptions (Nastasi & Hitchcock, 2008, pp. 257–259).

1. *Program success is dynamic and multidimensional*. That is, success encompasses acceptability, **social validity**, integrity, **implementer competence**, **sustainability**, **institutionalization**, and changing intended outcomes (as depicted in Figure 4.1). Formative evaluation should

Figure 4.1 Comprehensive Mixed-Methods Participatory Evaluation

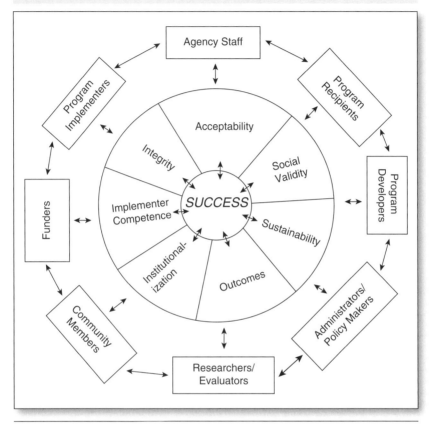

SOURCE: Nastasi, Moore, and Varjas (2004, p. 136). Copyright 2004 American Psychological Association. Adapted with permission. The use of APA information does not imply endorsement by APA.

NOTE: This model depicts the complexity of program evaluation within a participatory culture-specific program framework. Success is defined by the integration of multiple components, based on perspectives of multiple stakeholders. Determination of program success depends on the systematic integration of qualitative and quantitative data, gathered via mixed methods design. Readers are encouraged to adapt the figure when conceptualizing their own application of CMMPE, for example, substituting or adding stakeholder groups based on relevance to the setting.

address all of these dimensions as they relate to program monitoring and adaptation. Summative evaluation should address these dimensions as they relate to documenting and explaining program outcomes.

2. *The definitions and perspectives of program success are likely to vary among stakeholders.* Thus, as depicted in Figure 4.1, the views of

program developers, evaluators/researchers, funders, implementers, recipients, and related stakeholders are critical to determining success.

3. *Program evaluation has multiple purposes.* In this chapter, we discuss formative evaluation for the purposes of monitoring implementation in terms of acceptability, integrity, implementer competence, social validity, immediate impact (intended and unintended), and capacity for sustainability and institutionalization and for informing adaptations to address one or more of these dimensions (e.g., social validity, sustainability) or otherwise improve a program. Summative evaluation addresses these same dimensions as they relate to outcomes (i.e., to explore process–outcome relationships) and judging overall success and value of the program.

4. *Comprehensive program evaluation requires mixed qualitative–quantitative methods.* As we describe and illustrate in the current and subsequent chapters, the multiple perspectives and purposes inherent in the CMMPE necessitates the use of both qualitative and quantitative evaluation research methods.

5. *Comprehensive program evaluation requires participation of stakeholders.* That is, the involvement of stakeholders as partners in the process of formative and summative evaluation helps ensure that the diversity of views is reflected in the findings and facilitates ownership and sustainability of the program.

6. *Comprehensive program evaluation requires advanced planning and is integral to program implementation.* Evaluation planning is considered a part of program development. Furthermore, program monitoring and adaptation during implementation are guided by data-based decision making.

The subsequent sections of this chapter describe and illustrate the application of CMMPE to program monitoring and evaluation of the multiple dimensions of program success depicted in Figure 4.1.

MONITORING PROGRAM IMPLEMENTATION

The purpose of program monitoring is to document and assess the dimensions of program success during implementation. Using CMMPE, program developers, implementers, and evaluators engage in a participatory process of gathering data from multiple stakeholders, using qualitative and quantitative methods, and then examining data to inform decisions about continued implementation or need for program modifications and support for implementers. The primary goal of this formative evaluation process is to enhance the likelihood of program success through an iterative monitoring process, coupled with the provision of additional supports or modifications as warranted based on evaluation data. In this section, we define each dimension of success, identify relevant evaluation questions, and describe applications of mixed methods evaluation.

Program Acceptability

Acceptability refers to the perspectives of stakeholders regarding program feasibility (Is the program feasible given the resources?), importance (Does the program meet the needs of the target population?), probable success (Will the program likely achieve intended outcomes?), and congruence with stakeholder worldviews (Are the program philosophy, conceptual basis, and goals consistent with the values and beliefs of stakeholders?). Thus, the intent of assessing acceptability is to determine the extent to which stakeholders (those with vested interests and resources) support the program and thus are likely to facilitate its implementation and sustainability. Examples of mixed methods techniques to evaluate acceptability include (a) rating scales, with items relevant to the dimensions of acceptability, administered to multiple stakeholders; (b) interviews (individual or group) with key stakeholders (e.g., administrators, implementers, funders); and (c) observations of program implementation (e.g., to document implementer and recipient reactions).

Social Validity

Related to acceptability is the social validity dimension, which refers to the extent to which the program goals/objectives and intended outcomes are socially valued within the target context or everyday lives of recipients. Social validity also refers to the cultural relevance of program goals and outcomes—that is, consistency with the values, beliefs, behavioral norms, and "language" (concepts, terminology) of the target group. Relevant questions include the following: Are the program goals or intended outcomes (knowledge, beliefs, attitudes, behaviors, skills, competencies) relevant to the daily lives of program recipients? Does the program reflect cultural norms and values of the target group? As one might expect, social validity is "in the eye of the beholder"; thus, different stakeholders are likely to have varying perspectives about the social value or cultural relevance of an intervention. For example, teachers might view a behavior management program as relevant to classroom functioning, but parents might view the program as inconsistent with their disciplinary practices and irrelevant to the daily lives of children in their communities. Gathering data about perceived value and relevance from multiple stakeholders can help inform program developers about potential sources of resistance to program implementation and lead to subsequent communications about how to increase social validity. Mixed methods techniques might include (a) rating scales to examine perceived value and relevance; (b) interviews, both formal and informal, with stakeholders; and (c) observations of normative behaviors in natural contexts (e.g., classrooms, neighborhood, or peer group) to determine compatibility with program goals. **Program acceptability** and validity are considered prerequisites for integrity and sustainability, dimensions we explore in subsequent sections. That is, if stakeholders do not value program goals and outcomes, view the program as irrelevant to everyday life, or find the program difficult to implement given the available resources, they are less likely to implement the program as designed or to sustain program efforts.

Program Integrity

Program integrity (fidelity, adherence) refers to the extent to which the program is implemented as designed. Critical to promoting program integrity is the implementation of "deep structure" or core program elements that are theoretically linked to outcomes (Colby et al., 2013; see also Chapter 2). "Surface structure" or superficial elements are of less importance to integrity and are potentially subject to modification. Thus, evaluating program integrity requires documenting the core and superficial (adaptable) elements of program implementation. Evaluating program integrity serves multiple purposes: (a) to document core and adaptable elements, (b) to facilitate the examination of process–outcome links, (c) to guide program adaptations, and (d) to facilitate program transferability to other contexts. Furthermore, detailed documentation of program implementation can enhance understanding of core elements and the conditions necessary for effective programming, thus contributing to implementation science (as discussed in Chapter 2). Examples of mixed methods techniques include (a) implementer or recipient documentation and ratings of each program session, (b) observations of program implementation, (c) interviews with program implementers about the challenges and needed modifications, and (d) interviews with program recipients about core program components and activities.

Implementer Competence

As discussed in Chapter 2, the knowledge, attitudes, and skills of the implementer are critical to effective implementation and, thus, success of interventions. Program developers must ensure that implementers have the necessary competencies to implement the program with integrity and to adapt the program to meet the cultural and contextual needs of the recipients. Thus, a necessary component of program implementation is staff (implementer) training and monitoring. Evaluation of implementer competence can be conducted as part of initial and follow-up trainings and through ongoing monitoring of program implementation. The key evaluation questions include the following: What implementer competencies are necessary to carry out the intervention? Does the implementation staff have the requisite knowledge, attitudes, and skills for carrying out the intervention? What training and support are needed to ensure implementer competence? These questions should encompass competencies related not only to program content and activities but also to cultural competence of implementers (as defined in Chapter 2). Examples of mixed methods for assessing implementer competence include (a) written tests and rating scales to assess knowledge and attitudes; (b) cognitive application using hypothetical situations (e.g., to test knowledge of relevant skills); (c) behavioral application to hypothetical situations through role play; (d) implementer self-ratings of knowledge, attitudes, and skills relevant to specific sessions or components of the program; (e) observation of intervention sessions to assess skill level; and (f) individual or group interviews to assess perceived challenges and engage in problem solving. The latter three approaches (d, e, and f) could be used as part of a consultation approach to supporting implementers (see Nastasi et al., 2004); that is, evaluators/program developers observe, provide corrective feedback, and engage in collaborative problem solving to address challenges. This process also can inform program adaptation based on the experiences of implementers. (For a full discussion of a participatory consultation approach to staff development within PCSIM, see Nastasi et al., 2004.)

Program Impact

Program impact refers to the "outcomes" or effects of the intervention, both intended and unintended. Intended outcomes are linked to program goals and objectives; for example, what skills are recipients expected to acquire based on the goals of the program? Unintended outcomes refer to program effects that are not planned (i.e., not linked to goals and objectives). Program impact can occur at multiple levels; for example, interventions can result in changes in recipients, implementers, related stakeholders, and context. That is, changes in the program recipients could influence how they interact with others and influence norms relevant to specific relationships or contexts. For example, a bullying prevention program could change the nature of peer interactions and create a more peaceful school environment. Conversely, a group intervention program for "bullies" may increase the level of bullying due to peer influence and lead to a more threatening school environment (an iatrogenic effect). In both instances, the impact on peers and environment may not have been intentional, yet it is still of importance. Although questions about outcomes are typically the goal of summative evaluation, attention to program impact during implementation is critical to informing modifications and promoting appropriate progress toward program goals and objectives Essential questions during this formative phase are as follows: What are the observed impacts of the program on recipients, implementers, related stake-holders, and social contexts? How can what was learned from the observed impacts be used to improve the program? These questions can be addressed using mixed methods such as (a) periodic evaluation of immediate impact (e.g., formal assessment of changes in knowledge or attitudes following a specific number of sessions), (b) tracking changes in skills or behaviors through observation on a regular basis (e.g., daily or weekly), (c) formal or informal reports from stakeholders about observed impact (e.g., teacher reports of changes in social interactions among students, or decrease in schoolwide reports of bullying incidents), and (d) individual or group interviews with different stakeholder groups (recipients, implementers, etc.) about perceived impact at individual, group, and/or contextual levels. The perceived and actual changes that occur as a function of program implementation are likely to influence perceptions of acceptability, social validity, and potential for sustainability of the program.

PROGRAM ADAPTATION

Program adaptation refers to the process of modifying program features to meet the individual, cultural, and contextual needs of the target population. As discussed in an earlier section (and in Chapter 2), a critical consideration is whether needed modifications will affect deep (core) or surface (superficial) structure elements (see also Colby et al., 2013). Whereas surface elements (e.g., specific activities or materials) are more easily adapted, changes in core elements (e.g., the use of cognitive–behavioral strategies) can alter the theoretical underpinnings of the intervention and are more likely to affect outcomes. For example, changing an intervention from an individualistic approach (e.g., changing self-concept or enhancing self-esteem) to a collectivist approach (e.g., changing how one perceives the self in relationship to other people) based on the cultural norms and beliefs of the target population is likely to require rethinking of the target outcomes (e.g., behavior to support one's self-concept vs. behavior to improve social relationships) as well as the conceptual foundations of the intervention.

Another distinction in program adaptation (discussed in Chapter 2) is *designer versus implementer adaptations*—that is, whether modifications are done by the program designer or the individuals implementing the program (see also Colby et al., 2013). Ideally, the designers and implementers can collaborate on program adaptations, particularly changes that involve core (deep structure) elements. It is more typical that implementers will make surface structure changes in the normal course of programming to accommodate needs and resources. In this section, we discuss the use of data-based decision making (i.e., relying on formative evaluation) to inform program adaptations, whether conducted by designers or implementers. Furthermore, we recommend continued formative evaluation of adaptations to examine all program dimensions (acceptability, integrity, impact, etc.) to ensure success of the modified program.

The formative evaluation data relevant to the· key dimensions—acceptability, social validity, integrity, implementer competence, impact, and capacity for sustainability and institutionalization—provide the basis for decisions about program adaptations. Periodic review of formative data by stakeholders is advisable as part of ongoing program monitoring. Ideally, this process is participatory and involves multiple stakeholders who review data and generate potential solutions to enhance program success. What is most critical in this process is that stakeholders use mixed methods data to examine the measured impact of the intervention and determine which factors (e.g., acceptability, integrity) account for outcomes. That is, outcomes as well as process–outcome relationships are examined based on formative evaluation data (i.e., data collected to date), and these findings provide the basis for decision making. For example, analyses might indicate significant relationships between implementer competence and outcomes, in which case changes to training and support for implementers would be instituted to facilitate implementer competence, or in the case of poor outcomes, to develop the necessary competencies. Similarly, if specific intervention activities are found to have poor acceptability by recipients or implementers, and if these predict poor outcomes, then program activities are modified accordingly. Or, if data indicate that program activities are not being implemented appropriately, then efforts would be instituted to support program implementation. Thus, each dimension of success (depicted in Figure 4.1) is considered as formative data are reviewed, and then relevant adaptations are instituted. Program evaluation continues after modifications, as part of an ongoing monitoring process, to facilitate continued attention to all program dimensions and to determine if program adaptations enhance program impact.

DETERMINING OVERALL PROGRAM SUCCESS

As depicted in Figure 4.1, program "success" involves multiple dimensions and is not solely dependent on measured outcomes. Evaluating overall program success—the central goal of summative evaluation—involves assessing outcomes as well as the relationship between outcomes and other program dimensions (acceptability, integrity, etc.). Furthermore, summative evaluation requires attention to questions about program validity (e.g., internal, external, consequential), questions that we explore in depth in Chapter 5.

Assessing outcomes at the end of an evaluation is sometimes straightforward enough. In the context of an RCT, the key question is whether a treated group outperformed a control group on some dependent variable. But from there, a number of considerations arise. One must wonder about proximal versus distal outcomes, their social and consequential validity, and if any were unintended. Finally, to better understand outcomes, their processes must be evaluated (typically, this means assessing mediating and moderating factors).

Proximal outcomes are of course those that are somewhat immediate to the evaluation. If, for example, a new teaching technique were investigated, achievement scores on some test would be a proximal outcome. But there are a number of more distal concerns as well. Does improved achievement yield better life circumstances such as improved job prospects or salary? In high-income countries, this is generally a reasonable expectation. But in some other settings, the relationship might not be so clear, and researchers might want to focus on outcomes such as immediate physical health. For example, under-standing the basic science of bacteria is a great academic goal, but it might be more practical to help people see that their health may be improved if they drink water from an inspected well rather than more nearby sources such as a river where people bathe and do laundry. This leads to the important issues of social and consequential validity.

Consequential validity has been of some interest in psychometrics (Messick, 1989, 1994, 1995). Across his body of work, Messick expanded some aspects of construct validity to focus on understanding the consequences of measurement and unintended goals. If, for example, some cultural group is harmed by the results of its testing, then this calls into question the validity evidence supporting the use of the measure. This is no small or abstract issue when considering ongoing tensions associated with standardized testing in the United States over potential social injustices (e.g., promoting continued social and economic inequities). As researchers who are interested in culturally rel-evant program evaluation, we are also interested in careful understanding of how well an outcome measure is suited to a setting and the consequences of poor measurement.

Critical to understanding potential social and political issues associated with evaluation is the assessment of social validity from the perspective of summative MMR evaluation. Consider, for example, behavioral modification and compliance. Improved behavior and compliance represent socially valued outcomes in most settings, but the degree of compliance will vary by culture. In the United States, for example, total compliance is anathema to other ideas such as individualization, self-determination, and free will. If an overzealous compliance agenda were applied in schools, the outcomes would probably not be socially valid. If it were realized, a consequence is that children exposed to the program would not be adequately prepared to function in U.S. society. In this way, outcomes interact with fidelity (see Figure 4.1): The poor social validity would likely undermine program effectiveness because stakeholders would probably reject it. It may also be the case that interventionists wish to focus on an outcome that is not immediately valued by some stakeholders (recall, for example, the idea about algebra from Chapter 1 where one might want to focus more on the generalization of algebraic thinking beyond the rote memorization of facts); doing so represents the additional set of challenges that entails changing perceptions about what is important. Needless to say, open-ended, exploratory work that entails interpretation of interview statements, observed behavior, and documents like newspaper accounts may be critical for assessing whether an outcome is valued. In this sense, we hope that the role of deep qualitative inquiry in outcome selection or development is self-evident, particularly if one is involved in culturally relevant programming.

A final point about outcomes is that it is necessary to understand factors that alter or influence them. In a quantitative sense, this involves mediators and moderators. *Mediators* might be assessed by asking questions about the relationship of a treatment effect to dosage or fidelity, whereas *moderators* might, for example, focus more on whether some group experiences stronger outcomes than another (e.g., if males experience better mental health outcomes compared with females). These considerations are not inherently quantitative in orientation; we just use the *mediator* and *moderator* terms for convenience, and understanding such influences is promoted by CMMPE. Any strong qualitative understanding of context will entail understanding of whether subgroups or different stakeholders have different viewpoints about a set of outcomes or experience program effects in different ways. Moreover, qualitative methods can help facilitate the identification of program processes that influence or explain program outcomes. For example, consider a situation in which teachers who were most likely to implement the program with fidelity were also those who expressed the highest levels of acceptability and perceived social validity; their students also experienced the greatest gains on program outcomes. These connections became evident in interviews with teachers and were confirmed through statistical analyses.

CAPACITY FOR SUSTAINABILITY AND INSTITUTIONALIZATION

Both of these dimensions deal with the likelihood that stakeholders and organizations can continue intervention programming beyond a particular project period (typically, when external program developers and funders cease their involvement). Program *sustainability* addresses the extent to which implementers can continue the program without external support—that is, that they have necessary skills and motivation to sustain program efforts. Of course, sustainability depends on other dimensions such as acceptability, social validity, integrity, implementer competence, and perceived outcomes.

Institutionalization refers more broadly to the capacity of the organization or system to continue specific or related program efforts over time and the extent to which programming has become integral to the system. Related questions for these dimensions include the following: Does the organization have the necessary infrastructure and capacity (e.g., policies, finances, staff) to continue programming? Does the organization have the capacity (e.g., staff competence) to adapt interventions to meet changing population, cultural, and contextual needs? Are the organizational leaders and other stakeholders committed to program continuation and willing to commit needed resources? Again, the level of institutionalization is likely to be influenced by perceptions of acceptability and social validity and observed individual and contextual/ organization impacts. Thus, administrators are more likely to commit resources (time, money, and staff) to programming if they view a positive impact on the recipients, the implementers, and the overall climate of the organization. For example, if an antibullying program addresses student discipline (behavior) problems that plague the school, teachers have developed skills needed to prepare students in alternative interpersonal interactions, the level (frequency, intensity) of student bullying has declined, and the school has a more peaceful climate, then the principal is more likely to view the program as successful and commit necessary resources for continuation.

Formative evaluation (during program implementation) of sustainability and institutionalization focuses on the capacity of the implementers and the organization. Thus, related to the aforementioned questions, evaluators are interested in whether stakeholders are both committed to program continuation and recognize what resources are necessary for long-term sustainability. Mixed methods evaluation techniques that specifically address these dimensions can include key stakeholder rating scales and interviews and observations of staff interactions (e.g., faculty meetings) that reflect the views of the program and its perceived long-term value. Given the link to other program dimensions (e.g., acceptability, social validity, outcomes), data on sustainability and institutionalization can be collected as part of the evaluation of these dimensions. Furthermore, sharing data with organizational leaders and other key stakeholders about program success (e.g., as member checking) can facilitate discussion and decision making about the long-term continuation of programming following summative evaluation.

AN ILLUSTRATION

To illustrate the application of CMMPE for program monitoring and adaptation, we draw from a 12-year (2001–2013) intervention research and development program conducted in the slum communities of Mumbai, India.[1] The program, titled *Research and Intervention for Sexual Health: Theory to Action* (RISHTA, which means "relationship" in the Hindi and Urdu languages), was an interdisciplinary public health project to reduce sexually transmitted infections among married men and women. The primary goal was to develop and test culture-specific interventions to be delivered in health care and community settings. The project involved (a) development and evaluation of multiple interventions, including the integration of health education and risk reduction in primary care for men, delivered by medical practitioners; (b) individual counseling for women visiting an urban health care facility, delivered by mental health professionals; (c) group-based couples' intervention for married heterosexual couples, delivered in community settings by community educators; and (d) community education conducted by peer educators, religious leaders, and community agencies. The general approach to

---

[1] The research and intervention program known as *RISHTA* (meaning "relationship" in Hindi/Urdu and an acronym for *Research and Intervention on Sexual Health: Theory to Action*), has included three NIH-funded projects, spanning 12 years (2001–2013): (a) Men's Sexual Concerns and Prevention of HIV/STI (RO1MH64875; PI, S. Schensul; Co-PIs, B. Nastasi, R. Verma, 2001–2007); (b) supplement, Assessing Women's Risk of HIV/STI Transmission Within Marriage in India, funded by the U.S. Office of AIDS Research of NIH (2002–2006); and (c) Prevention of HIV/STI Among Married Women in Urban India (R01MH075678; PI, S. Schensul; Co-PIs, R. Verma, B. Nastasi, N. Saggurti, S. Maitra, R. Aras, A. Pandey, J. Schensul, A. Mekki-Berrada, 2007–2013). Publications from these projects include Davis et al. (2014), Kostick et al. (2010), Kostick, Schensul, Singh, Pelto, and Saggurti (2011), Mehrotra, Schensul, Saggurti, Burleson, and Maitra (2014), Nastasi et al. (2013), Nastasi et al. (2014), Nastasi and Hitchcock (2009), Nastasi, Saggurti, Schensul, Verma, and Gandhi (2007), Saggurti et al. (2013), Schensul et al. (2007), Schensul, Mekki-Berrada, Nastasi, and Saggurti (2006), Schensul, Mekki-Berrada, Nastasi, Singh, et al. (2006), Schensul, Nastasi, and Verma (2006), Schensul, Saggurti, et al. (2009), Schensul, Verma, and Nastasi (2004), and Schensul, Verma, Nastasi, Saggurti, and Mekki-Berrada (2009). The illustration in this chapter is drawn from unpublished documents related to work conducted with married couples in the third project.

program development was consistent with the PCSIM (Nastasi et al., 2004; described in Chapter 2) and involved the use of MMR to inform intervention development and evaluation.

We describe the evaluation of one component of the 12-year program, the couples' intervention, to illustrate the application of MMR to guide program implementation and adaptation. The six-session intervention program (Nastasi, Maitra, & Members of the RISHTA Intervention and Research Team, 2013) was culturally constructed based on existing theory (e.g., cognitive–behavioral, social construction) and several years of formative research to understand the psychological, relational, and social–cultural factors that influenced sexual risk of the target population of married men and women. The program objectives included (a) enhancing knowledge, attitudes, and skills related to marital communication and conflict resolution; (b) reducing tension; (c) decreasing sexual risk; and (d) improving the quality of marital relationship. Sessions were structured so that men and women met separately for the first four sessions (focused on enhancing knowledge, attitude, and skills) and then as couples in the last two sessions (focused on application through experiential activities). All sessions were cofacilitated by same-gender educators. Program implementers received specialized training and support from program designers, including initial training relevant to the program content and process, and ongoing supervision, consultation, and follow-up training throughout the project implementation. The intervention was delivered to multiple groups of participants over 2.5 years.

Evaluation followed principles of CMMPE, as articulated in an earlier section, with formative evaluation focused on program monitoring and adaptation. The components of program evaluation included (a) acceptability, (b) social validity, (c) integrity, (d) implementer competence, (e) impact/outcomes, and (f) capacity for sustainability and institutionalization. In addition, data were collected from recipients, implementers, and through direct observation by program evaluators/designers. Methods for data collection included (a) session observations, (b) postsession interviews, (c) rating scales, (d) session logs, (e) consultation with implementers, and (f) immediate posttest measure of program outcomes. Summative evaluation also included 6-month and 1-year outcome assessments and community surveys. As groups were initiated throughout the 2.5-year intervention period, data from earlier groups (including findings from immediate posttests) could inform adaptations for later groups.

Table 4.1 illustrates the application of multiple mixed methods (observation, interview, rating scales, session logs, consultation, and self-report questionnaires as posttests) to evaluate, from multiple stakeholder perspectives (recipient, implementer, and designer/evaluator), the multiple dimensions of success: acceptability, social validity, integrity, implementer competence, impact, and capacity for sustainability and institutionalization. The scope of the evaluation may seem daunting until one looks more closely at how the evaluation was conducted. That is, each data collection method encompassed multiple components of success (as shown in Table 4.1), and ongoing data collection informed consultation with implementers, thus adding to the immediate value of data collection.

Narrative observations were conducted in all sessions by one of the implementation staff (not involved in implementing the respective session) and were conducted by a program evaluator in 10% of the sessions. In addition, program designers (who also provided consultation and follow-up training) observed the sessions periodically. These observations were designed to yield data on all dimensions of success. To facilitate observations, program designers developed guidelines that provided (a) general observation requirements (e.g., detailed narrative of verbal and nonverbal behavior and seating arrangements), (b) detailed process and content components for each session (e.g., required activities for each session), (c) indicators of implementer competence, and (d) indicators of recipient and implementer acceptability and social validity. Program implementers completed semistructured session logs that included (a) documentation of specific activities; (b) ratings of activity completion, effectiveness, and adaptations; (c) explanation of difficulties/adaptations; (d) self-ratings of implementer competence; (e) ratings of recipient and implementer acceptability and social validity; and (f) general comments.

Following 10% of the sessions across the 2.5-year duration, program recipients were interviewed by project evaluators using a semistructured interview format, to evaluate acceptability, social validity, and session integrity. At program conclusion (i.e., following six sessions), semistructured interviews were conducted with recipients and implementers to evaluate acceptability, social validity, integrity, implementer competence, perceived impact, and sustainability. In addition, program recipients completed self-report questionnaires as posttests to assess program outcomes (e.g., program-related knowledge, attitudes, and skills).

Table 4.1 Application of Comprehensive Mixed-Methods Participatory Evaluation to the Evaluation of Married Couples' Sexual Risk Prevention Program

	Narrative Observation[r,i,d/e]	Interviews[r,i]	Rating Scales[r,i]	Session Logs/ Notes[i,d/e]	Consultation Sessions[i,d/e]	Immediate Posttest[r]
Acceptability	X	X	X	X	X	X
Social validity	X	X	X	X	X	X
Integrity	X	X	X	X	X	X
Implementer competence	X	X	X	X	X	X
Impact	X	X	X	X	X	X
Sustainability/institutionalization capacity	X	X	X	X	X	

SOURCE: The information in this table is drawn from unpublished work conducted with married couples in the following project: *Prevention of HIV/STI Among Married Women in Urban India* (Principal Investigator [PI], S. Schensul; Co-PIs, R. Verma, B. Nastasi, N. Saggurti, S. Maitra, R. Aras, A. Pandey, J. Schensul, A. Mekki-Berrada R01MH075678, 2007–2013). See Footnote 1 (p. 94) for further description; additional information about the study can be obtained from the first author, Nastasi.

NOTE: *r* = recipient perspective; *i* = implementer perspective; *d/e* = program designer/evaluator perspective. This table depicts the use of mixed methods (narrative observation, interviews, rating scales, sessions logs/notes, consultation sessions, posttest questionnaire) to assess components of program success (acceptability, social validity, integrity, implementer competence, impact, sustainability, and institutionalization capacity) from the perspectives of multiple stakeholders (program recipients, implementers, and designers and evaluators).

Throughout implementation, program designers conducted regular follow-up sessions for the purposes of consultation, supervision, and training. These sessions provided the opportunity to gather data from implementers about all dimensions of program success and to discuss the need for adaptations to address implementation challenges. On the basis of these sessions, as well as ongoing data collection, program designers in collaboration with implementers made decisions about adaptations. An example of an adaptation that was a response to feedback from recipients and implementers was an increased focus on sexual knowledge. That is, program recipients expressed an interest in learning more about sexuality and sexual risk, and implementers observed more limited knowledge than expected. Similarly, based on session observations and implementer feedback, program designers provided additional training for implementers to enhance knowledge and skill related to the presentation and discussion of sexuality.

Although beyond the focus of this chapter, the extensive collection of formative evaluation data provided the basis for mixed methods analysis of program success and examination of process–outcomes relationships. Furthermore, formative evaluation contributed to the development of a manual (Nastasi et al., 2013) that was distributed to service providers and policymakers during local and national dissemination conferences. These conferences focused on sharing evaluation data and discussing issues regarding capacity for sustainability and institutionalization.

CONCLUSION

The purpose of this chapter was to describe the application of mixed methods to the evaluation of intervention programs. We introduced the CMMPE as the conceptual and procedural foundation for program evaluation using multiple dimensions and multiple perspectives to define program success. The CMMPE is especially helpful when program developers and evaluators are interested in understanding intervention processes and outcomes and their relationship. CMMPE also facilitates the use of evaluation to inform program monitoring and adaptation. Furthermore, this model can facilitate the participation of multiple stakeholders and help ensure program effectiveness, sustainability, and institutionalization. We illustrated the application of CMMPE to the evaluation of a community-based prevention program. In the next chapter, we examine issues related to the validity of intervention programs, which are typically applied to evaluating program outcomes but have relevance to the multiple dimensions reflected in CMMPE.

Key Terms

- **Comprehensive Mixed-Methods Participatory Evaluation (CMMPE):** A model for evaluation that depicts the complexity of program evaluation within a participatory culture-specific program framework. Success is defined by the integration of multiple components, based on perspectives of multiple stakeholders. Determination of program success depends on the systematic integration of qualitative and quantitative data gathered via mixed methods design.
- **Formative evaluation:** Program evaluation for the purpose of monitoring implementation in terms of acceptability, integrity, implementer competence, social validity, immediate impact (intended and unintended), and capacity for sustainability and institutionalization and for informing adaptations to address one or more of these dimensions (e.g., social validity, sustainability) or otherwise improve a program.
- **Implementer competence:** The knowledge, attitudes, and skills of those delivering the program that are necessary to implement the program with integrity and to adapt the program to meet the cultural and contextual needs of the recipients.
- **Institutionalization:** The capacity of the organization to continue specific or related program efforts over time and the extent to which programming has become integral to the system.
- **Program acceptability:** The perspectives of stakeholders regarding program feasibility, importance, probable success, and congruence with stakeholder worldviews.
- **Program adaptation:** The process of modifying program features/ elements to meet individual, cultural, and contextual needs of the target population. It refers to both deep (core) and surface (superficial) structure features and to designer and implementer adaptations.
- **Program impact:** The intended or unintended effects of the intervention on recipients, implementers, related stakeholders, or context. It is also referred to as program outcome.

- **Program integrity:** The extent to which the program is implemented as designed. It is also referred to as fidelity or adherence.
- **Social validity:** The perspectives of stakeholders about the value and cultural relevance of program goals and intended outcomes within the target context and everyday lives of program recipients.
- **Summative evaluation:** Program evaluation for the purpose of determining the success or value of an intervention. Summative evaluation focuses not only on short- and long-term program outcomes (intended and unintended) but also on program acceptability, integrity, implementer competence, social validity, and capacity for sustainability and institutionalization. Summative evaluation also addresses questions about the relationship between process (e.g., integrity, implementer competence) and outcomes.
- **Sustainability:** The extent to which implementers have the necessary skills and motivation to continue intervention efforts without external support.

Reflective Questions and Exercises

1. Identify an intervention you are interested in conducting with a specific population and context (e.g., you might select an EBI you identified through a literature review or a manualized treatment that is commercially available). Answer the following questions:
   a. Has the intervention been validated for your intended population and context?
   b. What are the core (deep structure) and adaptable (surface structure) elements of the intervention?
   c. What information is necessary to determine if the program is culturally and contextually appropriate to the intended setting and population?

2. Based on responses to #1, develop a data collection plan consistent with CMMPE (Figure 4.1) to accomplish the following:
   a. Determine what adaptations are needed to make the program culturally and contextually relevant.
   b. After adapting the program, conduct formative evaluation to examine the dimensions of success in order to inform further program modification.
   c. Conduct an outcome evaluation.

For a, b, and c, be sure to identify the types of data you would collect to address the multiple dimensions of success depicted in Figure 4.1, determine the informants, and develop a time line for data collection.

3. You have been asked to develop a formative evaluation plan for a community-based health promotion program (choose a health topic of interest). Develop the following:

   a. An interview protocol to assess acceptability, social validity, integrity, perceived implementer competence, and perceived impact from the perspective of program implementers.

   b. Guidelines for observing acceptability, social validity, integrity, implementer competence, and perceived impact during program sessions.

References

Colby, M., Hecht, M. L., Miller-Day, M., Krieger, J. L., Syvertsen, A. K., Graham, J. W., & Pettigrew, J. (2013). Adapting school-based substance use prevention curriculum through cultural grounding: A review and exemplar of adaptation processes for rural schools. *American Journal of Community Psychology, 51,* 190–205. doi:10.1007/s10464-012-9524-8

Davis, L. M., Schensul, S. L., Schensul, J. J., Verma, R., Nastasi, B. K., & Singh, R. (2014). Women's empowerment and its differential impact on health in low income communities in Mumbai, India. *Global Public Health: An International Journal for Research, Policy and Practice.* Advance online publication. doi:10.1 080/17441692.2014.904919

Kostick, K. M., Schensul, S. L., Jadhav, K., Singh, R., Bavadekar, A., & Saggurti, N. (2010). Treatment seeking, vaginal discharge and psychosocial distress among women in urban Mumbai. *Culture, Medicine and Psychiatry, 34,* 529–547. doi:10.1007/s11013-010-9185-8

Kostick, K. M., Schensul, S. L., Singh, R., Pelto, P., & Saggurti, N. (2011). A methodology for building culture and gender norms into intervention: An example from Mumbai, India. *Social Science & Medicine, 72*(10), 1630–1638. doi:10.1016/j.socscimed.2011.03.029

Mehrotra, P., Schensul, S. L., Saggurti, N., Burleson, J. A., & Maitra, S. (2014). The WHO concept of sexual health applied to an urban poor community in Mumbai, India. *International Journal of Sexual Health.* Advance online publication. doi:10.1080/19317611.2014.942487

Messick, S. (1989). Validity. In R. L. Linn (Ed.), *Educational measurement* (3rd ed., pp. 13–103). Upper Saddle River, NJ: Merrill/Prentice Hall.

Messick, S. (1994). The interplay of evidence and consequences in the validation of performance assessments. *Educational Researcher, 23,* 13–23.

Messick, S. (1995). Validity of psychological assessment: Validation of inferences from persons' responses and performances as scientific inquiry into score meaning. *American Psychologist, 50,* 741–749.

Nastasi, B. K., & Hitchcock, J. H. (2008). Evaluating quality and effectiveness of population-based services. In B. J. Doll & J. A. Cummings (Eds.), *Transforming school mental health services: Population-based approaches to promoting the competency and wellness of children* (pp. 245–276). Thousand Oaks, CA: Corwin Press with National Association of School Psychologists.

Nastasi, B. K., & Hitchcock, J. (2009). Challenges of evaluating multi-level interventions. *American Journal of Community Psychology, 43,* 360–376. doi:10.1007/s10464-009-9239-7

Nastasi, B. K., Maitra, S., & Members of the RISHTA Intervention and Research Team. (2013). *Narrative prevention counseling (NPC) for married women and couples: Promoting sexual health, psychological well-being and healthy marital relationships through individual counseling* (A manual developed as a part of the RISHTA project: Research and Intervention in Sexual Health: Theory to Action). New Delhi, India: International Center for Research on Women.

Nastasi, B. K., Moore, R. B., & Varjas, K. M. (2004). *School-based mental health services: Creating comprehensive and culturally specific programs.* Washington, DC: American Psychological Association.

Nastasi, B. K., Saggurti, N., Schensul, S. L., Verma, R. V., & Gandhi, M. (2007). *Addressing gupt rog: Narrative prevention counseling for STI/HIV prevention: A guide to AYUSH and allopathic practitioners.* New Delhi, India: Population Council.

Nastasi, B. K., Schensul, J. J., Schensul, S. L., Mekki-Berrada, A., Pelto, B., Maitra, S., . . . Saggurti, N. (2015). A model for translating ethnography and theory into culturally constructed clinical practice. *Culture, Medicine and Psychiatry, 39,* 92–109. doi:10.1007/s11013-014-9404-9

Saggurti, N., Schensul, S. L., Nastasi, B. K., Singh, R., Burleson, J. A., & Verma, R. K. (2013). Effects of a health care provider intervention in reduction of sexual risk and related outcomes in economically marginal communities in Mumbai, India. *Sexual Health.* Advance online publication. doi:10.1071/SH13076

Schensul, S. L., Hawkes, S., Saggurti, N., Verma, R. K., Narvekar, S. S., Nastasi, B. K., . . . Risbud, A. (2007). Sexually transmitted infections in men in Mumbai slum communities: The relationship of prevalence to risk behavior. *Sexually Transmitted Diseases, 34*(7), 444–450. doi:10.1097/01.olq.0000249776.92490.3

Schensul, S. L., Mekki-Berrada, A., Nastasi, B. K., & Saggurti, N. (2006). Healing traditions and men's sexual health in Mumbai, India: The realities of practiced medicine in urban poor communities. *Social Sciences & Medicine, 62,* 2774–2785. doi:10.1016/j.socscimed.2005.11.003

Schensul, S. L., Mekki-Berrada, A., Nastasi, B. K., Singh, R., Burleson, J. A., & Bojko, M. (2006). Men's extramarital sex, marital relationships and sexual risk in urban poor communities in India. *Journal of Urban Health: Bulletin of the New York Academy of Medicine, 83,* 614–624. doi:10.1007/s11524-006-9076-z

Schensul, S. L., Nastasi, B. K., & Verma, R. K. (2006). Community-based research in India: A case example of international and interdisciplinary collaboration. *American Journal of Community Psychology, 38*(1–2), 95–111. doi:10.1007/s10464-006-9066-z.

Schensul, S. L., Saggurti, N., Singh, R., Verma, R. K., Nastasi, B. K., & Mazumder, P. G. (2009). Multilevel perspectives on community intervention: An example from an Indo-US HIV prevention project in Mumbai, India. *American Journal of Community Psychology, 43,* 277–291. doi:10.1007/s10464-009-9241-0

Schensul, S. L., Verma, R. K., & Nastasi, B. K. (2004). Responding to men's sexual concerns: Research and intervention in slum communities in Mumbai, India. *International Journal of Men's Health, 3*(3), 197–220.

Schensul, S., Verma, R. K., Nastasi, B. K., Saggurti, N., & Mekki-Berrada, A. (2009). Sexual risk reduction among married women and men in urban India: An anthropological intervention. In M. Inhorn & R. Hahn (Eds.), *Anthropology and public health: Bridging differences in culture and society* (2nd ed., pp. 362–396). New York, NY: Oxford University Press.

⚜ FIVE ⚜

USE OF MMR TO ADDRESS VALIDITY CONCERNS IN PROGRAM EVALUATION

Learning Objectives

The key objectives of this chapter are for readers to do the following:

- Consider common questions associated with summative evaluation that have implications for CMMPE
- Understand how MMR designs can enhance assessment of experimental design validity
- Understand how MMR can promote understanding of generalization and transferability

INTRODUCTION

In Chapter 4, we discussed the application of MMR to evaluation for the purpose of monitoring and adapting interventions during implementation and for determining program success. We presented the CMMPE (see Figure 4.1) as a conceptual and procedural model for guiding formative and **summative evaluation** of the multiple dimensions of success and from the perspective of multiple stakeholders. As depicted in Figure 4.1, outcomes are one dimension of program success. However, even as we examine the effects of the interventions during summative evaluation, it is still important to examine the influence of other dimensions of success (e.g., acceptability, integrity). Only by considering the broader definition of program success can we understand and explain what contributed to outcomes and thereby facilitate generalization, transferability, or **translation** of EBIs. In this chapter, we explore the application of MMR to answer questions about validity (causal, social, consequential) and generalization (also, transferability and translation) of findings. Most important to our discussion, we hope that the information presented here helps readers to think through cultural and contextual matches between intervention work, program evaluation, and setting.

CONCEPTUAL AND PROCEDURAL CONSIDERATIONS

When thinking about the application of MMR to program evaluation, it is important to consider that there are many types of models that inform design, ranging from relatively straightforward mixing of qualitative and quantitative design to fairly complex multistage programs of research that are iterative (early studies influence later design, research question formulation, and theory refinement) and intentionally synergistic (as in the idea that the whole product, or set of findings, is greater than the sum of its component parts). Nastasi, Hitchcock, and Brown (2010) summarize several different models, or typologies. An example of how a more complex model has been used to evaluate a culturally specific program is provided at the end of this chapter (see also Figure 2.3). Leading up to the example, concerns around issues of summative evaluation, causality, outcomes, and generalization of findings are described in light of straightforward applications of mixing in the hope of demonstrating to readers the idea that weaknesses in one form of inquiry can be addressed by the strength of another. This can be done via fundamental mixing concepts (see Greene, Caracelli, & Graham, 1989) like *triangulation* of evidence, whereby qualitative and quantitative findings can be examined for convergence; *complementary* application, where one approach is more suited than another to collect and interpret data (e.g., qualitative methods tend to be better at exploration and in-depth understanding of perceptions, quantitative methods tend to be better at gathering data from large samples); and *development*, meaning later studies can be informed by prior ones.

How Do These Considerations Relate to MMR and Evaluation?

Evaluation determines the merit, worth, or value of things; evaluators identify values and/or standards that apply to what is being evaluated, conduct empirical studies, and integrate conclusions with the standards into an overall evaluation or set of evaluations (Scriven, 1991). This definition of evaluation is broad, and evaluations are subclassified in a variety of ways (see, e.g., Nastasi & Hitchcock, 2008). One way to classify evaluation work is to consider if it is formative or summative in nature. Again, the former tends to focus on program improvement and refinement, which can entail making adaptions to promote program acceptability, sustainability, and its social validity and capacity to deliver the program with integrity, whereas the latter entails judging the overall worth of a program. To further distinguish between the two, Scriven (1991) offers the following quote: "When the cook tastes the soup, that's formative; when the guests taste the soup, that's summative" (p. 169). In our experience, although evaluations can take on a singular formative or summative focus (indeed, some of our own work can potentially be classified as one or the other), many projects endeavor to do both. Oftentimes, stakeholders ask some variant of the question: "Does the program work?" They may concurrently ask, "How can it be improved?" But in our experience, the first question is often the fundamental one in the minds of stakeholders, and it often comes with underlying and sometimes unarticulated hopes to generate a causal answer. That is, did exposure to the program (or policy, intervention, product, etc.) *cause* some desired outcome? This opens the door to a fairly long-standing literature about causal inference.

Causal Inference and Validity

Causal inference is perhaps best understood in the context of the validity typology described by Shadish, Cook, and Campbell (2002), which is rooted in Campbell's refinements that have developed over the past several decades (e.g., Campbell, 1957; Campbell & Stanley, 1963). Briefly, the typology includes the following: internal, external, statistical-conclusion, and construct validity. *Internal validity* deals with whether there is a causal relationship between two variables (e.g., a treatment exposure and some outcome). *External validity* refers to whether this causal relationship persists across different settings, people, outcomes, measures, and so on. *Statistical-conclusion validity* deals with inferences about the covariation between two variables of interest, which in this case would apply to treatment exposure and an outcome. *Construct validity* deals with inferences about a construct that can be made from observations taken from a sample and from design details. (Recall that we discussed social and consequential validity in Chapter 4.) These various inferences may be best thought of in terms of continua and not dichotomous concepts. That is, it is not fully correct to think in terms of whether one may or may not have internal validity; rather, internal validity may be quite strong, fairly good, weak, and so on. Some organizations such as the U.S. Department of Education's What Works Clearinghouse (2013) promote internal-validity categorizations so as to simplify policy decisions, and this seems reasonable, but researchers do not necessarily have to rely on such categorizations when thinking through evidence for the purposes of their own work.

When assessing causal evidence, one can consider the sundry threats to validity such as sample loss (attrition), regression to the mean, history, matura-tion, selection, and so on (details below). There are threats to other forms of validity as well (e.g., small sample sizes will generally lead to low statistical power in the absence of a powerful effect, and this undermines statistic-conclusion validity). Keeping in mind that this text promotes the use of MMR, we hope that readers will appreciate the point that establishing a causal argu-ment is an exercise in logic. In this sense, there is nothing inherently statistical about the process of inferring causation, and the sort of hard reasoning that qualitative researchers use can be applied (Maxwell, 2004). Indeed, we rou-tinely infer causation in the day-to-day navigation of our worlds (e.g., a fire caused the damage; this event caused the fire; "X" action led to, or caused, that person to be promoted in a job; relocating the restaurant closer to the stadium improved sales; larger schools tend to have better achieving students, so we should consolidate small, rural ones). The above parenthetical examples essentially represent causal conclusions, or inferences, that we make all the time. In the first couple of examples, there is no need to set up some hypothesis test and estimate a p value that is smaller than .05. Indeed, Shadish et al. (2002) make the point that human beings have been making reasonable causal inferences back when we were figuring out the properties of fire, well before the advent of hypothesis testing that relies on concepts like t and F distributions.

The last parenthetical example, dealing with school consolidation, does however require some pause because it represents a sort of causal attribution that can inform policy. Suppose it turns out that valid data show, in some given region, that achievement is indeed associated with school size where larger schools tend to have higher achieving students (this is dubious; see Howley, Johnson, & Petrie, 2011). Assume that this is a perfectly valid association, or correlation. Even with this assumption, any causal inference that the associa-tion exists because of a consolidation policy is likely wrong. After all, there is no education theory or causal mechanism, which we know of, that supports the idea that if a student who is struggling is then placed in a larger school, that student will necessarily improve. The reverse is also true. Why should we think that taking a high achieving student and placing her or him in a small school would yield a drop in performance? One might argue that large schools have better resources or perhaps that larger groups of economically well-off children normalize behaviors associated with achievement, and so on. Hence, students would in fact be better off in larger schools. If so, the explanation is not about the size of the school but instead about resource allocation and student grouping. Furthermore, suppose closing small rural schools meant that students in more isolated communities were expected to travel great distances to complete their education. Then, consolidating small schools might have pernicious outcomes and for little or no benefit. This is by the way not an abstract point. Readers of this book who reside in the United States can place "Closing Rural Schools" in the search engine of their choice and see, at least as of this writing, how prevalent a concern this can be (see also Howley et al., 2011).

This digression about school size serves a purpose toward discussing MMR, causal inference, and program evaluation. Readers should see a policy, or a program (in this case, school consolidation), as an organized human activity done with a purpose. If it can be thought of as a program, then we should also be worried about evaluating it. Furthermore, although statistics can be used to help understand causal presumptions behind the rationale for consolidation, getting them out in the form of a question is an exercise in logic, and often, good qualitative skills are needed to get policymakers to do so. First, in our experience, getting decision makers to articulate their reasons for an action can sometimes be a challenge that is surmounted by careful interviewing. Consolidation entails complex interplay between budgets, community politics, and education theory/programming. Second, data that most people would see as being qualitatively oriented can help illuminate program effects. After all, we might interview students who are asked to change schools, teachers who need to take on new students, or bus drivers with longer routes about their perception of the impacts of change. We might also participate in bus rides to observe and to explore intended and unintended consequences of a policy. In sum, we might use both quantitative and qualitative approaches to inquiry to understand some phenomenon, and as noted in Chapter 1, MMR principles are to use these different approaches in a thoughtful manner. In this sense, readers should understand that we see quantitative and qualitative applications as the norm in much of program evaluation and social science; they complement and inform each other. To us, methodological choices tend to focus not on whether to use mixed methods but rather how to use them in a planned, systematic manner in ways supported by models such as CMMPE.

Getting back to summative evaluation, this often entails or at least implies a causal question (Did the program work?). We find the majority of explanations pertaining to causal validity to be inherently logical, although some of it can be quite complex. Consider, for example, Shadish's (2010) comparison between Campbell's and Rubin's approaches[1] to causal inference (see also Rubin, 1974; Schneider, Carnoy, Kilpatrick, Schmidt, & Shavelson, 2007; Shadish et al., 2002), which indicates that the two are compatible, but full conceptual integration requires more work even though the two have been present for decades. Although it can take a long time to develop a command of several of the nuances, we think that much of the key logic behind causal inference can be described somewhat quickly. Furthermore, causal reasoning is easily aligned with MMR logic. This is not to suggest that we can be cavalier with our descriptions nor should readers rely only on this chapter, but we do think that much can be learned in a short time, assuming a careful read.

To understand summative program evaluation that focuses on whether an intervention or program works (in the sense that people who are exposed to it are better off in some way, such as whether consolidation yielded improved achievement), it is important to understand the general logic behind why a study can potentially be characterized as having strong internal validity. Recall that Shadish et al. (2002) described internal validity as the validity of an inference that there is a causal relationship between two variables. In a program evaluation setting, one variable may be a systematic introduction of a treatment (which is an independent variable) and the other variable, say, academic engagement (a dependent variable). Assuming that academic achievement appeared to increase after exposure to treatment, studies with strong internal validity, or what we can also call *causal evidence*, would demonstrate that the treatment being evaluated is the most plausible[2] reason for the observed improvement. Likewise, should there be no improvement, a study with strong

---

[1] Very briefly, Campbell and Stanley's (1963) framework (see also Shadish et al., 2002) uses a more logical approach to causation, whereas Rubin's has a more statistical orientation.

[2] The word "plausible" can be contrasted with "possible." Shadish et al. (2002) make the point that design need not rule out all possible rival explanations for an observed treatment effect, just the ones that are plausible.

internal validity would demonstrate that the program is not effective[3] (although no single study can be conclusive). There are of course many studies that yield causal evidence that allow decision makers to evaluate if a program worked, and these range from ones where any resulting evidence is so weak they may hardly be worth the effort (e.g., design without a clear counterfactual), to designs that can yield compelling findings (e.g., RCTs).

An example of a design that would yield evidence characterized by poor internal validity is the quasi-experiment that lacks a control group (Shadish et al., 2002). In the vernacular of research design, the qualifier *quasi* is somewhat equivalent to *almost* and should give the practitioner pause. In common language, if the reader were asked, "Would you like to date my friend? This is a quasi-nice person," then there would be reason for clarification. One should be skeptical and ask, "What do you mean by quasi?" before agreeing to a date. This same sort of skepticism applies when dealing with quasi-experiments because this is meant to denote the idea that there is an inherent threat to the internal validity of the study. In the case of a quasi-experiment with no control group, one might, for example, take a group of children who exhibit extreme behavior problems, confirm this with a pretest, introduce a treatment, and administer some posttest. Assume that the outcome measure used in the evaluation is an excellent one and assume further that there was indeed an unambiguous drop in problematic behavior after intervention exposure. In this case, the data themselves should not necessarily be questioned, but it is reasonable to question the inference for why such an improvement was observed. That is, if one inferred that the improvement for the drop was due to the treatment, a number of problems arise. The improved behavior may indeed be due to the treatment; on the face of it, this is a reasonable explanation. But there are also a number of plausible alternative explanations for the drop in observed behavior. These alternatives are referred to as *threats to internal validity*, and Shadish et al. (2002) have identified several. Until these explanations can be plausibly removed, internal validity would be poor, and decision makers should hesitate before buying into this seemingly effective program.

Threats to Internal Validity

As we concluded in the previous section, researchers need to rule out plausible alternative explanations for seeming causal relationships, or what

---

[3] In a context where a null hypothesis test of statistical significance is used, the null is retained.

Shadish et al. (2002) call threats to validity. One such alternative explanation is the so-called *history threat*. Some event may have occurred roughly when the treatment was introduced, which was in fact responsible for the improved outcomes. For example, among the group of children, perhaps there was a change in school staff and a new person who is great at managing problematic behavior started on the job. If so, what caused the improvement—the treatment or the new staff member? Of course, any number of events, which we might imagine could have influenced the behavior, may have occurred during the time of treatment onset; we cannot really rule out such a possibility in the absence of a control group. This is because if a control group was available, and we had reason to believe that its members would also experience such co-occurring events, but at the same time did not show improved behavior, then the history threat is less of a concern. The idea here is that these sorts of rival explanations need to be ruled out before we can afford credit to the program being evaluated. The plausibility of such rival explanations can be explored, even in the absence of a control group, by taking careful note of the students' environment (observation), examining records of how it may be different from the past (document analyses, interviewing staff members), and talking with the students themselves (interviewing). In this sense, internal validity can be markedly improved by adding in qualitative inquiry.

Another threat is a phenomenon referred to as *regression to the mean*, and this refers to the idea that extreme scores tend not to replicate. Suppose that out of a desire to be helpful to a school, an interventionist identifies children with the most problematic behavior on the basis of some schoolwide screening measure applied on a given day and conducts an intervention with this extreme group. Then suppose score drops are observed at some postintervention measurement occasion. Suppose again, behavior improves after intervention. This observation may be due to a treatment effect, but it may also be due to the regression to the mean phenomenon. Remember, this means that extreme scores tend not to repeat, and indeed it can be difficult to maintain highly disruptive behavior over time (the most concerted efforts to be disruptive have to be tiring). So regression to the mean may be as good an explanation for an observed improvement as was the introduction of the treatment, on the basis that extreme behavior is difficult for most people to maintain. Worse, small or even moderate drops in the level of problematic behavior might be construed as a treatment effect, but all that is really happening is that children were selected on the basis of having an especially bad time, and any observed improvement is not a function of the underlying reasons for poor behavior. Here again, a deep understanding of a group of students' history can help researchers assess this validity threat, and such an understanding can be better achieved via qualitative inquiry. Analyses of documents such as office discipline referrals and report cards can go a long way in understanding prior behavior, as can interviews with teachers, parents, and so on. Consistent with exploratory and emergent design, it may be critical to adopt open-ended questions in order to allow for discovery of behavior patterns.

To make matters worse in terms of making a causal argument, *both history and regression to the mean* are at the same time plausible explanations for an observed improvement. Furthermore, there are many other such threats to internal validity (e.g., students simply mature over the course of the study, the measurement itself may alter observed behavior, and the list goes on). Fortunately, several of these threats can be addressed by adding a control group. This is because if something like regression to the mean was the actual reason for the observed improvement in behavior, one would expect to see the pattern in both study conditions; that is, both the treated and untreated students would, on average, improve at comparable rates. Assuming however that any improvements occurred solely among the students who were treated, or if the treated group improves at a faster rate, then all of these other threats to validity are rendered less plausible. Indeed, the presence of a control group yields a clearer counterfactual, which can be thought of as what happens in the absence of a treatment (Shadish et al., 2002).

Even if a control group is included, most design specialists would still characterize such a study as a quasi-experiment in the absence of random assignment of participants to study conditions. The study would be much improved; that is, the design would have much better internal validity, but a rival explanation remains: The treated group may not be equivalent to the control group at the outset of the investigation. If this is true, then any observed benefit may be attributed to the differences between the two study groups and not the intervention itself. Suppose, for example, parents volunteered to have their children treated and children in the control group were placed there because their parents were less interested in trying something new. If at the end of the study the treated children showed improved behavior compared with those in the control group, one would not know if the observed outcome is due to the treatment; it is reasonable that the observed difference between study groups is due to preexisting familial differences. Given the design, the researcher cannot know the answer. This yields a new validity threat called *selection*. That is, the way in which participants are placed into study group (perhaps they self-selected) yields two groups that are not equivalent on some key characteristics such as motivation to improve, and this difference can explain treatment group improvements because these participants would have done better than those in the comparison regardless of whether the intervention helps.

The single best way to address such a problem, the selection threat, is to randomly assign children to have access to the therapy or be in a control condition. With such assignment, then, there are both considerable statistical theory and logic that allow one to argue that, on average, the children in the two conditions should be equivalent (Shadish et al., 2002). This is because chance dictates assignment; there is reason to believe that the groups are equal (on average) to each other. There may indeed be children of parents who are highly motivated to try novel treatments, but this would also be true in the control group because chance was used to determine which children were exposed to a treatment. This advantage is minimized with small sample sizes (because it is harder to achieve group equivalence) but a reasonably large sample of a homogeneous group that is randomly assigned to study conditions should provide the basis for solid internal validity (holding constant other aspects of design). The use of randomization yields the RCT design (see Shadish et al., 2002),[4] which, in the vernacular of social science design, equates to an experiment (no quasi add-on is needed; getting back to the above dating analogy, the person is just described as nice with no qualifier). If such a design is well implemented and children in the intervention group were performing better than their counterparts in the control condition, then exposure to the intervention stands as the most plausible explanation for the

---

[4] The U.S. Department of Education (2003) has in the past several years referred to RCTs as the *gold standard* of research. This enviable moniker is clearly meant for studies with a causal question, and we agree with this distinction so long as readers keep in mind that RCTs have little use when a causal question is *not* at hand. After all, how would randomization of study participants help researchers understand important questions, such as factors that promote unsafe sexual practices and decisions to stop schooling or drug use? Furthermore, when a causal question is at hand, there are a number of other approaches that can be reasonably applied to support causal inference; these include single-subject designs, case studies that utilize pattern matching, quasi-experiments that use strong baseline equating procedures, the regression discontinuity design, and so on. We do not think that the researchers who initially used the *gold standard* language in the context of RCTs were in any way confused about these issues, but our perception is that there have been wider misunderstandings about when the design can be useful.

observed improvement. Ideally, a next step then would be to treat the control children, who would receive the intervention with the benefit of decision makers now having strong evidence that it works. Again, there are a number of additional threats to internal validity, and it is our belief that the best source for reviewing these is Shadish et al. (2002), and we hope readers will take an interest because we cannot fully cover the issues here. What is important for the current discussion is the idea that it is important to understand when causal questions arise and to think through whether evidence is supported by a design that allows for an argument that some program, treatment, policy, and so on *works* in the sense that these yield better outcomes than what can be expected from the status quo. This should also be done in the presumed mechanism for causing change.

Cultural Considerations and MMR Considerations

Now we return to the idea of accounting for culture. None of the prior discussion pertaining to causality has any special connection to culturally relevant programming. Nor do programs that are designed to be relevant to a particular culture happen to be free of the need for causal evidence when a causal question is at hand. But here again, we argue that MMR work can be especially helpful for examining causal investigations when dealing with culturally specific interventions. Use of randomization is consistent with MMR applications in general, and it is certainly possible to add randomization components in a model like CMMPE. At the most basic of research method integration levels, RCTs can, and often do, benefit from qualitative work (see also Donovan et al., 2002; Grissmer, Subotnik, & Orland, 2008). Consider, for example, the aforementioned matter of sample loss, or attrition. This is a well-known threat to the internal validity of otherwise well-conceived RCTs. Say, for example, 100 children were randomly assigned to have access to a treatment, so that 50 were treated and 50 were not. Say, further, at posttest that 20 children in the control condition did not yield any outcome data (they drop out of the study or otherwise do not show up for a posttest). If subsequent analyses of data show that treated children did not perform any better than their control counterparts on an outcome measure (i.e., it looks like the treatment did not make a difference), there is clearly a plausible rival explanation at hand that threatens the internal validity of the study: Data from the 20 children may change the findings. In other words, one might make an argument that a treatment was ineffective on the basis of the collected data, but it is equally plausible that the unmeasured children in the control condition would have performed poorly and their absence masks a treatment effect. Unanticipated attrition can potentially be addressed via a number of statistical procedures (Enders, 2010), but there is a clear argument that it can be best to avoid sample loss in the first place.

Another threat, demoralization, may interact with attrition (studies contend with multiple threats at once). Children may have conceptualized their assignment to a control condition in such a way that they did not want to bother to continue with the study, and so it can be worthwhile to understand their perceptions. Thus, several advantages can be gleaned from interviewing study participants. At the outset, it can help to understand their suitability for a study before random assignment. If, for example, we learn that a potential participant is not interested in the research question, or perhaps finds the treatment to be objectionable, then it may behoove researchers to not include the individual in the study. Furthermore, imagine trying to explain the purpose of a study to a group in an unfamiliar culture; in this sense, it can be critical to understand the shared knowledge, beliefs, attitudes, and so on of the group before proceeding. Consider again some of the formative steps in CMMPE. Understanding the acceptability, social validity, integrity, and cultural competence needs of a program can go a long way toward convincing stakeholders of the merit of a study and preventing attrition.

We are not the only ones who argue that RCTs can be improved via qualitative methodology. Consider the following quote: "Whenever resources allow, field experiments will benefit from including qualitative methods both for the primary benefits they are capable of generating and also for the assistance they provide to the descriptive causal task itself" (Shadish et al., 2002, p. 478). Now consider another definition of MMR: "research in which the investigator collects and analyzes data, integrates the findings, and draws inferences using both qualitative and quantitative approaches or methods in a single study or program of inquiry" (Tashakkori & Creswell, 2007, p. 4). An inherent strength of applying qualitative components is that this can open the door for using the strengths of one aspect of the "mixed" design to play to the weaknesses of other. Again, such interplay of design strengths and weaknesses is a hallmark of mixed methods thinking (Johnson & Onwuegbuzie, 2004). Think about the interplay of randomization and interviewing in the context of attrition. Randomizing participants to study conditions sets the stage for an opportunity to establish clear, causal evidence, but the procedure cannot, of course, provide information about why participants may drop out of a study.

Furthermore, researchers may have little prior information about the reason for attrition for any particular person; hence, they may wish to explore the thoughts and feelings of people to understand what it is that might contribute to study discontinuation. Here, we see a clear example of qualitative techniques bolstering randomization, and vice versa: Whereas the latter technique is great for supporting causal inference, the former is well suited to understanding motivations and perceptions.

Of course, the use of multiple techniques opens the door to cross-method triangulation. As an example, Nastasi, Hitchcock, Varjas, et al. (2010) conducted an ethnographic study in Sri Lanka to develop a culturally specific, school-based intervention technique.[5] Outcome measures were based on prior ethnography and were used to measure impacts in the trial. That is, ethnographic work was conducted not just to understand context but also to develop culturally specific interventions and outcome measures. The study used hierarchical linear models (see Raudenbush & Bryk, 2002) to investigate program impacts because, although the intervention was individually administered in an after-school program, the intervention had an academic–social component and students interacted within classrooms during the school day. Hence, it may have been the case that the assumption of independent errors may have been violated. On the face of it, standard statistical approaches like a *t* test could not be validly applied. Having said that, the previous ethnographic work suggested that student interactions may not have been particularly salient because public education classrooms in Sri Lanka can be large (50 or more students), as was the case in this school, and there is generally a competitive atmosphere, which limits the quantity and quality of student interactions. Indeed, teachers tend to not slow down for students who do not maintain a command of the material. Furthermore, interventionists were confident that the after-school content and material were unlike anything the school had experienced before (i.e., making use of cooperative learning groups), so the degree of dependence (i.e., size of intraclass correlations[6]) would be either nonexistent or quite small. It turned out that classroom grouping did account

---

[5] This is the study we describe in more detail at the conclusion of the chapter and in Chapter 6.

[6] An intraclass correlation (ICC) is a ratio of within-cluster variance to total population variance (Bloom, 2005). For example, in a two-level model where schools are assigned to treatment and control conditions, grouping of students within schools is a form of clustering. In this case, the clustering accounted for by school grouping relative to the population variance would yield an ICC. A zero ICC is the case where each individual observation is independent, allowing for standard analyses such as independent *t* tests.

for very little variance, promoting a sense of confidence since this result was consistent with qualitative expectations. This represents a kind of cross-method triangulation that yielded evidence that overall conclusions about classroom structure were reasonable.

There are many other ways in which MMR can support causal inference in RCTs, and we continue to work out ideas. For now, we hope that this discussion demonstrates the application of MMR to RCTs, which in turn show how the use of these procedures can inform a common question in summative evaluation. Undergirding much of the discussion is the point that summative program evaluation can always benefit from MMR. But if evaluation is done in highly familiar settings, the need for such approaches may be partially diminished. From our experience, however, the use of MMR becomes essential when working in novel contexts and when we seek clear evidence of treatment effects. We will return to this issue when describing an example toward the end of the chapter. But first, we set the stage for MMR application when thinking about generalization of findings.

SAMPLING, EXTERNAL VALIDITY, AND TRANSFERABILITY CONSIDERATIONS

Once a finding is established, how does it apply outside of the context of a study? The goal of much research is to learn something that can be generalized to a broader set. Under what conditions can the results of a study be appropriately generalized beyond the specific sample used in the study? The answer to this question is related to the sampling design of the study—how the sample of participants is selected from a population of interest. The following discussion will apply equally to studies that are nonexperimental (e.g., survey study) as well as experimental (or quasi-experimental) designs in which hypotheses are formulated and tested. However, in the latter case, it is important to keep clear the distinction between *selection* and *assignment.* Assignment refers to how study participants are assigned to condition (e.g., treatment or control) and random assignment is one option, whereas sampling (or selection) refers to how the study participants are selected to be in the study in the first place, prior to being assigned to a condition. In this book, we avoid the use of the word *selection*, except for specific cases (e.g., referencing the selection threat to internal validity), because it can mean two things: (1) a researcher selects someone to be in a study (i.e., sampled) or (2) from there the researcher selects the person to be treated or not (i.e., assigned); and we have found this to yield unnecessary confusion.

The primary requirement for being able to generalize the results from a sample to a larger population is that the sample be *representative* of the population. This means that the sample looks like the entire population on all variables (observed and unobserved) of interest. The only design in which generalizability can be fully and unconditionally assumed is the use of a *census*, in which the sample is really not a sample at all but is instead the entire population of interest. This might be feasible when the population of interest is very narrowly defined (e.g., when a study is only concerned with the results of teachers within a single school), but in most cases, conducting a census will not be feasible as this would require enormous resources while dealing with a population that likely changes over time.

A common alternative is *simple random sampling*[7] in which each and every member of the population of interest has an equal, nonzero probability of being selected for the sample. This is the basis for statistical (or probabilistic) generalization. This type of sampling does not ensure that the sample is representative of the population for any particular variable. However, via use of the central limit theorem, it is possible when using simple random sampling to describe statistically the probabilistic degree of representativeness of the sample on both observed and unobserved variables. This allows the development of standard errors and confidence intervals to describe mathematically the degree to which the study results can be generalized to the larger population of interest.

Although simple random sampling is often a desirable design feature with many benefits, it also has certain limitations. The first is that while the procedure, which allows one to understand the degree of confidence that results from a sample, can be applied to a broader population, this is only a probabilistic statement. One can examine how representative the sample is of the population, but it is not possible with simple random sampling to ensure a priori how representative the sample will be on any given variable. A second limitation of such sampling is in terms of subpopulation generalizability. This is an issue that we think is often not considered or understood when selecting

---

[7] More specifically, we use this term to refer to simple random sampling without replacement, as opposed to simple random sampling with replacement (e.g., Groves et al., 2009).

a sampling design and is germane to research focused on microcultures, sub-groups, and so on. Even if one were to have a sample that was representative of the overall population for key variables, it does not necessarily follow that the sample would be representative for important subpopulations on those variables. If there are selected subpopulations of interest for which it is impor-tant to have generalizability, then simple random sampling will not be sufficient.

Both of these limitations can be addressed through the use of *stratified random sampling*. In this design, strata are defined based on the variables that need to be representative, and then, each stratum is sampled separately, such that the percentage of the overall sample within each stratum matches the percent in the population. Within each stratum, simple random sampling is applied, so that other observed and unobserved variables are sampled with the statistical benefits provided by simple random sampling (Groves et al., 2009). For example, we imagine that most K–12 education research that entails probabilistic generalization in Saudi Arabia would need to randomly sample study participants within each gender because schools are split by this characteristic.

Finally, it is worth noting that there are a variety of other complex sam-pling designs, which have various implications for the representativeness and generalizability of the results. Consider that the use of group-randomized designs in which classrooms or schools, instead of students, are randomly assigned to condition, are becoming increasingly common. This requires con-sidering both the representativeness of the clusters being sampled, as well as the representativeness of the overall population of students who make up those clusters.

Transferability and Ecological Systems Theory

In qualitative work, researchers often rely on transferability (Lincoln & Guba, 1985) and naturalistic generalization (Stake, 1995). *Transferability* deals with how applicable research findings may be to other settings. This is generally done by the consumer of the research; that is, in probabilistic gener-alization, the onus is on the research team to specify the population to which a sample can be generalized and to consider the degree to which error under-mines generalization. In transferability, the onus is on the reader or consumer, but the researchers need to sufficiently describe the context of the study so that readers have the tools needed to think through if the findings apply to some new situation. Transferability is promoted via techniques like thick description (Brantlinger, Jiminez, Klingner, Pugach, & Richardson, 2005), which entails sufficiently describing the context, quotes, field notes, and procedures so that readers can judge the degree to which results can apply and even be replicated in some new setting. The general advice is, of course, to describe as much as possible about the original research so that readers can make their own judgments. When describing naturalistic generalization, Stake (1995) suggests providing an opportunity for readers to have vicarious experience in that description, so that readers can feel what it might be like to have been part of some phenomenon. Hellström (2008) describes the idea of organizing findings by highlighting priorities in case descriptions that promote **transfer**.

Recall that EST (Bronfenbrenner, 1989) is a root approach for understanding cultural concerns in our own work. EST may yield concrete steps for promoting transfer and translation of research (translation is discussed below). Again, the idea behind EST is that people are influenced by interactions in multiple contexts: microsystems, exosystems, macrosystems, mesosystems, and chronosystems. Nastasi, Moore, and Varjas (2004) borrow from EST when conceptualizing the PCSIM (see Chapter 2) that emphasizes the importance of developing culturally specific and participatory consultation. In this sense, EST can be applied as a kind of method for helping researchers design studies in a way that accounts for different settings. The model considers ecology but adds in complexities that arise from the cultural experiences of stakeholders within systems while also broadening beyond Bronfenbrenner's focus on human development. There is therefore no reason for using the exact systems Bronfenbrenner describes when examining culture, but a key idea is to understand the broader ecology, which means attempting to describe different system levels and how they interact. This provides a guiding theory when conceptualizing data collection and analytic schemes. This entails identifying key stakeholders and understanding their roles, how they interact at different levels and between levels, and how change in one level can affect the needs of an individual or more generally alter an entire system.

Attention to ecology promotes looking for multilevel systems, how they interact, and what elements of a system are likely to be highly sensitive to change across time. Details need to be worked out, but this lens suggests that transfer might be facilitated by describing the ecologies of varying systems that at least share reasonably common characteristics. (Also recall our earlier discussion about implementation science in Chapter 2.) In the case of many applications of education research, this may well apply. This is because schools are indeed variable in nature; no two schools are exactly alike. But they also share common entities: In the United States, for example, they are typically part of some larger district (even if a whole district, in essence, conducts its business in one building); they have in common similar staff titles with similar responsibilities, mission to the community, and of course, students. From a microsystem point of view, researchers can describe interactions between students and teachers, recognizing that an exosystem calls attention to issues such as district policies, mesosystem descriptions might call attention to interactions between staff and leaders, and a macrosystem lens can consider issues such as federal law, state politics, and so on. A chronosystem point of view might motivate description of key events such as the enactment of a law such as the *No Child Left Behind Act* or some more local but pivotal events such as the hiring of a new and highly effective leader, failure to pass an important tax levy, and so on.[8] In the end, transfer needs thick description and requirements for such description will vary by study, but we find it intriguing that EST has served well with thinking through cultural nuances, and schools, for all of their variability, share characteristics that can be assessed when applying EST. We also think that this applies to a number of institutional settings that are common in many cultures (e.g., hospitals, government bodies, etc.), and application of EST can promote logical generalization.

Logical Generalization

Whether by qualitative transferability, naturalistic generalization, or probabilistic generalization (i.e., using statistical inference), the application of program evaluation findings, or otherwise, requires some thinking in terms of how findings from a study can be logically applied to some other setting or context. Here again, we see no reason for why culturally relevant interventions or program evaluations differ from any other type of social science inquiry, except for the fact that MMR applications may promote logical generalization if phenomena are understood from qualitative, quantitative, and mixed perspectives. That is, MMR reasoning can yield more mileage because one can

---

[8] For further illustration, we discuss the issue of multilevel evaluation applied to community-based health risk prevention work in Nastasi and Hitchcock (2009).

think about probabilistic generalization (if the design allows for it), transferability, and logical generalization, all at once. Recall that external validity deals with the degree to which a causal inference can be held across new study participants, settings, and so on. Perhaps a basic principle is that the more conditions in a study differ from the point to which one might generalize, the harder the task. But in our experience, generalization in the social sciences, in the standard sense of the word, can suffer from misapplication of logic. As noted in prior chapters, overgeneralization is problematic and offers a central justification for this book; many assume that some approach tailored in the United States easily applies in other settings. The reverse is also true. Some might argue that generalization is not possible because of a small sample size, a nonrandom sample was drawn from a population, or the method that was used, such as a case study or qualitative applications. That is, the sort of thinking we encountered, and probably will continue to encounter, is that findings drawn from whole classifications of methods cannot be generalized. But this does not ring true (see Shadish, 1995; Yin, 2009). First, summative evaluations that use primarily quantitative techniques have no special affordances when it comes to statistical generalization, in the absence of random or at least systematic sampling. For example, exceedingly few RCTs entail use of random sampling (Hedges, 2013). This should not be surprising. Think of how many school principals or other education leaders might react if they were informed that their schools were sampled from some population and therefore must participate in a study. In systems with very strong hierarchies, where some central government compels study participation, this might be possible, but almost all of the time researchers will be pushing their luck with this approach to sample recruitment. School leaders will typically need to be convinced of the merits of study participation, and even if they agree in principle, they may not be in a position to join a study in a given year. Hence, many RCTs use a volunteer sample. Yet we use RCT evidence. The implication here is that decision makers engage in at least logical generalization all of the time.

So what about case studies? Can data from these be generalized? Consider that any number of cases in medicine might yield some (fortunately) rare finding about the effects of a virus, bacterium, injury, or parasite, but we nevertheless do not question the idea that they offer findings that are easily generalized. Take the use of nasal irrigation (or a neti pot), which is done to ward off or ameliorate the symptoms of the common cold. For those who are unfamiliar with the practice, one puts a small amount of water in a container that looks like a teapot. Water is poured from the opening of the container into one nostril, thus irrigating the sinuses, and the water is then released from the other nostril (consult your favorite search engine to obtain an image; it is said that a picture is worth a thousand words). We raise the practice here because there were two tragic cases in the United States, in 2011, where the use of publicly available water exposed neti pot users to an amoeba called *Naegleria fowleri*, leading to their deaths (Yoder et al., 2012). This particular strain of amoeba causes death by entering the nose and traveling along an olfactory nerve to the brain and subsequently yielding damage. This conclusion, that *N. fowleri* caused the deaths, required research and case investigations of reported physical symptoms, water samples, and what the two cases have in common. This work entails a sample size of two, yet it is inherently logical that these findings, rare as they may be, inform public policy and messaging pertaining to the practice of nasal irrigation. This is because it stands to reason that any other users of the practice put themselves at risk of amoeba exposure without putting in safeguards such as boiling water to sterilize it before use. Our point here is that we do not discount findings from small samples and lack of random sampling, just as we cannot just accept findings, without critical thinking about generalization issues, when these characteristics are in place.[9]

How does one think through generalization issues? Shadish (1995) provides some guidance when he described five principles of generalization relevant to the application of RCT and ethnographic evidence: proximal similarity, heterogeneity of irrelevancies, discriminant validity, empirical interpolation/extrapolation, and explanation (these all can work in tandem). Briefly, generalization is simply easier when the conditions of research match up to the setting where findings are to be applied, that is, *proximal similarity*. To the next principle, when findings hold up across different times, settings, and measures that should be irrelevant to the finding, the *heterogeneity of irrelevancies* principle applies. The cases of amoeba infection can generalize widely in part because race, nationality, the time in which one lives, and so on are largely irrelevant to a number of medical concerns. This relates to *discriminant validity*, which deals with the idea that a construct produced a finding. If the victims of the bacteria infection passed away from some other ailment, then the

---

[9] As an aside, the idea of generalizing findings from very small samples should be counterbalanced with the notion of theory confirmation. The nasal irrigation example used here has elements of both; the two cases help confirm what is known about the particular amoeba. The cases also yield a form of logical generalization in that people who engage in the practice have learned that they may be putting themselves at risk if using untreated tap water.

generalization from the case is harder to make. *Interpolation and extrapolation* entail projecting observed findings to new values; generalization is easier if the strength of some observed relationship between variables changes as circumstances vary. For example, in some of our work in Sri Lanka (Nastasi, Hitchcock, Varjas, et al., 2010; see also Chapter 6), we found that an after-school program that promoted an understanding of emotion–cognition–behavior connections related to stressful relationships was associated with greater confidence of adjusting successfully to stress as well as evidence of effective coping (problem solving, social support). We might therefore assess if this mechanism holds true as we explore different forms of coping. If the relationship does indeed hold, we will have corresponding evidence that the treatment can generalize to new applications. The idea of *explanation* as a function of logical generalization applies when full understanding of a relationship between sets of variables ensues with a level of exactness that allows for more ready generalization. Getting back to the tragic cases where users of neti pots passed away, identifying the amoeba as the cause of death represents the sort of explanation that is needed to promote logical generalization. This sounds simple enough, but appreciate how hard it might be to dole out generalizable advice in the absence of the exact explanation. The issues of whether to use a neti pot, when, under what circumstances and the type of water source, age of the users, and so on could have been considered as contributions to understanding the cases, but identification of the culprit is what yielded information that is easily generalized.

In the context of culturally relevant programming and evaluation, such issues of generalization equally apply. Generalization and transferability considerations can help critical readers assess if some intervention developed in another time and place can apply. At the same time, these ideas will help researchers describe what aspects of their work might apply to other cultures and settings. See again Figure 4.1. If evaluators have data on how the various stakeholder groups contributed (or not) to the different evaluation constructs to promote success, it stands to reason that researchers can better promote transfer and think through logical generalization.

Translation

To this point, our focus was on reviewing issues of generalization and transferability and suggesting the application of ecological systems to promote these concerns. A closing topic focuses on the idea of *translation* of research; that is, dissemination and deployment of research to the same or other populations (Nastasi et al., 2004). Or put another way, consideration of how research findings translate to practice, or in medical terms, getting findings from a lab to bedside treatment, is a critical issue that will also be influenced by cultural factors. In the PCSIM model, translation can be greatly facilitated via the participatory process where stakeholders are active members in the research process. So presumably when an intervention is tested, stakeholders know its features and have firsthand knowledge of how it will work within a given school. Nastasi et al. (2004) describe three phases of translation: dissemination, deployment, and theory development. *Dissemination* is the process where findings are communicated and interpreted. *Deployment* covers those factors that need to be addressed in order to have a reasonable chance to replicate findings after adoption. *Theory development* in the context of PCSIM entails reflection of how practice and personal theory of school operations can be updated after the consultative research process. When considering findings from external studies, theory development might entail considering how findings alter thinking about localized service delivery. For example, if some favored intervention appears to "not work," this should motivate teachers to think about whether and how conclusions might affect their own practice. Consideration of whether findings might generalize or transfer to their setting in rural schools could inform this process. Sample key questions that cover these points include the following:[10]

- What has been learned?
- Who are the target participants?
- Do findings transfer/generalize to our setting?
- What are the necessary conditions and resources for deployment?
- What requisite skills are needed to implement the intervention?
- What written and oral dissemination materials are needed for adoption?
- What challenges are involved with adoption?
- What is needed to secure stakeholder buy-in?
- What opportunities might come from adoption?
- How do findings inform current practice?

---

[10] These are summarized from a longer list of questions and issues discussed in Nastasi et al. (2004).

PULLING IT ALL TOGETHER: AN EXAMPLE

To concretize the key ideas in this chapter (i.e., the application of MMR to summative evaluation and causality, external validity, transferability, and translation) and those discussed in Chapter 4 (i.e., understanding moderators, socially valid outcomes), consider the aforementioned RCT led by Nastasi and colleagues (Nastasi, Hitchcock, Varjas et al., 2010). They conducted an ethnographic study in Sri Lanka to develop a culturally specific, school-based intervention technique. Outcome measures were based on prior ethnography and were used to measure impacts in the trial. That is, ethnographic work was conducted not just to understand context but also to develop culturally specific interventions and outcome measures. The intervention itself was rooted in Bronfenbrenner's (1989) ecological model and understanding stress and coping as facets of a culturally specific mental health model. Details on the model development are available in Nastasi et al. (2004). Two key points follow: First is that the intervention development, associated outcome measures, and its evaluation not only used MMR applications, this was done as part of a systematic program of research conducted across several years and substudies (Nastasi, Hitchcock, Sarkar et al., 2007). The second is that the overall program of research followed an integrated, synergistic MMR model articulated by Nastasi, Hitchcock, & Brown (2010). Recall that MMR models and typologies can be conceptualized along a continuum of complexity in terms of how systematically quantitative and qualitative inquiry approaches are integrated. Simple multistrand studies can be conducted, whereby some design that is best aligned with quantitative reasoning is complemented by a qualitative add-on, or vice versa. Such complementarity is described throughout this chapter. These sorts of multiple-strand approaches represent the very "DNA" of MMR studies, and in many cases, such approaches are perfectly adequate for addressing a research question. But for this example, we go beyond such integration because we have found that more complex models are needed for culturally relevant intervention development and evaluation (as an aside, do not equate *more complex* with *better*; the integration models we work with were borne out of necessity and not some inherent love of abstraction, and some of the most rigorous research entails simple design).

Iterative models are recursive, and dynamic, in that the knowledge gained from early phases influence later design choices. The RCT described here certainly followed this approach because it was initially understood that aspects of Sri Lankan culture revealed via exploratory work would necessarily alter programmatic thinking (Nastasi, Hitchcock, Sarkar, et al., 2007; Nastasi, Varjas, Sarkar, & Jayasena, 1998). The notion of synergistic models can be understood from the basic idea of synergy, and that is, the whole is greater than the sum of its parts. The Nastasi, Hitchcock, Varjas, et al. (2010) RCT tested an intervention that was rooted in a model of mental health that was derived from extensive interviewing, observations, surveying, document analyses, and time spent in the culture that helped yield an understanding of what Sri Lankan youth found to be stressful and how they cope with stress. From there, this led to conceptualization of an intervention that might yield better outcomes. But a concurrent complexity was the finding that measuring outcomes across large numbers of children in a psychometrically sound manner, which were socially valid and proximally tied to the intervention, required generating culturally specific measures (Hitchcock et al., 2005; Nastasi, Hitchcock, Burkholder, et al., 2007). Hence, one strand of the work entailed measurement development where ethnographically informed themes that were used to generate items were factor analyzed to see if the underlying constructs could be understood using qualitative and quantitative approaches. Consistent with the idea of the whole research agenda being greater than the sum of its quantitative and quali-tative parts, understanding of the cultural constructs was refined by using both approaches. Indeed, a basic consideration was that qualitative steps were needed to even know what questions to include on an instrument, and wide dissemination of the instrument helped establish what was gleaned from interviews, focus groups, document analyses, and observations, which appeared to be relevant to a larger sample of survey respondents. Together, this is consistent with cross-method triangulation and meta-inference (Nastasi, Hitchcock, & Brown, 2010). In sum, the intervention and outcome measures that were relevant to children in the culture (not just the ones exposed to the intervention) were the product of a program of research where findings were revealed across different stages.

To obtain some summative evaluative information, a group of children were randomly assigned to access the intervention, or not. This represents a key point because, to justify wider use of the procedures and to show that it makes a difference, a design that could yield strong causal data was warranted. One hundred and twenty children were randomly sampled from within Grades 6 to 11 from one school (i.e., *n* = 120) and then randomly assigned to be exposed to the intervention in an after-school program or to a no-treatment control group.

Overall, we found important treatment effects. We were unable to gather data on 8 children yielding an analytic sample of 112 students. This represents a form of attrition. We were not overly concerned about this biasing the impact estimate (i.e., in this case, attrition was a minimal threat to internal validity), because if we imputed the best possible scores for missing control children and the worst possible scores for missing treatment children (on outcome measures that could be summarized by a single score), we still found statistically significant and meaningful treatment effects. As noted above, we analyzed data in a manner that accounted for student clustering. We also had several outcome measures and accounted for inflated Type 1 error by using various statistical corrections (details are beyond the scope of this chapter; please see the source citation, Nastasi, Hitchcock, Varjas, et al. [2010] RCT, for details).

The RCT findings were supported by additional measures conducted within the intervention group. We collected narratives of how 51 students responded to and coped with stress. Overall, children exhibited a number of sophisticated strategies that were consistent with intervention goals and, judging from our prior work, were unlikely to have been achieved in the absence of the intervention. Interviews with other stakeholders (administrators and teachers) supported the social validity and acceptability of the program. Treated students were also asked to complete a *life ecomap*, wherein they were asked to graphically depict important relationships in their lives and depict if these relationships were characterized by stress or support or both, and then to provide a narrative of stressful and supportive experiences.[11] Analysis of the ecomaps and related narratives demonstrated understanding of stress and coping consistent with that measured on outcome instruments and with program goals.

Recall the above discussion of moderators. Statistical analyses identified an interesting pattern: On one measure of emotional distress, we identified a gender by treatment interaction, whereby treated girls yielded lower scores than their control counterparts and the opposite was true of boys. This might indicate that the treatment was harmful, but an MMR perspective yields a more nuanced and, we think, accurate idea—that is, treated girls understood their situation better than did girls in the control condition (keep in mind that prior qualitative work compelled us to consider this possibility). The issue

---

[11] We found the ecomap activity to be consistent with the collectivist culture that emphasizes understanding of the self in relationship to others. An example of an ecomap that illustrates this concept is included in Chapter 6.

here is that Sri Lankan culture has different behavioral expectations for females and males; females are socialized to feel responsible for the welfare of others, especially in close relationships (e.g., family, peers). Our interpretation of the treatment effect is that girls became more aware of this issue as they considered their responsibilities in various stressful situations, yielding a complex cultural consideration where we need to consider potential cultural change versus more immediate coping.[12] A key take-home point here is that this provides an example of a synergistic and iterative application of method integration that helps us understand a key moderator.

In terms of external validity and generalization, random sampling did occur, but it was from within one school. Hence, probabilistic generalization should strictly stop at the population of students in that school at the time of the study. But we think that logical generalization can go well beyond that, and our argument is rooted in programmatic MMR investigation. First, we found that the intervention appeared to work and was certainly accepted in other Sri Lankan contexts, and it was informed by a number of culturally laden constructs that still exist as of this writing. That is, we are confident that notions of stress and coping have not changed very much in the past few years even though the country was affected by the tsunami tragedy (see Jayasena, Borja, & Nastasi, 2015; Nastasi, Jayasena, Summerville, & Borja, 2011), and this is drawn from prior ethnographic work. Whether this bears out to be empirically true of course warrants further study. We do of course recognize some limitations; chief among them are that the study was done at the time of civil war, and Northern provinces of the country where fighting occurred may entail markedly different conceptualizations of the key constructs (throughout most of our work there, these regions were not accessible). But here again, logical generalization of the treatment effect can be done more confidently with the benefit of MMR applications. That is, as we consider principles of generalization to different settings, and across time (recall chronosystems from EST), we can do so with greater clarity because we have an experimental

---

[12] This is a highly complex topic both in terms of ethics and research design. As to the former—ethics—we had the support of the Sri Lankan government (provincial ministry) and other stakeholders (e.g., educators) to provide the sort of help described. So long term, we feel comfortable with potential cultural change, just as we would invite some changes to our native cultures. In terms of the latter, more nuanced measurement and replication are needed, and we hope to conduct more studies in the country.

and quantitative sense of the treatment effect as measured by culturally informed measures and because we have an ethnographic sense of why the treatment should have worked. We return to discussion of this work in Chapter 6, in which the program of research and development in Sri Lanka is used to illustrate the application of PCSIM and CMMPE over the course of a multiyear project that covered the full scope of program development, evaluation, and translation.

CONCLUSION

The purpose of this chapter was to introduce an MMR perspective and application on issues of summative program evaluation with causal questions, considerations in outcome measure selection and development, and generalization and translation concerns. These issues are of broad interest to the social sciences, and thinking through them all can be challenging. It is also a challenge to think through these issues when dealing with culturally relevant program evaluation. But what can help is an awareness of iterative and synergistic MMR design models. We do not think that these models necessarily have to be maintained in working memory during design. What is important is to always remain cognizant of the logic and rationale for mixing of methods. But from there, we think that MMR models and approaches can be used to guide program evaluation, in general, and when attending to culture, in particular.

Key Terms

- **Summative evaluation:** Program evaluation for the purpose of establishing the effects (outcome) or overall value of a program, and the process–outcome relationships as they relate to explaining program effects.
- **Transfer:** Helping consumers of research understand if findings from a particular program evaluation are likely to be relevant to their circumstances.
- **Translation:** Dissemination and deployment of research to the same or other populations.

Reflective Questions and Exercises

1. Is there any reason why researchers should *not* consider generalization in its various forms as well as transferability and translation when conducting their own work? When doing applied research, how might these issues be communicated with policymakers and other stakeholders?

2. Find a published article describing causal evidence pertaining to an intervention. Evaluate the degree to which it addressed basic threats to causal validity. How would you characterize the evidence in terms of the various kinds of generalizations described in this chapter?

References

Bloom, H. S. (2005). Randomizing groups to evaluate place-based programs. In H. S. Bloom (Ed.), *Learning more from social experiments: Evolving analytic approaches* (pp. 115–172). New York, NY: Russell Sage Foundation.

Brantlinger, E., Jiminez, R., Klingner, J., Pugach, M., & Richardson, V. (2005). Qualitative studies in special education. *Exceptional Children, 71,* 195–207. doi:10.1177/001440290507100205

Bronfenbrenner, U. (1989). Ecological systems theory. In R. Vasta (Ed.), *Annals of child development* (Vol. 6, pp. 187–249). Greenwich, CT: JAI Press.

Campbell, D. T. (1957). Factors relevant to the validity of experiments in social settings. *Psychological Bulletin, 54,* 297–312.

Campbell, D. T., & Stanley, J. C. (1963). *Experimental and quasi-experimental designs for research.* Chicago, IL: Rand McNally.

Donovan, J., Mills, N., Smith, M., Brindle, L., Jacoby, A., & Peters, T. (2002). Improving design and conduct of randomized trials by embedding them in qualitative research: ProtecT (prostate testing for cancer and treatment) study. *British Medical Journal, 325,* 766–770. doi:10.1136/bmj.325.7367.766

Enders, C. K. (2010). *Applied missing data analysis.* New York, NY: Guilford Press.

Greene, J. C., Caracelli, V. J., & Graham, W. F. (1989). Toward a conceptual framework for mixed method evaluation designs. *Educational Evaluation and Policy Analysis, 11,* 255–274.

Grissmer, D. W., Subotnik, R. F., & Orland, M. (2008). *A guide to incorporating multiple methods in randomized controlled trials to assess intervention effects.* Retrieved from http://www.apa.org/ed/schools/cpse/randomized-control-guide.pdf

Groves, R. M., Fowler, F. J., Couper, M. P., Lepkowski, J. M., Singer, E., & Tourangeau, R. (2009). *Survey methodology* (2nd ed.). Hoboken, NJ: Wiley.

Hedges, L. V. (2013). Recommendations for practice: Justifying claims of generalizability. *Educational Psychology Review, 25*(3), 331–337. doi:10.1007/s10648-013-9239x

Hellström, T. (2008). Transferability and naturalistic generalization: New generalizability concepts for social science or old wine in new bottles? *Quality & Quantity, 42,* 321–337. doi:10.1007/s11135-006-9048-0

Hitchcock, J. H., Nastasi, B. K., Dai, D., Newman, J., Jayasena, A., Bernstein-Moore, R., . . . Varjas, K. (2005). Illustrating a mixed-method approach for validating culturally specific constructs. *Journal of School Psychology, 43,* 259–278. doi:10.1016/j.jsp.2005.04.007

Howley, C., Johnson, J., & Petrie, J. (2011). *Consolidation of schools and districts: What the research says and what it means.* Boulder, CO: National Education Policy Center. Retrieved from http://nepc.colorado.edu/files/PB-Consol-Howley-Johnson-Petrie.pdf

Jayasena, A., Borja, A. P., & Nastasi, B. K. (2015). Youth perspectives about the factors that contribute to psychological well-being in Negombo, Sri Lanka. In B. K. Nastasi & A. P. Borja (Eds.), *Handbook of psychological well-being in children and adolescents: International perspectives and youth voices.* New York, NY: Springer.

Johnson, R. B., & Onwuegbuzie, A. J. (2004). Mixed methods research: A research paradigm whose time has come. *Educational Researcher, 33*(7), 14–26. doi:10.3102/0013189X033007014

Lincoln, Y. S., & Guba, E. G. (1985). *Naturalistic inquiry.* Beverly Hills, CA: Sage.

Maxwell, J. A. (2004). Causal explanation, qualitative research, and scientific inquiry in education. *Educational Researcher, 33*(2), 3–11. Retrieved from http://www.jstor.org/stable/3699970

Nastasi, B. K., & Hitchcock, J. H. (2008). Evaluating quality and effectiveness of population-based services. In B. J. Doll & J. A. Cummings (Eds.), *Transforming school mental health services: Population-based approaches to promoting the competency and wellness of children* (pp. 245–276). Thousand Oaks, CA: Corwin Press with the National Association of School Psychologists.

Nastasi, B. K., & Hitchcock, J. H. (2009). Challenges of evaluating multi-level interventions. *American Journal of Community Psychology, 43,* 360–376. doi:10.1007/s10464-009-9239-7

Nastasi, B. K., Hitchcock, J. H., & Brown, L. M. (2010). An inclusive framework for conceptualizing mixed methods design typologies: Moving toward fully integrated synergistic research models. In A. Tashakkori & C. Teddlie (Eds.), *Handbook of mixed methods in social & behavioral research* (2nd ed., pp. 305–338). Thousand Oaks, CA: Sage.

Nastasi, B. K., Hitchcock, J. H., Burkholder, G., Varjas, K., Sarkar, S., & Jayasena, A. (2007). Assessing adolescents' understanding of and reactions to stress in different cultures: Results of a mixed-methods approach. *School Psychology International, 28*(2), 163–178. doi:10.1177/0143034307078092

Nastasi, B. K., Hitchcock, J., Sarkar, S., Burkholder, G., Varjas, K., & Jayasena, A. (2007). Mixed methods in intervention research: Theory to adaptation. *Journal of Mixed Methods Research, 1,* 164–182. doi:10.1177/1558689806298181

Nastasi, B. K., Hitchcock, J. H., Varjas, K., Jayasena, A., Sarkar, S., Moore, R. B., Albrecht, L. (2010). School-based stress and coping program for adolescents in Sri Lanka: Using mixed methods to facilitate culture-specific programming. In K. M. T. Collins, A. J. Onwuegbuzie, & Q. G. Jiao (Eds.), *Toward a broader understanding of stress and coping: Mixed methods approaches* (pp. 305–342). Charlotte, NC: Information Age.

Nastasi, B. K., Jayasena, A., Summerville, M., & Borja, A. (2011). Facilitating long-term recovery from natural disasters: Psychosocial programming in tsunami-affected schools of Sri Lanka. *School Psychology International, 32,* 512–532. doi:10.1177/0143034311402923

Nastasi, B. K., Moore, R. B., & Varjas, K. M. (2004). *School-based mental health services: Creating comprehensive and culturally specific programs.* Washington, DC: American Psychological Association.

Nastasi, B. K., Varjas, K., Sarkar, S., & Jayasena, A. (1998). Participatory model of mental health programming: Lessons learned from work in a developing country. *School Psychology Review, 27*(2), 260–276.

Raudenbush, S. W., & Bryk, A. S. (2002). *Hierarchical linear models: Applications and data analysis methods* (2nd ed.). Thousand Oaks, CA: Sage.

Rubin, D. B. (1974). Estimating causal effects of treatments in randomized and non-randomized studies. *Journal of Educational Psychology, 66,* 688–701.

Schneider, B., Carnoy, M., Kilpatrick, J., Schmidt, W. H., & Shavelson, R. J. (2007). *Estimating causal effects using experimental and nonexperimental designs* (Report from the Governing Board of the American Educational Research Association Grants Program). Washington, DC: American Educational Research Association.

Scriven, M. (1991). *Evaluation thesaurus* (4th ed.). Newbury Park, CA: Sage.

Shadish, W. R. (1995). The logic of generalization: Five principles common to experiments and ethnographies. *American Journal of Community Psychology, 23*(3), 419–428.

Shadish, W. R. (2010). Campbell and Rubin: A primer and comparison of their approaches to causal inference in field settings. *Psychological Methods, 15*(1), 3–17. doi:10.1037/a0015916

Shadish, W. R., Cook, T., & Campbell, D. (2002). *Experimental and quasi-experimental designs for generalized causal inference.* Boston, MA: Houghton Mifflin.

Stake, R. (1995). *The art of case research.* Thousand Oaks, CA: Sage.

Tashakkori, A., & Creswell, J. W. (2007). Editorial: Exploring the nature of research questions in mixed methods research. *Journal of Mixed Methods Research, 1,* 207–211. doi:10.1177/1558689807302814

U.S. Department of Education. (2003). *Identifying and implementing educational practices supported by rigorous evidence: A user friendly guide.* Retrieved from http://ies.ed.gov/ncee/pdf/evidence_based.pdf

What Works Clearinghouse. (2013). Procedures and standards handbook (Version 3.0). Retrieved from http://ies.ed.gov/ncee/wwc/documentsum.aspx?sid=19

Yin, R. K. (2009). *Case study research: Design and methods.* Thousand Oaks, CA: Sage.

Yoder, J. S., Straif-Bourgeois, S., Roy, S. L., Moore, T. A., Visvesvara, G. S., Ratard, R.C., Beach, M. J. (2012). Primary amoebic meningoencephalitis deaths associated with sinus irrigation using contaminated tap water. *Clinical Infectious Diseases, 55*(9), e79–e85. doi:10.1093/cid/cis626

❖ SIX ❖

MMR MODEL APPLICATION

A Full Example

Learning Objectives

The key objectives of this chapter are to provide the readers with illustrations of the following:

- Application of mixed methods to develop and evaluate intervention programs
- Use of mixed methods to address culture and context in program design, implementation, adaptation, and evaluation
- Use of a participatory and recursive research intervention process (PCSIM) to address culture and context in program development and evaluation

INTRODUCTION

The purpose of this chapter is to illustrate the application of MMR to the development and evaluation of culturally relevant intervention programs. To do this, we draw on a multiyear program of research in Sri Lanka that exemplifies the use of MMR to inform development, implementation, adaptation, and evaluation of culture-specific interventions for promoting psychological well-being of school-age populations. This chapter brings together the multiple phases of the work, many of which have been described in prior publications (see the References). This chapter integrates the full scope of the research, as a representation of MMR for intervention development and evaluation, and thus provides a complete picture for readers of the PCSIM process described in Chapter 2 (see Figure 2.2), from conceptualization to adaptation. In addition, this program of research illustrates the application of MMR to program development, implementation, and evaluation, as described in Chapters 3 through 5. Furthermore, at the heart of this research program was a commitment to culturally relevant construction in partnership with stakeholders to ensure that the program reflected the culture and context of the target population. To accomplish our long-term goals, we engaged in a recursive (denoted by the symbol: ←→) research-intervention process that involved sequential, concurrent, and recursive integration of qualitative and quantitative methods (see Nastasi, Hitchcock, & Brown, 2010).

The structure of this chapter follows the PCSIM process depicted in Figure 6.1. The primary focus is on the application of MMR in respective phases to illustrate the progression from project conceptualization to translation. Within each section, we describe MMR design and methods with a brief presentation of findings for respective phases. The intent is to summarize the multiyear project, with reference to more detailed sources for interested readers.

CONTEXTUAL AND CULTURAL CONSIDERATIONS

The work in Sri Lanka started as an effort to explore culturally relevant constructs related to psychological well-being of children (Nastasi, Moore, & Varjas, 2004; Nastasi, Varjas, Sarkar, & Jayasena, 1998). The efforts in the early phases of the PCSIM process (see Figure 6.1 and Table 6.1), initiated in 1995, focused on exploring the literature, practices, and policies relevant to mental health, or psychological well-being, of children and adolescents (Phase I); gaining an understanding of the culture and context in which we planned to work (Phase II); and establishing partnerships with key stakeholders (Phase III). These phases typically constitute *entry* into the new culture and context. We viewed our entry as an immersion into the target culture and context facilitated by MMR. In Phases I and II, we used a concurrent mixed methods approach, with qualitative methods as dominant (i.e., QUAL + quan). Thus, our conceptualization and understanding of the culture relied primarily on qualitative data collection (see Table 6.1), supplemented by quantitative data from government

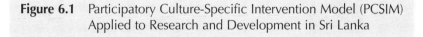

Figure 6.1 Participatory Culture-Specific Intervention Model (PCSIM) Applied to Research and Development in Sri Lanka

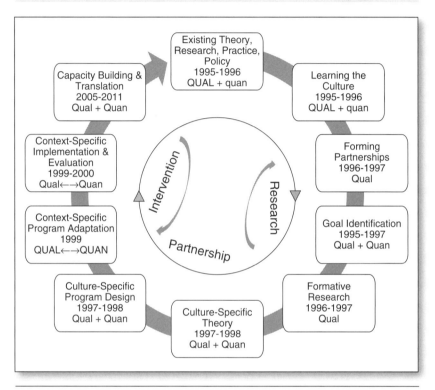

SOURCE: From Nastasi, Moore, and Varjas, K. M. (2004). Copyright 2004 by the American Psychological Association. Adapted with permission. The use of APA information does not imply endorsement by APA.

NOTE: The 10 phases of the model (as depicted in Figure 2.2) were applied during a program of research and development in Sri Lanka that spanned two decades. The specific dates and MMR design relevant to each phase are depicted. Notation for design: Qual = qualitative methods; Quan = quantitative methods; QUAL or QUAN refers to the dominance of one methodology over the other, qual or quan refers to the secondary use of methodology; > = followed by [sequential design]; + = concurrent with [concurrent design]; >/+ = sequential or concurrent; ←→ = recursive/interactive design.

documents. Phase III relied primarily on qualitative methods and overlapped with other phases (I–V). Although depicted as occurring across 2 years, the formation of partnerships continued throughout the multiyear project as we entered new contexts within the country and initiated new phases of the work. However, the primary partnership for the duration of our work was formed in these early years, with Dr. Asoka Jayasena, an educational sociologist and

Table 6.1 Participatory Culture-Specific Intervention Model (PCSIM) Applied to Research and Development in Sri Lanka

Project Phase (Timeline)	MMR Design[a]	Types of Data Collected	Outcomes/Application	Relevant Publications
Phase I (1995–1996) Conceptualization: theory, research, practice, policy	QUAL + quan	Participant observation Key-informant interviews Individual interviews Group interviews/meetings Artifacts Government documents (e.g., policies, data) Professional literature	Development of conceptual model of PWB[b] (see Figure 6.2)	Nastasi et al. (1998) and Nastasi et al. (2004)
Phase II (1995–1996) Learning the culture	QUAL + quan	Participant observation Key-informant interviews Individual interviews Group interviews/meetings Artifacts Government documents (e.g., policies, data) Professional literature Local media Secondary data analysis[c]	Contributed to development of culture-specific framework and identification of PWB needs and resources	Nastasi et al. (1998) and Nastasi et al. (2004)

Phase	Type	Methods	Outcomes	References
Phase III (1996–1997) Forming partnerships	Qual	Key-informant interviews Individual interviews Group interviews/meetings	Identified key partners and stakeholders at local and provincial levels	Nastasi et al. (1998), Nastasi et al. (2004), Nastasi and Jayasena (2014), and Nastasi, Varjas, Bernstein, and Jayasena (2000)
Phase IV (1995–1997) Goal identification	Qual + Quan	[Informed by data collected in Phases I–III]	Formulation of short- and long-term goals with key partners and stakeholders	Nastasi et al. (1998) and Nastasi et al. (2004)
Phase V (1996–1997) Formative research	Qual	Participant observation Key-informant interviews Individual interviews Group interviews Artifacts	Culture-specific definitions of constructs depicted in conceptual framework; identification of PWB needs and resources; development of culture-specific measures of PWB	Hitchcock and Nastasi (2011), Nastasi et al. (1998), Nastasi et al. (2004), and Varjas, Nastasi, Moore, and Jayasena (2005)
Phase VI (1997–1998) Culture-specific theory	Qual + Quan	[Informed by data collected in Phases I–V; dissemination workshop products]	Modification of conceptual model to integrate culture-specific definitions	Nastasi et al. (1998), Nastasi et al. (2004), and Varjas et al. (2005)

(Continued)

Table 6.1 (Continued)

Project Phase (Timeline)	MMR Design[a]	Types of Data Collected	Outcomes/Application	Relevant Publications
Phase VII (1997–1998) Culture-specific program design	Qual + Quan	[Informed by data collected in Phases I–VI]	Design of school-based promotion program (curriculum); design of PWB measures; development of teacher training materials	Nastasi, Hitchcock, Varjas et al. (2010)
Phase VIII (1999) Context-specific implementation and adaptation	Qual ←→ Quan	Participant observations Individual interviews Group interviews Mixed method session logs (implementers) Mixed method session ratings (participants) Curriculum products Culture-specific self-report and teacher-report measures	Piloting, revision, and validation of PWB measures; initial implementation, piloting, and adaptation of program curriculum and teacher training materials for specific school context	Hitchcock et al. (2005), Hitchcock et al. (2006), Hitchcock and Nastasi (2011), Nastasi, Hitchcock, Burkholder et al. (2007), Nastasi, Hitchcock, Varjas et al. (2010)
Phase IX (1999–2000) Context-specific implementation and evaluation	Qual ←→ Quan	Participant observations Individual interviews Group interviews Mixed method session logs (rating scales + narrative) Curriculum products Culture-specific self-report measure (pre-post)	Formative and summative evaluation of PWB program; documented program acceptability, social validity, integrity, and outcomes	Nastasi, Hitchcock, Sarkar et al. (2007) and Nastasi, Hitchcock, Varjas et al. (2010)

142

| Phase X (2005–2011) Translation and capacity building | Qual + Quan | (2005–2008) Participant observations Individual interviews Group interviews Elicitation techniques (ecomaps + narratives) Mixed method session logs (rating scales + narrative) Curriculum products

(2010–2011) Focus groups Individual interviews Participant observations Ecomaps Culture-specific self-report measures | Translation of intervention program to post-tsunami context to facilitate long-term recovery (2005–2008)

Testing of conceptual framework in culturally different community in Sri Lanka (2010–2011)

Planning for new wave of mixed method data collection to examine long-term applicability of cultural constructs and intervention program components (2015–2016) | Jayasena, Borja, and Nastasi (2015), and Nastasi et al. (2011) |

a. Qual = qualitative methods; Quan = quantitative methods; > = followed by [sequential design]; + = concurrent with [concurrent design]; >/+ = sequential or concurrent; ← → = recursive/interactive design; QUAL or QUAN = dominant qualitative or quantitative research method, respectively; qual or quan = secondary/ supplementary research method.

b. PWB = psychological well-being.

c. Data for secondary analysis (qualitative and quantitative) were derived from a previous research project conducted in the same community, with focus on sexual risk among older adolescents and young adults (see Nastasi et al., 1999).

teacher educator from the University of Peradeniya, Sri Lanka. She became a cultural broker (facilitating interpretation and navigation of culture and context) and partner (with the book's first author) in the research intervention process.

The outcomes of Phases I and II were an initial understanding of culture and context, identification of needs and resources related to psychological well-being of children and adolescents in Sri Lanka, and development of a culture-specific model for guiding our work on psychological well-being (depicted in Figure 6.2). Our understanding of Sri Lanka was informed by multiple sources, including qualitative data collection (e.g., observations, interviews), data from government sources (e.g., national census), ongoing interactions with the cultural broker, and reading of professional and popular literature about the history and culture.

Figure 6.2   Conceptual Model of Psychological Well-Being

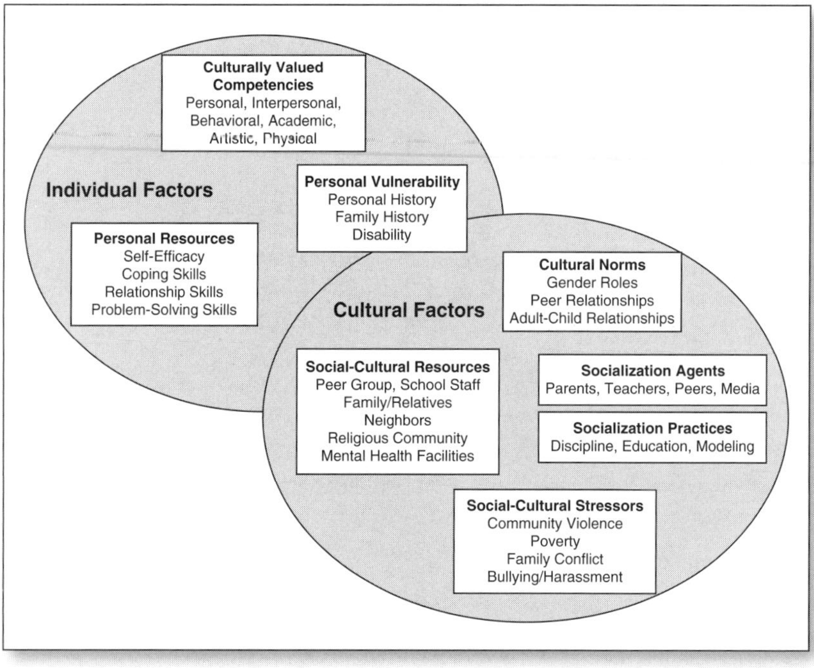

SOURCE: © 1998 by the National Association of School Psychologists, Bethesda, MD. Reprinted with permission of the publisher. www.nasponline.org

NOTE: This model of psychological well-being, based on existing theory and research, guided formative research to identify culture-specific definitions of key constructs and subsequent development of the culture-specific model of psychological well-being for Sri Lanka.

Sri Lanka, a low- to middle-income country, is an island off the southern tip of India, with a democratic socialist government. The population numbers an estimated 20 million and includes several ethnic and religious groups. The majority ethnic group is Sinhalese, followed by Sri Lankan Tamils, Indian Tamils, Ceylon Moors, and Veddhas (a relatively isolated indigenous group). The primary religious group is Buddhist (70%), followed by Hindus (13%), Muslims (10%), and Catholics and other Christians (6% and 1%, respectively) (Sri Lanka Department of Census & Statistics, 2012). The primary, and official, language is Sinhala; other languages spoken include Tamil, Vedda, and English. At the time we began our work, the country was engaged in a civil war, initiated by a rebel Tamil group and largely centered in the Northern and Eastern Provinces; the 30-year war ended in 2009. The culture of the country has been influenced historically by colonization by the Portuguese, Dutch, and (most recently) British. Sri Lanka became an independent country in 1948. The government provides free education and health care, which likely contribute to the reported high literacy and low infant mortality rates, respectively (Karunathilake, 2012). Our work was centered in the Central, Southern, and Western Provinces; the ongoing conflicts in Northern and Eastern Provinces prohibited safe entry. The primary research and development work was conducted in the Central Province, with subsequent translation to Southern and Western provinces.

Our initial research revealed a significant need for services combined with limited resources related to the promotion of psychological well-being of children and adolescents (see Nastasi et al., 1998, for details). First, mental health in the country was organized within a psychiatric framework, and the only services available were provided within medical care facilities for those with moderate to severe mental health problems by the country's fewer than 20 psychiatrists. Services related to mental health promotion, prevention, and early intervention, consistent with a public health models (e.g., Hess, Short, & Hazel, 2012), were nonexistent. Second, Sri Lanka's suicide rate (highest among young adults, ages 20–30 years) was the second highest in the world and the highest in Asia (Communication Center for Mental Health, 1995). Third, the government of Sri Lanka provided free health care and education to its population; thus, community health care facilities and schools were opportune contexts for reaching children and adolescents. Finally, ongoing policy discussions supported schools as the potential site for addressing mental health (psychological well-being) of children and adolescents. For example, a Ministry of Health report (Abeyasinghe & Ratnayake, 1996) cited schools as the potential context for addressing reported mental health concerns such as suicide, aggression, sexuality, and alcohol and other drug abuse. Concurrently, the country's educational system was in a period of reform.

At the conceptual level, our work was guided by Bronfenbrenner's (1989) ecological development perspective (described in Chapter 2 and depicted in Figure 2.1) and a conceptual framework (Figure 6.2) derived from current theory and research on factors that influence mental health at individual and population levels (e.g., Elias & Branden, 1988). Thus, the model that guided our subsequent work was based on the assumptions that the person–ecology interaction was critical, and individual and cultural factors influenced psychological well-being of children and adolescents. The specific factors within individual and cultural domains were determined by a review of research literature in child development and mental health (see Figure 6.2; Nastasi & DeZolt, 1994; Nastasi et al., 1998; Nastasi et al., 2004). The *individual* factors included (a) *culturally valued competencies*, abilities or characteristics valued in the culture; (b) *personal vulnerability*, for example, related to personal or family history; and (c) *personal resources*, skills that facilitate adaptation to different contexts and/or coping with stressors. *Cultural* factors included (a) *social–cultural stressors*, risk factors in the child's ecology that increase the probability of psychological distress and related adjustment problems; (b) *social–cultural resources*, protective factors in the child's ecology that facilitate coping and adaptation and prevent adjustment difficulties; (c) *cultural norms*, culturally defined standards for guiding behavior; (d) *socialization agents*, key stakeholders in the child's ecology; and (e) *socialization practices*, the strategies used by agents to facilitate child development.

An outcome of Phases I to III was identification of long-term and short-term goals (Phase IV) that could guide our subsequent work. Informed by contextual and cultural considerations and the proposed conceptual model, project partners identified long-term goals related to development of school-based programming to promote psychological well-being of children and adolescents, and short-term goals related to conducting formative research to inform development of a culture-specific conceptual framework that would in turn lead to design, implementation, and evaluation of culture-specific programming.

PROGRAM DESIGN

As discussed in Chapter 3, MMR can inform the design of intervention programs. In this section, we describe the application of MMR during formative research in the Central Province of Sri Lanka and the resulting culture-specific explication of the conceptual framework for psychological well-being and initial program design (see Figure 6.1 and Table 6.1, Phases V–VII).

Formative research (Phase V) was conducted for the purpose of defining individual and cultural factors related to psychological well-being, as depicted in Figure 6.2. The research in this phase was conducted in the Central Province of Sri Lanka, centered in the urban community of Kandy, the country's second largest city, and the surrounding villages. The student population of the government-funded schools in the province was drawn from around the country, and students represented the religious, ethnic, and socioeconomic diversity of the country. We engaged in purposive sampling of schools and participants to represent religious, ethnic, and socioeconomic diversity. The target population was students of both genders in Grades 7 to 12 (i.e., adolescents) and grade-specific teachers and school administrators drawn from 18 schools. The data collection method was qualitative (ethnographic), with reliance on group (students, teachers) and individual (administrator) interviews, participant observation in schools and classrooms, and collection of artifacts related to school culture (e.g., school policies). The group interviews with students and teachers constituted the primary data set, with administrator interviews, observations, and artifacts as supplementary. In total, 51 focus group interviews were conducted, 33 with students and 18 with teachers. The student groups included 13 all-female groups, 16 all-male groups, and 4 mixed-gender groups. Teacher groups were typically mixed gender. Interviews were conducted in the participants' primary language (usually Sinhala) with back translation to English. Interviews were semistructured, using questions to elicit definitions of key individual and cultural constructs (depicted in Figure 6.2). For example, we asked questions about the sources of stress (e.g., what makes adolescents angry, scared, etc.), reactions to stressors, sources of support for coping with stressors, and consequences of stressful experiences. These questions helped us define the constructs of social–cultural stressors and resources and personal vulnerabilities and resources for this population. To identify culturally valued competencies, we asked questions about the expectations for children and adults in different roles (student, friend, citizen, teacher, and parent). Questions about parent and teacher roles also provided information relevant to socialization practices. Data across questions provided information relevant to cultural norms (e.g., gender-specific expectations, nature of adult– child interactions). Data were analyzed using a deductive–inductive process— that is, using a deductively derived coding scheme (based on the conceptual framework) along with inductive identification of culture-specific codes, themes, and patterns (see Nastasi, 2008; Nastasi & Borja, 2015). The findings were subsequently presented to a group of 10 educators, educational administrators, college students, and young adults from the Central Province for the purposes of member checking and generating recommendations for subsequent action at policy and practice levels (see Nastasi et al., 1998).

The findings from formative research, along with qualitative and quantita- tive findings from prior phases (I–IV), informed the development of a culture- specific model of psychological well-being (i.e., Figure 6.2 with factors defined by data). The explication of the model constituted Phase VI activities. This model, along with the findings from formative research, informed the design of an intervention program (Phase VII). The three components of the program were (1) a school-based intervention curriculum to promote psycho- logical well-being, (2) self- and teacher-report measures of perceived compe- tence and stress and coping that could be used for population-based assessment as well as program evaluation, and (3) training materials to prepare teachers to implement the curriculum.[1] In developing each of these components, we relied on data from our formative research. For example, in developing the measure of stress and coping, we constructed scenarios (situations) that had been identi- fied in formative data as common sources of stress (e.g., academic pressure) and constructed response options from the data to depict feelings, coping strategies, sources of support, and resultant adjustment difficulties for respec- tive situations (see Nastasi, Hitchcock, Burkholder, et al., 2007).[2] In addition, collective cultural norms, evident in formative research data, influenced the types of activities included in the intervention curriculum. For example, in contrast to the individualistic focus on the "self" and self-development evident

---

[1] Information about the intervention and copies of related materials can be obtained from the first author.

[2] As described in Nastasi, Hitchcock, Burkholder, et al. (2007), the development of this instrument involved a sequential mixed methods design, whereby we generated themes and items from qualitative inquiry and then compared and contrasted quantitative factors with these inductively derived themes.

in social–emotional curricula for U.S. populations, the data from the Sri Lankan population supported a cultural conception of self in relationship to others and development of self as a social process. This subsequently informed our use of the "ecomap"[3] activity as a primary stimulus for generating information and discussion of cultural expectations, stressors, and coping (see Nastasi, Hitchcock, Varjas, et al., 2010).

Ecomaps are graphic representations (drawings) of one's social network. Students are asked to draw themselves in the center and then, surrounding them, all the important people in their lives. They are then asked to label each relationship as stressful, supportive, or combination (stress + support, or ambivalent). Subsequently, students are asked to label each relationship by role (parent, friend, teacher, etc.). Finally, students are asked to respond to questions about associated feelings for each relationship and to construct two stories, one about a stressful experience and one about a supportive experience for the depicted relationships. The stories should include a narrative about what happened, how the situation is related to stress or support, and associated feelings, thoughts, and actions. Students had opportunities throughout the curriculum to draw ecomaps specific to different ecological contexts—family, school, peer group, and general "life" ecomap; the latter was constructed at program initiation and again at program conclusion. Figure 6.3 provides an example of an ecomap by one of the students in the intervention program, produced at program conclusion. Note that the ecomap reflects different ecological contexts; although students were not necessarily instructed to arrange in that manner, they were asked to reflect on the ecomaps constructed throughout and develop one that reflected all aspects of their lives. (Additional information about ecomap administration and data analysis procedures can be obtained from the first author.)

PROGRAM IMPLEMENTATION AND ADAPTATION

The implementation and adaptation of the components of the intervention program (curriculum, measures, teacher training) were facilitated through a recursive, Qual ←→ Quan, application of MMR in Phase VIII (see Table 6.1

---

[3] Recall from Chapter 3 that we described ecomaps as a mixed methods elicitation technique that yields both qualitative and quantitative data.

Figure 6.3   Ecomap

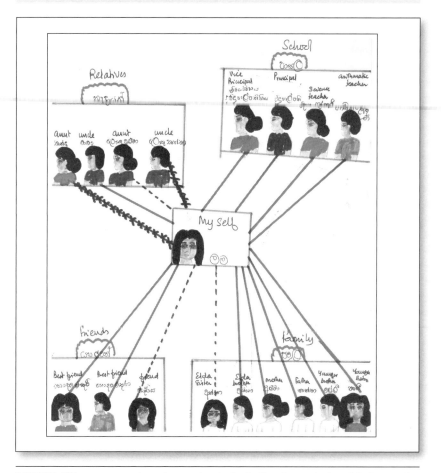

SOURCE: This ecomap was drawn by a student in Grade 10 at the conclusion of the intervention program conducted in the Central Province of Sri Lanka (see Nastasi, Hitchcock, Varjas, et al., 2010, for details about the intervention program).

NOTE: This depicts what we have called a "life ecomap", that is, reflecting important relationships across the person's ecology. The *ecomaps* were used as stimuli to facilitate discussion of "self" in relationship to others and examination of the concepts of stress, support, reactions to stress and support (emotional, cognitive, behavioral), coping strategies, and consequences of stressful experiences for personal adjustment. Although we have subsequently applied ecomaps for both intervention and data collection in other cultures, in Sri Lanka, we capitalized on the congruence with collective cultural norms (i.e., viewing self in relationship to others). In this drawing, note the depiction of relationships within specific ecosystems (consistent with EST, Bronfenbrenner, 1989): friends, school, family, and extended family (relatives). The lines connecting self to each person indicate that the relationship is perceived as stressful (XXX), supportive (—), or ambivalent (combination of stress and support, - - - -). Students labeled the ecomaps in their primary language (in this case, Sinhala), and they were subsequently translated to English.

and Figure 6.1). This phase involved piloting of program components and initial implementation and adaptation to ensure contextual and cultural fit. Although the components were designed based on formative research with the target population, the match to culture and context still needed to be confirmed through initial implementation and data collection. The determination of fit for the curriculum and teacher training was based on participant observations of sessions, individual and group interviews with implementers, collection of session logs (completed by observers and implementers), session ratings (completed by participants), and examination of curriculum products (e.g., ecomaps). In addition, the self-report pretest of stress and coping provided additional data about the participant population. Mixed methods data collection continued during the initial implementation of the curriculum, and modifications were made based on data relevant to program acceptability, social validity, integrity, and impact (see Chapter 4, Figure 4.1).

Examples of modifications resulting from participant and implementer responses (reflected in session ratings and logs, respectively) and participant observations include the following. First, modifications of curriculum activities were made to maximize the focus on self in relationship to others through use of ecomaps at multiple points in the curriculum. Second, ecomaps provided the "contexts" for identification of stressful situations and facilitation of coping responses in curriculum activities. Third, because of teacher difficulty and lack of experience with small group activities (despite current focus in the country on cooperative learning), additional support and consultation on how to facilitate group process were provided. Fourth, because detailed session descriptions in the curriculum manual presented challenges for application, teachers were provided with brief session guides to facilitate ease of implementation (see Nastasi, Hitchcock, Varjas, et al., 2010).

Also included in Phase VIII of the PCSIM process was the piloting, revision, and validation of the psychological well-being measures of perceived competence and stress and coping (see Hitchcock et al., 2005; Hitchcock et al., 2006; Nastasi, Hitchcock, Burkholder, et al., 2007). Measures were translated to Sinhala, piloted for understanding, and revised accordingly. Then the self-report and teacher-report measures were administered in Central Province schools for the purposes of validation. A recursive MMR data analysis procedure was used for validation (described in Hitchcock et al., 2005; Hitchcock et al., 2006; Hitchcock & Nastasi, 2011). This process involved the integration of findings from factor analysis of quantitative data and reanalysis of qualitative data from Phase V to ensure that the factors reflected the cultural constructs identified in the formative research phase.

In the next section, we extend the discussion of the application of mixed methods to program implementation to include both formative and summative evaluation. Consistent with the focus in Phase VIII, we continued to use a recursive mixed methods design as the basis for documenting implementation and evaluating program effectiveness.

PROGRAM EVALUATION

Phase IX involves context-specific program implementation and evaluation (see Figure 6.1 and Table 6.1). In our work in Sri Lanka, we used a recursive Qual ←→ Quan process similar to that employed in the previous phase. Indeed, the formative evaluation process that informed program adaptations continued throughout program implementation. The intervention program was implemented in a single school with 120 students (60 intervention, 60 control) using an RCT to assess program effectiveness (see Nastasi, Hitchcock, Varjas, et al., 2010). The program included 18 sessions that were cofacilitated by teachers from the participating school and graduate students in teacher education from a local university. The purpose of the program was to facilitate development of effective strategies for coping with culturally and contextually relevant stressors (e.g., school, family, peer group). The curriculum was structured so that students had the opportunity to identify culturally valued competencies and context-specific stressors and supports, practice coping strategies, and engage in peer support.

The purposes of evaluation during Phase IX were to document program implementation, and evaluate program acceptability, social validity, integrity, and outcomes. Extending the work of Phase VIII, evaluation was both formative and summative. Thus, formative evaluation continued to inform program adaptation (e.g., increase support for implementers, make minor modifications in program activities), and summative evaluation documented the multiple components of program success (acceptability, integrity, outcome, etc.). The mixed methods applied during Phase IX included session observation, interviews with implementers, session logs (implementers) and ratings (participants), curriculum products, and the measure of stress and coping administered pre- and postintervention. These methods were designed to provide multiple sources of information regarding program acceptability, social validity, integrity, and impact from the perspectives of participants, implementers, and researchers. For example, the combination of observations, interviews, and session logs and ratings informed program acceptability, social validity, and integrity. Moreover, curriculum products and the self-report measure of stress and coping informed program outcomes. Quantitative findings (pre- and post-self-report measure) indicated that students in the intervention program (compared with control) reported lower levels of anticipated adjustment problems when faced with stressful situations (see Nastasi, Hitchcock, Varjas, et al., 2010, for a full report of findings). In addition, males in the intervention (compared with control) reported lower levels of anticipated distress, whereas females in the intervention (compared with control) reported higher levels of anticipated distress in response to stressful situations. Qualitative analysis of student narratives about stressful situations suggested that, by the end of the intervention, students had developed strategies for effective coping that relied on problem solving through individual and communal efforts. In contrast to quantitative findings that suggested lack of impact on perceived helpfulness of social supports, qualitative findings indicated that the program enhanced the use of natural supports such as those provided by peers and teachers. The integration of qualitative and quantitative findings in this study demonstrated the value of mixed methods evaluation for both documenting and explaining program outcomes.

PROMOTING TRANSLATION AND CAPACITY BUILDING

The final phase of PCSIM is focused on translation of culture-specific programming to other contexts within the same general culture, and capacity building within the target context and culture to facilitate continued efforts by stakeholders. To illustrate Phase X, we draw on subsequent research and development efforts in Sri Lanka that occurred following the December 2004 Tsunami (see Nastasi, Jayasena, Summerville, & Borja, 2011). The first of these efforts occurred 15 to 18 months after the tsunami and focused on translating the psychological well-being program that was developed and tested in the Central Province (Phases VII–IX). For this phase, we chose two coastal communities in the Southern Province that had been affected by the tsunami. Our goal was to facilitate long-term recovery through promotion of psychological well-being. Working with a nongovernmental organization, research-intevention partners (Nastasi & Jayasena) selected two government-funded schools in the Southern Province and initiated relationships with school administrators, teachers, and parents of students in Grades 1 to 10. To some extent, prior stages of the PCSIM were repeated; for example, we wanted to explore theory, research, practice, and policy relevant to post-disaster recovery (Phase I revisited), learn the culture of the target communities (Phase II revisited), initiate new partnerships (Phase III revisited), and identify goals for the program (Phase IV). In addition, we conducted brief formative data collection through individual meetings with school adminis-trators and separate group discussions with teachers and students to determine level of need, resources, and potential modifications of the existing program (brief Phase V). Based on revisiting Phases I to V, we modified the interven-tion program by reducing the number of sessions to 10, increasing the focus on identifying and understanding feelings, and adding a focus on environ-mental stressors and related communal support. In addition, we expanded the teacher training sessions and developed a parent education component. The program evaluation was both formative and summative, using mixed meth-ods consistent with those used in the earlier iteration. Given the resistance of the school staff to use of an RCT design and formal pre–post measures, program evaluation relied on qualitative and quantitative data collected during program implementation. Furthermore, qualitative analysis of student ecomaps and narratives collected during each session facilitated our under-standing of the types of stressors experienced by students following a natural disaster (see Nastasi et al., 2011). The findings of this analysis confirmed the utility of the ecomap as a context for discussion and problem solving related to stressful situations and indicated that, 15 to 18 months following a disas-ter, students were contending with both developmentally relevant stressors and those related to long-term recovery. Data also confirmed earlier findings about common stressors and natural supports obtained from the general population in the Central Province.

A subsequent translation phase of the research and development pro-gram in Sri Lanka was conducted in a coastal community in the Western Province, in 2010–2011 (see Jayasena et al., 2015). The purpose of this project was to examine the cultural and contextual relevance of the concep-tual model initially developed in the Central Province and subsequently applied in the Southern Province. The target community, the second largest in the province, is a fishing community with a unique history linked to earlier colonization by the Portuguese and Dutch. Most distinctive is the majority ethnic–religious group of Sinhalese Roman Catholics (recall the majority group of Sri Lanka is Sinhalese Buddhist). The research conducted in this community is best described as concurrent Qual + Quan, using participant observation, focus groups, individual interviews, ecomaps, and self- and teacher-report measures of stress and coping. The target population was male and female students in Grades 6 through 13, and their parents, teachers, and school administrators. An initial report of study findings can be found in Jayasena et al. (2015).

Finally, to facilitate capacity building and translation across time and context, current plans are under way to reinitiate the PCSIM process in the Central Province. The purposes of the proposed work are (a) to examine the applicability of the conceptual model developed in the 1990s to the current context; (b) to test the model across developmental levels and religious, ethnic, and socioeconomic diversity; (b) to conduct further validation of measures of psychological well-being and extend their application to parent- and teacher-report forms; and (c) to extend the application of the intervention program to a broader population. In addition, the intent of future work is to enhance capacity within the country to conduct similar research and intervention efforts. Consistent with the work described in this chapter, future efforts would involve the application of MMR to facilitate a recursive research-intervention process and to ensure cultural and contextual specificity.

CONCLUSIONS

The purpose of this chapter was to illustrate the application of MMR to development and evaluation of intervention programs. Drawing on a multiyear program of research, we provided examples of the use of mixed methods designs within the PCSIM. The program of research yielded a number of studies whose findings guided subsequent studies as well as practical applications. As illustrated in Figure 6.1 and Table 6.1, the phases of the PCSIM process involved research that relied on qualitative, quantitative, and/or mixed methods. Furthermore, as we have described elsewhere (Nastasi, Hitchcock, & Brown, 2010; Nastasi,

Hitchcock, Sarkar, et al., 2007), the multiyear cycle of conceptualization to translation is an example of an iterative mixed methods approach in which the design morphs as one phase informs the next. As depicted in Figure 6.1, the design varied from Qual (Phases III and V), to Qual + Quan (IV, VI, VII, X) or QUAL + quan (I and II), to synergistic integration Qual ←→ Quan (Phases VII and IX). Thus, within the PCSIM cycle, one might characterize phases as single studies (monostrand) and multiple phases as examples of multistrand research. We return to the discussion of mixed methods designs in monostrand versus multistrand research in Chapter 8. In the next chapter, we address the challenges of using MMR for intervention development and evaluation and provide some strategies for addressing challenges based on our experiences.

Reflective Questions and Exercises

1. Develop a plan for applying PCSIM to develop and evaluate an intervention program related to your area of study. Be sure to outline the steps for each of the 10 phases of PCSIM.

2. Consider the plan you developed in response to #1. Identify how your program plan differs from existing approaches (described in research literature) to interventions in your discipline or specialty.

3. Using the illustration from this chapter, critique the application of PCSIM in terms of the use of MMR to
   a. inform program development and evaluation,
   b. facilitate attention to culture and context, and
   c. contribute to program adaptation.

4. Identify evidence-based interventions within your own area of study and discuss the extent to which and how the program developers addressed culture and context. Generate strategies for adapting the program to another culture and context.

References

Abeyasinghe, R., & Ratnayake, P. (1996). *Youth needs and their health problems*. Colombo, Sri Lanka: Ministry of Health, Family Health Bureau.

Bronfenbrenner, U. (1989). Ecological systems theory. In R. Vasta (Ed.), *Annals of child development* (Vol. 6, pp. 187–249). Greenwich, CT: JAI Press.

Communication Centre for Mental Health. (1995). Suicide: The Sri Lankan syndrome. *CCMH Journal of Mental Health, 2*(4), 4–5.

Elias, M. J., & Branden, L. R. (1988). Primary prevention of behavioral and emotional problems in school-aged populations. *School Psychology Review, 17,* 581–592.

Hess, R. S., Short, R. J., & Hazel, C. E. (2012). *Comprehensive children's mental health services in schools and communities: A public health problem solving model.* New York, NY: Routledge.

Hitchcock, J., & Nastasi, B. K. (2011). Mixed methods for construct validation. In P. Vogt & M. Williams (Eds.), *Handbook of methodological innovation* (pp. 249–268). Thousand Oaks, CA: Sage.

Hitchcock, J. H., Nastasi, B. K., Dai, D. C., Newman, J., Jayasena, A., Bernstein-Moore, . . . Varjas, K. (2005). Illustrating a mixed-method approach for identifying and validating culturally specific constructs. *Journal of School Psychology, 43*(3), 259–278. doi:10.1016/j.jsp.2005.04.007

Hitchcock, J. H., Sarkar, S., Nastasi, B. K., Burkholder, G., Varjas, K., & Jayasena, A. (2006). Validating culture- and gender-specific constructs: A mixed-method approach to advance assessment procedures in cross-cultural settings. *Journal of Applied School Psychology, 22,* 13–33. doi:10.1300/J370v22n02_02

Jayasena, A., Borja, A. P., & Nastasi, B. K. (2015). Youth perspectives about the factors that contribute to psychological well-being in Negombo, Sri Lanka. In B. K. Nastasi & A. P. Borja (Eds.), *Handbook of psychological well-being in children and adolescents: International perspectives and youth voices.* New York, NY: Springer.

Karunathilake, I. M. (2012). Health changes in Sri Lanka: Benefits of primary health care and public health. *Pacific Journal of Public Health, 24,* 663–671. doi:10.1177/1010539512453670

Nastasi, B. K. (2008). Advances in qualitative research. In T. Gutkin & C. Reynolds (Eds.), *The handbook of school psychology* (4th ed., pp. 30–53). New York, NY: Wiley.

Nastasi, B. K., & Borja, A. P. (2015). Promoting psychological well-being globally: Project approach to data collection and analysis. In B. K. Nastasi & A. P. Borja (Eds.), *Handbook of psychological well-being in children and adolescents: International perspectives and youth voices.* New York, NY: Springer.

Nastasi, B. K., & DeZolt, D. M. (1994). *School interventions for children of alcoholics.* New York, NY: Guilford Press.

Nastasi, B. K., Hitchcock, J. H., & Brown, L. M. (2010). An inclusive framework for conceptualizing mixed methods design typologies: Moving toward fully integrated synergistic research models. In A. Tashakkori & C. Teddlie (Eds.), *Handbook of mixed methods in social and behavioral research* (2nd ed., pp. 305–338). Thousand Oaks, CA: Sage.

Nastasi, B. K., Hitchcock, J. H., Burkholder, G., Varjas, K., Sarkar, S., & Jayasena, A. (2007). Assessing adolescents' understanding of and reactions to stress in different cultures: Results of a mixed-methods approach. *School Psychology International, 28*(2), 163–178. doi:10.1177/0143034307078092

Nastasi, B. K., Hitchcock, J., Sarkar, S., Burkholder, G., Varjas, K., & Jayasena, A. (2007). Mixed methods in intervention research: Theory to adaptation. *Journal of Mixed Methods Research, 1*(2), 164–182. doi:10.1177/1558689806298181

Nastasi, B. K., Hitchcock, J. H., Varjas, K., Jayasena, A., Sarkar, S., Moore, R. B., . . . Albrecht, L. (2010). School-based stress and coping program for adolescents in Sri Lanka: Using mixed methods to facilitate culture-specific programming. In K. M. T. Collins, A. J. Onwuegbuzie, & Q. G. Jiao (Vol. Eds.), *Research on stress and coping in education: Vol. 5. Toward a broader understanding of stress and coping. Mixed methods approaches* (pp. 305–342). Charlotte, NC; Information Age.

Nastasi, B. K., & Jayasena, A. (2014). An international partnership promoting psychological well-being in Sri Lankan schools. *Journal of Educational and Psychological Consultation, 24*(4), 265–282. doi:10.1080/10474412.2014.929965

Nastasi, B. K., Jayasena, A., Summerville, M., & Borja, A. (2011). Facilitating long-term recovery from natural disasters: Psychosocial programming for tsunami-affected schools of Sri Lanka. *School Psychology International, 32,* 512–532. doi:10.1177/0143034311402923

Nastasi, B. K., Moore, R. B., & Varjas, K. M. (2004). *School-based mental health services: Creating comprehensive and culturally specific programs.* Washington, DC: American Psychological Association.

Nastasi, B. K., Schensul, J. J., deSilva, M. W. A., Varjas, K., Silva, K. T., Ratnayake, P., & Schensul, S. L. (1999). Community-based sexual risk prevention program for Sri Lankan youth: Influencing sexual-risk decision making. *International Quarterly of Community Health Education, 18*(1), 139–155.

Nastasi, B. K., Varjas, K., Bernstein, R., & Jayasena, A. (2000). Conducting participatory culture-specific consultation: A global perspective on multicultural consultation. *School Psychology Review, 29*(3), 401–413.

Nastasi, B. K., Varjas, K., Sarkar, S., & Jayasena, A. (1998). Participatory model of mental health programming: Lessons learned from work in a developing country. *School Psychology Review, 27*(2), 260–276.

Sri Lanka Department of Census & Statistics. (2012). Population by religion according to districts, 2012. *Sri Lanka Census of Housing and Population.* Retrieved from http://www.statistics.gov.lk/PopHouSat/CPH2011/index.php?fileName=pop43&gp=Activities&tpl=3

Varjas, K., Nastasi, B. K., Moore, R. B., & Jayasena, A. (2005). Using ethnographic methods to inform development of culture-specific interventions. *Journal of School Psychology, 43*(3), 241–258. doi:10.1016/j.jsp.2005.04.006

☘ SEVEN ☘

IMPLEMENTATION AND EVALUATION CHALLENGES

Learning Objectives

The key objectives of this chapter are for readers to do the following:

- Consider common challenges in program implementation and evaluation in cross-cultural settings
- Comprehend the idea that one can work in a different culture without necessarily leaving a country
- Understand the possible solutions for the various challenges described

INTRODUCTION: COMMON CHALLENGES IN PROGRAM IMPLEMENTATION AND EVALUATION

At this point, it is our hope that readers have a strong understanding of how any number of contextual and cultural factors should be expected to influence intervention development, service delivery, and program evaluation. Furthermore, readers should now see how to harness MMR applications to generate culturally specific interventions and program evaluation models. A wide variety of options exist, ranging from simple, parallel designs that use strengths associated with one form of inquiry to compensate for weaknesses of another when engaged in either intervention development or program evaluation to highly integrated, iterative, and multistep procedures (see Chapter 6) that can be implemented across a program of research and likely not a single study.

Complex approaches can be more easily pursued by consulting models and figures that promote planning for months or even years ahead. Although we think that the concepts described in earlier chapters yield the knowledge base needed to carry out culturally specific intervention development and evaluation, a task that remains is to offer an overview of the numerous challenges that accompany such efforts. In our own work, we have not always handled these challenges as well as we would have liked, and we expect that, in any given research effort, problems will sometimes arise that will undermine the rigor and quality of inquiry. But we also expect that such challenges can be minimized to a degree by understanding what they are. The purpose of this chapter is to review such challenges; this review primarily describes challenges in the abstract so that readers might consider how the general rule applies to their own efforts.

ESTABLISHING AND MAINTAINING PARTNERSHIPS

Of all the challenges reviewed in this chapter, those around partnering may be the most dynamic, complex, and far reaching. Partnership plays a critical role in PCSIM, beginning with the initial *entry* into the new culture and context (Phases I–III), as described in Chapter 6. Anyone will appreciate that it can be hard to make it through some family gatherings without argument or at least discomfort, much less through large-scale projects. And as readers can intuitively understand even without the benefit of this book, dealing with cultural differences can at times be highly complex. Indeed, a few theorists point out that dealing with new cultural norms and differences can be so complex that it is hard to understand their influence when delivering services (e.g., Sue, 1998). For those of us who embrace such opportunities, we understand that misunderstandings arise with little trouble, and there are times when patience is needed by all parties. Even in scenarios where researchers are dedicated to helping others, there are numerous examples where such altruism can be unwanted or even construed as insulting. This can happen without necessarily having to cross international borders. Within the United States, for example, decades of research and service have been allocated to the rural areas of the country, and some have observed that when interventionists assume that there is a deficit in the culture in which they are operating (i.e., something is wrong) and make no effort to build on existing strengths, then stakeholders may reject any efforts of help. Furthermore, assuming a deficit of this sort can serve to legitimize the status quo and thus serve to strengthen some of the very structures an interventionist might seek to change (see also Johnson, Shope, & Roush, 2009; Johnson & Strange, 2007). These same challenges can of course occur when working in any cultural context that is different from one's own. Similar criticism can be made of well-meaning individuals or groups coming from more affluent backgrounds and seeking to intervene in low-income urban communities in the United States. As we noted in Chapter 1 of this book, some intervention may even make matters worse precisely because of a lack of cultural understanding or some unexamined assumption that some group should be more like the culture to which the interventionist belongs.

In short, it can be easy to be clumsy, and intervention can potentially be iatrogenic without careful attention to cultural nuance. Ironically, it may actually be easier to make such errors when familiarity increases because one can be all the more cavalier. A U.S. researcher might, for example, be fairly cautious about cultural nuances and differences when working in, say, India but not as quickly recognize the need for caution when working in, say, high-poverty districts in New Orleans. Of course, a typical U.S. researcher is likely much better equipped in the latter case because of language familiarity, widespread recognition of some of the troubles the city has contended with in the past, and so on. But still such familiarity would entail having sufficient reason for ignoring or otherwise being unaware of issues like long-standing differences among different ethnicity groups, how schools in the city operate, religious influences in social science settings, and so on.

An initial solution for much of this is to embrace the idea of partnering, both with other researchers and with local staff. A general strategy that has been recognized for some time among qualitative researchers is to identify **gatekeeper**s (e.g., Jezewski, 1990; Jezewski & Sotnik, 2001; Lincoln & Guba, 1985) and **cultural brokers** (e.g., Lincoln & Guba, 1985). People in the *gatekeeper* role have some sort of local authority or other capacity that can be used to garner interest in and commitment to planned work. Gatekeepers may also play a role in protecting area organizations and stakeholders and bar or undermine access to needed samples, institutions, and other resources (i.e., they serve a gatekeeping function); hence, it is often necessary to not only identify gatekeepers but also convince them of the value of the proposed research (think again about aforementioned constructs like *acceptability* and *social validity*). The gatekeeper role has, incidentally, been recently recognized in other literatures, such as advice around the planning and conduct of RCTs (e.g., Gallo et al., 2012). *Cultural brokers*, by contrast, provide guidance about local norms, values, and practices that can help researchers better navigate the context. They may even help researchers refine their questions, and this process is promoted by engaging in emergent design approaches. The role of gatekeepers and cultural brokers are not necessarily mutually exclusive, and indeed, people in these positions may even be considered as formal partners in any given study. Dr. Asoka Jayasena (see Chapter 6), for example, facilitated and helped maintain a multidecade collaboration that, on balance, has proven to be a stable program of research despite deep and fundamental differences in culture, vast travel distances, minimal funding, and highly different languages. In this work, she served in all three capacities (cultural broker, gatekeeper, and partner).

Once partnerships are established, this by definition means working with other people, but it can be difficult to maintain relationships. The authors of this text have, between them, some experience in mixed methods intervention and evaluation in four countries and more than a few cross-national collaborations. In some of these efforts, there were ventures that did not yield useful outcomes because a partnership did not thrive. Problems can sometimes stem from partnerships that feel forced because of an agreement made at some higher level in a hierarchy without gaining full *acceptance* (e.g., a principal agrees to research but not the teachers). Recall that acceptability is a formal construct that can be empirically assessed, and it can pay dividends to understand the degree to which key stakeholders might not agree with some aspect of a study.

Another facet worth considering is that partnerships will naturally alter over the course of a study. One might, for example, spend considerable time with research methodologists when planning, then work with local stakeholders when collecting data, and finally work together with people in leadership roles when disseminating findings. Planning for these sorts of natural breaks and changes are needed to maintain role clarity and proper management of resources. In short, partnership building and maintenance is critical for ongoing program success. It is necessary to find stakeholders who have local capacity to effect change and have enough of an understanding of research purpose to help set the stage for wider team building. Furthermore, many of these principles apply to issues of stakeholder commitment, especially when involved with participatory work.

GAINING AND MAINTAINING
STAKEHOLDER COMMITMENT

The second author of this book once saw an opportunity to engage in long-term research in a highly unusual school district. The district was small, serving approximately 400 students across Grades K to 12 and remote, serving a widespread rural community. The district also was unusually successful with respect to obtaining external resources (e.g., grants) and a teaching corps with intense commitment. The initial gatekeeper, a school principal, was highly supportive of applying initial qualitative inquiry to better understand some of the rare, if not unique, challenges and opportunities students in the district faced and how teachers worked to generate the best possible educational experience. There were not many teachers in the school, and a handful took a real interest in starting a study that would tell the story of their work. The project was, however, ultimately abandoned because full stakeholder commitment was not gained, and this led to a loss of commitment by those who were initially interested. There may have been two interacting difficulties. The key one was that a series of local articles were produced that had nothing to do with the planned research that some staff viewed as bad press for the high school, and some key players became concerned about how an external group might characterize the overall district in a public report. A second issue that came up was lack of understanding of the design. One science teacher, who understood data to be numerical and research to be adherence to the scientific method through formal hypothesis testing, had real difficulty understanding some of the exploratory and emergent design approaches associated with initial qualitative work. Later discussion revealed that this teacher did not recognize interview responses and documents to be forms of data. It also happened that this person was an excellent teacher and a charismatic leader, albeit an informal one, for the school. The perception that the design was not clear to this person with the worry that more bad press may result from the work ultimately undermined stakeholder commitment to a point where it was judged that the research should not proceed.

We tell this story to demonstrate the importance of gaining stakeholder buy-in, maintaining it, and taking the time to seek out informal leaders in a given context to talk through concerns before they become entrenched. It is also important to attend to the dynamic nature of research and monitor if perceived threats emerge when planning. In the above example, the so-called bad press occurred after initial entry into the setting and probably snowballed in importance when the issue of public reporting was discussed. This scenario, which occurred nearly 20 years before this writing, might have had a more favorable outcome with the presentation of big picture models such as PCSIM and the possible benefits of the work to the local group. This sort of communication would have been easier if there were greater resources for researchers to spend more time in the district, hear about concerns, and identify benefits of proceeding from a host of stakeholders. A final thought here is that some of our work has been generated because we were asked to pursue it by local stakeholders. As we noted above, sometimes the desire to help may be perceived as an insult, and even when asked to begin work, intervention is never an easy task. A general set of considerations is to avoid deficit-based thinking and identify the strengths that can be built on in a local setting and rely heavily on the participatory emphasis of the models described in previous chapters. Participatory models should, by design, promote buy-in because stakeholders will have a say in how research is conducted and possibly develop their own skill sets.

FORMING SUSTAINABLE DECISION-MAKING TEAMS

The application of mixed methods work has a known difficulty, which is that few people hold the requisite skills to conduct all strands of research (e.g., Onwuegbuzie, 2007; Onwuegbuzie & Johnson, 2006). That is, few people are able to handle advanced qualitative inquiry, statistical analyses, and fully integrated mixing of methods. Furthermore, most efforts to develop and evaluate culturally specific interventions will require large research teams to handle data collection, and it is highly unlikely that any of these efforts can be done without a group of partners and gatekeepers. Hence, teams (with both researchers and stakeholders) need to be formed and sustained. With regard to team formation, it is important to ensure that individuals with local knowledge and sufficient standing with stakeholders to open doors are available and included in key decision making.[1] As to the latter point, sustaining a team, a

---

[1] It may be necessary to allocate resources (i.e., time, meeting spaces, team-building activities) to develop a shared, collaborative vision that can guide team activities. This can of course come from informal socializing as well as from formal activities like meetings and retreats. For further information on team building, see Friend and Cook (2013), Nastasi, Moore, and Varjas (2004), and Stone, Patton, and Heen (2010).

constant threat to functioning is staff turnover. As noted in Chapter 6, some projects take a long time to carry out, and it is thus necessary to assume that some people will drop out of a project. It is also possible that a staff member may still formally be involved in a project but because of a job change (e.g., a promotion), it is difficult for the key person to be as involved. Of course, while working with multi-organizational efforts, it is to be expected that some new staff may be added into the mix, and they may not always have the same appreciation of the original plans. These challenges can be met with careful communication about changes in plans, and it is generally good management advice to avoid making any single person indispensable to the project. It is also necessary to maintain good consulting skills and attend to changing priorities. Culturally specific intervention may bring with it cultural change, and it is thus important to remain vigilant about changes in priorities. It is also necessary to keep staff engaged as time passes.

ADDRESSING STAFF DEVELOPMENT NEEDS

Staff engagement segues to staff development needs. In initial project stages, it is important not to underestimate training. We have found some cultures to be taken with a particular type of inquiry (typically quantitative), and some local stakeholders may be somewhat cavalier about their own abilities and eschew training. This can be especially true with tasks like interviewing and observations, whereby the need for careful and systematic application of these techniques might potentially give way to poor rigor and confusion. Another irony here is that sometimes the very sort of initial understanding of a data collection procedure (we all understand interviewing to a degree) can undermine training because some people may not take seriously how little they, in fact, know. Another aspect of training is that many times graduate students will be involved in the work, and there will be a need for thoughtful development opportunities.

An answer for much of these concerns is to keep in mind that the approaches described in the book tend to be long term and broken into natural component parts. Initial projects that entail teamwork might thus involve highly concrete and straightforward tasks that can be completed while skills are refined and people become used to working with each other. If there is doubt about capacity, then there are different models for capacity building related to evaluation (**evaluation capacity building [ECB]**) approaches[2] (e.g., Labin, Duffy, Meyers,

Wandersman, & Lesesne, 2012; Preskill & Boyle, 2008), which can be generalized to include intervention implementation skills. Contemporary ECB models generally call attention to basic questions, including "What capacity needs to be promoted, for whom, and why?" This in turn promotes needs assessment activities that have to be informed by the nature of the intervention to be implemented, the evaluation questions to be pursued, and the long-term goals, such as whether the vision is for local staff to completely take over evaluation work over time. This information will inform process activities like when and how to provide training, as well as how to assess outcomes from a capacity-building perspective. The work of Labin et al. (2012) focuses on an integrative ECB model (which again can be conceptually generalized to other staff development concerns such as implementation capacity) and lists the following questions:

> What are the needs preceding ECB efforts? What strategies are being used for ECB and what implementation variables are being reported? What evaluation approaches and methods are being used to assess ECB efforts? What outcomes of ECB are being reported at the individual and organizational levels? (p. 312)

Labin et al. (2012) further point out the importance of considering how development strategies vary by preexisting resources and how training outcomes vary by strategy. There are of course other types of ECB models, but we find the work of Labin et al. to be appealing because the questions they pose can be applied conceptually to a broad range of staff development questions. Of course, there is value in turning staff development into its own evaluation research project that may or may not be pursued by an external team of researchers. This in turn represents yet another facet of partnering and yields additional questions about resources.

RESOURCE ACQUISITION AND ALLOCATION

Clearly resource allocation is a concern for any research project. A key challenge for this sort of work is that financial support can be harder to come by

---

[2] Other sources of information about capacity building can be found in international research and development—for example, Eade (1997).

with initial foci on exploration and piloting. It may also be the case that the work is to be done in high-poverty environments, but this is not always the case. A general principle to consider here is to match the funding need to the immediate study scope. It is our hope that this book will inspire and otherwise promote programmatic thinking and not just focus on singular studies. Of course, obtaining support for a program of research can seem overwhelming. As we have indicated, the planning of multi-phase programs of research, using models such as PCSIM, evolves as data are collected and decisions are made with partners. And funding agencies are reasonably reluctant to fund such emerging designs. Funding agencies and academic decision makers reasonably want to see results before offering money, time, and resources. Such results first should come in the form of learning important aspects of a target setting or culture and/or generating findings that should yield important outcomes for stakeholders. In the current academic environment, studies must also be published if researchers hope to be afforded the time, space, and resources to carry out their work.

All of this is made possible and even facilitated by switching back and forth between programmatic thinking and the scope of a single study. In other words, it can help to remain cognizant of the difference between seeking funding for a stage within a program of research instead of trying to seek multiyear support in a dynamic environment where partners and priorities are likely to change. Consider that most documents, whether of a grant application or a manuscript to be published, should begin with a review of what is already known so as to justify a set of research questions and end with conclusions that generally describe what is next. Both sets of concerns are easier to think about and communicate by attending to and describing one's program of study. In terms of resource allocation, be sure to have someone on a team who can think through fiscal choices and time lines. Grant funds should be thought of in light of a *burn rate*, where one attends to the rate of resource expenditure relative to a given goal. If a step is going to take too much money, time, or effort, then careful accounting must be taken to understand how critical the step is to the study. In our experience, resources are always tight, so attending to expenditures will often yield ideas on how to save money, obtain free help, or pursue matching gifts. Here again, articulating how a specific study fits within a program of research, to the best of our knowledge, can lead to better arguments for why the work should be funded.

CREATING VERSUS ADAPTING EXISTING EBIs

EBIs and their application represent a popular topic in the current literature and represent major social investments during the past several years. An example of this is the *What Works Clearinghouse*, funded by the U.S. federal government, which is a major project that purports to identify EBIs in education and promote their use (What Works Clearinghouse, 2008). Clearly, much of the justification for the steps described in this book is predicated on the assumption that there is no existing EBI for a particular culture or context, or if there is one, it is not easily adapted. Given some of the examples in Chapter 1, it is important indeed to be vigilant about erroneously assuming that an EBI can be readily used in a new culture, but so long as the assumption is reasonable, we fully endorse taking advantage of prior work. It may very well be the case that intervention development is not where resources need to be spent, but rather, researchers should focus on concerns such as acceptability and social validity. Thinking through this requires careful consideration of the constructs at work (e.g., the nature of the intervention and the outcomes on which it operates), embedded within the target culture, while applying principles of logical generalization and transferability. These considerations all form a complex question: *Can the EBI work here?* The answer may be *yes*. In this sense, we are not at odds with this way of thinking about the EBI movement and indeed consider ourselves to be a part of it. And, as we discussed in Chapter 2, the question about adaptability of EBIs (i.e., translating science to practice) is at the heart of implementation science. Furthermore, we think that logical generalization (described in Chapter 5) and thinking through **inference quality** (described in a later section of this chapter) are underutilized when thinking through how existing interventions might be applied in new settings. We argue that it is critical to avoid being cavalier about cross-cultural assumptions, particularly when dealing with notions of mental health and education, which are inextricably linked with cultural norms, values, and expectations. And, as we have mentioned earlier, culture is always a local consideration, even when working in our own communities or country.

A real challenge then is thinking through the decision to create an intervention that is designed for use within a particular culture versus adapting something that already exists. Three broad principles apply here. The first is to keep an open mind. We worry that the effort that goes into intervention development may bias researchers against the process, but the rewards of making a real difference to a new group in a way that could not have been possible prior to the generation of a novel treatment are not trivial. A second principle is to pilot use of the EBI. If logic and available literature dictate that some intervention might be readily applied, try it on a small scale and formatively evaluate how well it worked while focusing on cultural fit, need for adaptation, and what elements can be adapted. This will lead to a third principle of distinguishing between surface and deep structure aspects of the intervention. That is, there may be some element that is easily negotiable (e.g., if therapy is offered in the morning vs. the afternoon) and others that are not (e.g., theory and experience show that dosage must be five times per week, otherwise the benefits will not be accrued). Navigating these efforts can yield valuable insights into the culture of interest and the constructs on which one hopes to operate, but again, the open mind principle must be followed. It is a recipe for trouble to walk into new settings with an a priori assumption that a favored theory explains what is needed or a favored approach need only be applied because it worked elsewhere.

THINKING THROUGH MMR DESIGN QUALITY

Another challenge is that it can be difficult to know how to best mix different approaches to inquiry and to judge the rigor of MMR studies. This is because there is an enormous variety of MMR design options (e.g., Nastasi, Hitchcock, & Brown, 2010); the need to understand quantitative, qualitative and MMR design (e.g., Johnson & Onwuegbuzie, 2004); a somewhat limited literature base that describes mixed methods inference quality (O'Cathain, 2010); and, we think, paradigmatic arguments about whether qualitative approaches are inherently better than quantitative ones, or vice versa (see also Lincoln & Guba, 1985; Newman & Hitchcock, 2011; Onwuegbuzie, 2012). As to the last point, arguing about design superiority, or rejecting a whole class of design options (e.g., "I only believe in quantitative design"), is a bit like arguing about whether a hammer is superior to a saw (see also Shadish, 1995). Whether it is better to use one tool or another depends on the immediate task at hand (and any carpenter would want to have access to both tools and more). We thus hope that readers see from prior chapters that both qualitative and quantitative ideas are both deeply rooted and inextricably tied together in our overall thinking about program design and evaluation. We fully agree that singular classes of methods for such work can be used, and sometimes it is even efficient to do so, but we do not embrace one type of inquiry out of some methodological fealty or worry that one approach is superior to another. Rather, we see research more as a monolithic endeavor with qualitative and quantitative components that are typically needed to best understand phenomena (see also Hitchcock & Newman, 2013; Nastasi & Hitchcock, 2009; Newman & Hitchcock, 2011). In other words, embracing MMR approaches permeates our thinking when dealing with cultural influences and evaluation, but we can also imagine cases where MMR might not be needed. But even if one is emancipated from the paradigm disagreements, the sheer variety of MMR designs and the need to understand so many specialized design issues does make it difficult to know if a particular approach was well executed.

In terms of the literature on MMR quality, O'Cathain (2010) points out a number of complexities. One is that there is not yet a shared language around what many think of as validity, rigor, credibility, trustworthiness, and so on. There is also some disagreement (we think it is minimal) around how to assess *inference quality*—that is, dealing with design quality and rigor behind interpretation (see also O'Cathain, 2010; Tashakkori & Teddlie, 2008), and the competing but also overlapping notion of **legitimation**, which deals with making judgments about the validity, trustworthiness, and rigor of both qualitative and quantitative work (Johnson & Onwuegbuzie, 2004; Onwuegbuzie & Johnson, 2006). Indeed, it seems that dealing with MMR quality is both a process and an outcome. Furthermore, O'Cathain (2010) points out that although major mixed method theorists offer design-specific criteria (e.g., Creswell & Plano Clark, 2007), these cannot be applied to all potential research questions where MMR can be used. In the end, even though mixed methods scholars have worked on a rich and multifaceted set of considerations around issues of MMR quality, ranging from assessing component designs (i.e., the degree to which a qualitative or quantitative part was done well), how well one aspect compensates for the strengths of another, the strength of meta-inference, concerns in generalization, and to even political considerations, we simply cannot rely on some simple recipe to follow that it should yield high-quality MMR designs.

But this does not mean that the challenge of thinking through MMR quality is insurmountable. The key, we think, is to focus on principles of research quality. We also see parallels with CMMPE and PCSIM ideas such as the cycle of research (recall Chapter 2) and existing frameworks about inference quality and legitimation. Consider the eight steps of Johnson and Onwuegbuzie's (2004) process model:

> (1) determine the research question; (2) determine whether a mixed design is appropriate; (3) select the mixed method or mixed-model research design; (4) collect the data; (5) analyze the data; (6) interpret the data; (7) legitimate the data; and (8) draw conclusions (if warranted) and write the final report. (p. 21)

By our way of thinking, MMR quality should emerge from the careful application of this process. But two critical points here are that one must begin with a *clear* question and not lose sight of how the question should inform *systematic* research design. Even if one needs to use an exploratory/emergent approach, where a full set of questions cannot be articulated at the beginning, it is still critical to pursue clarity, and this merits special attention, especially because emergent design is common in cross-cultural work. In the case where emergent design is to be used, clarity entails being open and up front that a final set of questions necessarily cannot be addressed at the beginning, why this is the case, and describing the design approaches that should lead to question refinement. When an emergent approach is not necessary, then it is critical to just be clear about the question to be answered, not losing sight of it, and thinking about design as a systematic approach for answering the question. Being systematic means having a plan, following it, and being cognizant of and rational about decisions to alter the plan during the course of the research. All this points to the preeminent importance of understanding one's question first and then coming up with a workable design that should, if followed correctly, yield answers. Determining if an MMR design is appropriate, and which one(s) to use, fits within the second and third stages of Johnson and Onwuegbuzie's (2004) process model. Addressing these points goes a long way toward promoting MMR quality, as well as when dealing with any other form of research inquiry, and is consistent with PCSIM and other ideas presented in this book.

All of this entails seemingly obvious points, but in our experience, one can be lost in a world of long-term planning and application, political pressures, multiple sources of advice, and changes in popularity to particular methodological approaches. As an example, through our role as professors, we have had students approach us with a dissertation idea that is predicated on a desire to use a particular type of design and not a question. That is, a student may say he or she wants to do a mixed methods study before a clear question is expressed. This can happen because MMR seems to be popular and dissertation ideas often start out in the abstract and are informed via a lot of different opinions offered by faculty and other students. But to our way of thinking, asking to use MMR without knowing the question is like a student expressing a desire to use a *t* test without first figuring out what one hopes to learn. A variant of people putting design preference before articulating a question occurs when we are asked something along the lines of: What is the best way to mix qualitative and quantitative designs? Without knowing more, this question cannot be answered. If a patient told a medical doctor that he or she does not feel well but gives no more detail, then even the best practitioner would not know how to proceed with treatment, and likewise, we cannot know how to engage in mixing without sufficient contextual information. So again, the research question at hand should drive the design (whether dealing with MMR or otherwise), and question clarity is a fundamental determinant of research quality and rigor.

The remaining procedural steps outlined by Johnson and Onwuegbuzie (2004) overlap nicely with CMMPE, PCSIM, and the cycle of research we described in Chapter 2. Some more work is needed to confirm some details, but we suspect the eight-step process model may be simply thought of as a more general variant of our approaches, with the difference being that our approaches are designed to specifically deal with culture and intervention work. If this is true, following the approaches we described is essentially in line with MMR ideas around thinking about MMR quality from a procedural perspective and the notion of legitimation.

This conceptual agreement is also true, at least at a surface level, when thinking about O'Cathain's (2010) initial framework for assessing MMR quality. The framework has seven domains: (1) planning quality, (2) design quality, (3) data quality, (4) interpretive rigor, (5) inference transferability, (6) reporting quality, and (7) utility. PCSIM explicitly requires a review of existing theory and learning of the culture, both of which are consistent with planning quality concerns. The PCSIM steps of forming partnerships, specifying research goals, formative research, local theory development, and implementation and evaluation are in no way at odds with O'Cathain's suggestions around design quality, data quality, and interpretive rigor. We also see conceptual connections between PCSIM's steps of capacity building and translation and transferability and report quality. Finally, although PCSIM is itself a cyclical model whereby the last stage of translation informs the next new set of questions, it also can be used within our broader cycle of research (see Figure 2.3), and this connects back to calls for the capacity to synthesize research. In sum, although there is much work to be done by the broader field in terms of providing guidance around the assessment of general MMR quality, we are encouraged by the principled agreement between how we think culturally specific intervention design and evaluation can be done and current ideas around MMR quality.

CROSS-CULTURAL SOCIAL SCIENCE RESEARCH HAS RECEIVED INADEQUATE ATTENTION

A final challenge we list is a broad one—the wider fields of the social sciences have not sufficiently attended to cross-cultural service delivery and intervention. This makes us worry about what we do not know, and we wonder if this lack of attention somehow contributes to more potentially uninformed attempts to intervene in new settings without attending to cultural nuances (see Chapter 1). Arnett (2008) reviewed six APA journals published across a period of several years (2003–2007, as well as 1988, 1993, and 1998, to look at trends over time) and found that U.S. authors and samples dominated psychology inquiry, prompting the observation that perhaps some journals might alter their names (e.g., "Journal of Abnormal American Psychology" [p. 604] in lieu of *Journal of Abnormal Psychology*). The prevailing point of this work is that although psychological research endeavors to understand human behavior, there is a serious gap given the focus on the U.S. and, to a lesser degree, European groups and cultures. This position is supported by other scholars in the field (e.g., Cole, 1996, 2006; Sue, 1999). Indeed, in 1998, Sue wrote,

> Yet, in the case of ethnic minority populations, no rigorous research has determined if psychotherapy is effective. If therapists need to base practice on research findings, and if psychotherapy and assessment tools have not demonstrated their effectiveness or validity, should psychotherapy continue to be offered to these populations? How can guidelines and standards for cultural competency be devised in the absence of research? (p. 443)

These scholars focus on psychology, but this equally applies to other social science settings, including education (see also Arnett, 2008; Cole, 1996). And of course, we argue that some of our own work and that of many others have begun to address the gap in recent years, but it is nevertheless the case that cross-cultural work has received inadequate attention, and this has been a long-standing concern. We see this lack of scholarship and empirical investigation as a challenge because of what we simply do not know in terms of how behavior, values, norms, and perceptions vary across cultural settings. We can think of a number of future directions (see Chapter 8), but even when just focusing on our own applications and ideas, it is clear that there is much work to do if, as a field, we see strong gains in our capacity to intervene in cross-cultural settings. Broad areas of inquiry like this simply need the efforts and attention of many scholarly groups, and per our judgment and that of other scholars, this has been lacking.

CONCLUSION

In this chapter, we have listed a number of challenges that can undermine general cross-cultural research, but we focused on intervention development, implementation, and evaluation. Only general ideas were offered in the abstract because it can be hard to know what types of partnering, stakeholder commitment, and resource needs might apply in a given scenario. Further complicating matters, we called attention to the possibility that an existing EBI may be applied and, determining if this is the case, will require close attention to the nature of the culture, the constructs at work, and piloting the intervention to initially confirm if it indeed may work. A broad overarching concern is that relatively little cross-cultural work has been pursued by others using contemporary methods. Although Cole (1996) argues that there is a long-recognized need for cultural psychology (and we add to this almost any social science endeavor)—there are guiding models such as Bronfenbrenner's EST, a deep experiential base from ethnography, and a promising application from mixed methods—we are still working in a field that is understudied.

Anyone who pursues similar work will thus likely find that it is not easy. However, it is our fervent hope that by presenting models such as PCSIM, along with recognition of the types of challenges one will likely run into, any attempts to engage in culturally specific intervention and evaluation work will be made easier and more rewarding. We are confident that a strong respect for attending to acceptability, feasibility, social validity, and so on, and studying these factors with rigor when you can, or at least remaining cognizant of these issues when you cannot empirically assess them, can make success a little easier to achieve. Above all, despite the numerous challenges, we hope readers will take solace in the fact that people who have lived through them find this sort of work to be rewarding, and we believe that we're making a difference.

Key Terms

- **Cultural brokers:** People who provide guidance about local norms, values, and practices that can help researchers better navigate the context. They may even help researchers refine their questions, and this process is promoted by engaging in emergent design approaches.
- **Evaluation Capacity Building (ECB):** An effort to promote the skills, knowledge, and motivation to conduct or use evaluation methods; this is a general definition from the literature that we think expands to intervention implementation.
- **Gatekeeper:** A person with some sort of local authority or other capacity that can help garner interest in and commitment to planned work. Gatekeepers may also play a role in protecting area organizations and stakeholders and bar or undermine access to needed samples, institutions, and other resources (hence their gatekeeping function).
- **Inference quality:** Assessing the design and interpretation of mixed methods studies.
- **Legitimation:** Assessing the validity, credibility, or trustworthiness of qualitative and quantitative data and inferences.

Reflective Questions and Exercises

1. Think of a time when you may have relied on a cultural broker and/or gatekeeper as you entered a new setting (e.g., a country that was new to you, a new school, job, etc.). How have cultural brokers and gatekeepers helped you? Have you ever served in these roles? How would you apply these experiences to a research project?

The next two items may be more concrete if you completed the exercises at the end of Chapter 6, where you were encouraged to develop a PCSIM plan.

2. As you consider developing and/or evaluating an intervention in the context of a target culture, consider who you may partner with; pay particular attention to potential cultural brokers and gatekeepers. How would you keep them engaged over time?

3. If you were to carry out a mixed methods project, who would be on your team? What skills are necessary to carry out the project? Do you have the requisite skills? What training would you need? Given the need to build capacity, how might you facilitate development of the necessary skills among stakeholders?

4. Find a published, empirical (i.e., it presents data) mixed methods paper. Consider issues around inference quality and, more generally, critique its design.

References

Arnett, J. J. (2008). The neglected 95%: Why American psychology needs to become less American. *American Psychologist, 63*(7), 602–614. doi:10.1037/0003-066X.63.7.602

Cole, M. (1996). *Cultural psychology: A once and future discipline.* Cambridge, MA: Harvard University Press.

Cole, M. (2006). Internationalism in psychology: We need it now more than ever. *American Psychologist, 61*(8), 904–917.

Creswell, J. W., & Plano Clark, V. (2007). *Designing and conducting mixed methods research.* Thousand Oaks, CA: Sage.

Eade, D. (1997). *Capacity-building: An approach to people-centred development.* Oxford, England: Oxfam.

Friend, M., & Cook, L. (2013). *Interactions: Collaboration skills for school professionals* (7th ed.). Upper Saddle River, NJ: Prentice Hall.

Gallo, A., Weijer, C., White, A., Grimshaw, J. M., Boruch, R., Brehaut, J. C., . . . Taljaard, M. (2012). What is the role and authority of gatekeepers in cluster randomized trials in health research? *Trials, 13.* doi:10.1186/1745-6215-13-116

Hitchcock, J. H., & Newman, I. (2013). Applying an interactive quantitative–qualitative framework: How identifying common intent can enhance inquiry. *Human Resources Development Review, 12*(1), 36–52. doi:10.1177/1534484312462127

Jezewski, M. A. (1990). Culture brokering in migrant farm worker health care. *Western Journal of Nursing Research, 12*(4), 497–513.

Jezewski, M. A., & Sotnik, P. (2001). *Culture brokering: Providing culturally competent rehabilitation services to foreign-born persons* (J. Stone, Ed.). Buffalo, NY: Center for International Rehabilitation Research Information and Exchange.

Johnson, R. B., & Onwuegbuzie, A. J. (2004). Mixed methods research: A research paradigm whose time has come. *Educational Researcher, 33*(7), 14–26. doi:10.3102/0013189X033007014

Johnson, J., Shope, S., & Roush, J. (2009). Toward a responsive model for educational leadership in rural Appalachia: Merging theory and practice. *Education Leadership Review, 10*(2), 93–103.

Johnson, J., & Strange, M. (2007). *Why rural matters: The realities of rural education growth*. Arlington, VA: Rural School and Community Trust.

Labin, S. N., Duffy, J. L., Meyers, D. C., Wandersman, A., & Lesesne, C. A. (2012). A research synthesis of the evaluation capacity building literature. *American Journal of Evaluation, 33*(3), 307–338. doi:0.1177/1098214011434608

Lincoln, Y. S., & Guba, E. G. (1985). *Naturalistic inquiry.* Beverly Hills, CA: Sage.

Nastasi, B. K., & Hitchcock, J. (2009). Challenges of evaluating multi-level interventions. *American Journal of Community Psychology, 43,* 360–376. doi:10.1007/s10464-009-9239-7

Nastasi, B. K., Hitchcock, J. H., & Brown, L. M. (2010). An inclusive framework for conceptualizing mixed methods design typologies: Moving toward fully integrated synergistic research models. In A. Tashakkori & C. Teddlie (Eds.), *Handbook of mixed methods in social & behavioral research* (2nd ed., pp. 305–338). Thousand Oaks, CA: Sage.

Nastasi, B. K., Moore, R. B., & Varjas, K. M. (2004). *School-based mental health services: Creating comprehensive and culturally specific programs*. Washington, DC: American Psychological Association.

Newman, I., & Hitchcock, J. H. (2011). Underlying agreements between quantitative and qualitative research: The short and tall of it all. *Human Resources Development Review, 10*(4), 381–398. doi:10.1177/1534484311413867

O'Cathain, A. (2010). Assessing the quality of mixed methods research: Toward a comprehensive framework. In A. Tashakkori & C. Teddlie (Eds.), *Handbook of mixed methods in social & behavioral research* (2nd ed., pp. 531–558). Thousand Oaks, CA: Sage.

Onwuegbuzie, A. J. (2007). Mixed methods research in sociology and beyond. In G. Ritzer (Ed.), *Encyclopedia of sociology* (Vol. 6, pp. 2978–2981). Oxford, England: Blackwell.

Onwuegbuzie, A. J. (2012). Introduction: Putting the mixed back into quantitative and qualitative research in educational research and beyond: Moving towards the radical middle. *International Journal of Multiple Research Approaches, 6*(3), 192–219.

Onwuegbuzie, A. J., & Johnson, R. B. (2006). The validity issue in mixed research. *Research in the Schools, 13*(1), 48–63.

Preskill, H., & Boyle, S. (2008). A multidisciplinary model of evaluation capacity building. *American Journal of Evaluation, 29*(4), 443–459. doi:10.1177/1098214008324182

Shadish, W. R. (1995). The logic of generalization: Five principles common to experiments and ethnographies. *American Journal of Community Psychology, 23*(3), 419–428.

Stone, D., Patton, B., & Heen, S. (2010). *Difficult conversations: How to discuss what matters most* (10th anniversary ed.). New York, NY: Penguin Books.

Sue, S. (1998). In search of cultural competence in psychotherapy and counseling? *American Psychologist, 53*(4), 440–448.

Sue, S. (1999). Science, ethnicity, and bias: Where have we gone wrong? *American Psychologist, 54*(12), 1070–1077.

Tashakkori, A., & Teddlie, C. (2008). Quality of inferences in mixed methods research. In M. Bergman (Ed.), *Advances in mixed methods research: Theories and applications* (pp. 101–119). London, England: Sage.

What Works Clearinghouse. (2008). *Procedures and standards handbook* (Version 2.0). Retrieved from http://ies.ed.gov/ncee/wwc/documentsum.aspx?sid=19

❧ EIGHT ❧

FUTURE DIRECTIONS

Learning Objectives

The key objectives of this chapter are for readers to do the following:

- Recall key topics discussed throughout the book
- Understand the gaps in our understanding of intervention science, particularly related to implementation and adaptation
- Consider future directions for applying MMR to intervention development and evaluation to address gaps in knowledge

INTRODUCTION

To frame discussion of future directions, we return to our rationale for application of MMR to intervention research and the limitations of existing models (discussed in detail in Chapters 1 and 2). Motivating our use of mixed methods in intervention and prevention work were the oft cited challenges related to translating EBIs to applied settings and the emerging field of implementation science. Questions about research-to-practice translation centered on (a) how to adapt interventions based on culture and context, (b) what conditions were necessary to replicate the stated outcomes of EBIs, and (c) how to achieve outcomes given the "uncontrolled" conditions and related challenges in natural settings. Answering these questions posed challenges to strict reliance on quantitative methods, and it contributed to the growing interest in qualitative and MMR designs across disciplines (e.g., social science, education, health science, medicine). We also identified challenges with a view that EBI entails relying only on prior research for addressing the evidence standard, rather than also generating one's own evidence when making localized judgments about intervention development and adaptation. We also see value in adopting APA's (2006) broader notion of EBP that allows for practitioner judgment, clinical expertise, and accounting for context and culture.

In Chapter 2, we explored existing models for conceptualizing interven tion research across these multiple disciplines and identified potential foci for application of MMR designs. As we noted, the proponents of these existing models (e.g., large-scale dissemination or scaling up, implementation science, planned adaptation) raised questions that could be addressed by mixed methods although they did not necessarily utilize MMR. We have presented examples of MMR applied to intervention development and evaluation, mostly drawing from our own work, but this is not to say that we are the only researchers engaged in such applications. As we portray in Chapter 2, MMR more appro- priately characterizes the future of intervention research rather than the present. In this chapter, we discuss the potential role of MMR in shaping the future and consider ways to extend existing models through mixed methods designs.

As you may recall from Chapter 2, we categorized existing models for intervention development as follows: (a) establishing an evidence base for intervention effectiveness (EBIs), (b) employing interventions within a systems framework, (c) facilitating effective implementation, (d) adapting programs to local culture and context, (e) promoting cultural competence of stakeholders in program development, and (f) using participatory models. Furthermore, we examined each model based on the extent to which the following factors were included: (a) cultural specificity or cultural (co-)construction, (b) program adaptation (i.e., the modification of program to local culture and context), (c) the application or applicability of MMR, and (d) partnership/collaboration with key stakeholders.

IMPLICATIONS FOR MODEL DEVELOPMENT

As we discussed in Chapter 2, all the existing models could be expanded through MMR to address the challenges of translation of research to practice, and proponents of some of the models support the use of MMR to address limitations. However, the application of MMR was only evident in participatory models such as PAR and its variants, CBPR (e.g., Jacquez, Vaughn, & Wagner, 2013; Lindamer et al., 2009), CBPAR (e.g., Maiter, Simich, Jacobson, & Wise, 2008), or PCSIM (Nastasi, Moore, & Varjas, 2004).

We concluded Chapter 2 with discussion of the use of MMR in intervention research to facilitate implementation, adaptation, and cultural grounding, within a systems framework, thus integrating features of existing models. Furthermore, we argued that complex MMR designs, particularly those that involve synergistic and participatory approaches such as the *synergistic partnership-based fully integrated mixed methods design model*, depicted in Figure 2.3 (Nastasi, Hitchcock, & Brown, 2010), are necessary to address the myriad questions related to implementation, adaptation, cultural grounding, and systemic factors in intervention research. You may recall that we described the model in Figure 2.3 as aspirational. To complete our argument for the use of MMR in intervention research, we return to discussion of mixed methods designs and the implications of models such as the synergistic partnership-based fully integrated mixed methods design.

APPLICATION OF MMR TO INTERVENTION DEVELOPMENT AND EVALUATION

Throughout the book, we provide examples of research that employed mixed methods for intervention design (Chapter 3); implementation, adaptation, and evaluation (Chapter 4); and the full process (Chapter 6). The illustration in Chapter 6 employed a multistrand, iterative, participatory approach in which each strand (single study) informed the next within a multiyear program of research. The synergistic mixing of methods was exemplified in implementation phases for the purpose of adaptation and evaluation, for example, in developing measures of psychological well-being, modifying the intervention to match cultural norms and implementer competencies, and evaluating program outcomes. As we noted, one of the intervention activities (ecomap) evolved into a synergistic mixed methods technique for data collection in future research. In this program of research, MMR also helped address issues related to ensuring cultural and contextual specificity of the intervention (e.g., informing cultural construction, adaptation to local context). Furthermore, we employed a partnership process, maintaining one key partnership throughout, establishing new partnerships in different phases of the work, and relying on key stakeholders to inform the process and outcomes. As we reflect on this work, we recognize the potential for extending application of MMR to advance development of culturally and contextually relevant interventions.

IMPLICATIONS FOR EXTENDING MIXED METHODOLOGY

A logical extension of mixed methodology is portrayed in the synergistic partnership-based fully integrated mixed methods design model depicted in Figure 2.3. Each phase of the research cycle could include a synergistic mixing of methods (Qual ⟵ ⟶ Quan), from study conceptualization to application of findings. This would require that the researcher plans each phase to include both qualitative and quantitative methods and make decisions based on the integration of those methods. For some phases, the mix is logical, for example, integrating Qual and Quan in data collection and analysis. Other phases may require extending our current practices, for example, as we decide how to examine and integrate worldviews of partners or existing theory, research, practice, and policy. (See Nastasi et al., 2010, for full discussion of the synergistic model.) Of course, how one uses mixed methods needs to be linked to the research questions.

Another consideration when applying mixed methods is whether the proposed research is monostrand (single study) or multistrand (series of studies; program of research). As we have illustrated in Chapter 6, mixed methods in multistrand research implies a mixing of qualitative and quantitative methods across the program of research, with each study informing the next. Thus, individual studies may rely solely on qualitative or quantitative and others may involve different approaches to mixing in terms of timing (e.g., concurrent, sequential), priority (dominant QUAL vs. QUAN), and integration (e.g., additive, explanatory, synergistic). These decisions are ideally guided by research purpose and questions. In practice, such decisions are also likely to be influenced by other factors such as the worldview and competencies of the researcher, or the acceptability and feasibility given the target population and context. We also propose that decisions about use of MMR could be guided by the current status of intervention research and how mixed methods might contribute to advancing the science of intervention development and evaluation.

ADVANCING THE SCIENCE OF INTERVENTION DEVELOPMENT AND EVALUATION: IMPLICATIONS FOR IMPLEMENTATION SCIENCE

As we discussed in Chapter 2, advancing the science related to development of effective interventions in psychology, education, public health, and medicine largely depends on enhancing our understanding of how to translate research to practice. The science related to establishing EBIs has been grounded in the use of RCTs to establish causal relationships between the *designed* intervention and its *intended* outcomes, through carefully controlled implementation and measurement of outcome variables. Although strong causal evidence is important, the shortcomings of much of EBI research have resulted in development of the field of implementation science, with a focus on understanding the conditions under which EBIs work, and thus trying to understand the contextual (process) variables that influence outcomes. The understanding of process–outcome relationships can be expected to facilitate effective translation of research to practice. What has emerged from work thus far in implementation science is the *recognition* of the myriad variables that determine the success of any intervention. What remains to be learned is the exact nature of these variables, how they influence outcomes, and how interventions should be modified to address variations in context and culture of the intended population. Although many implementation scientists recognize the limitations of nearly sole reliance on quantitative approaches such as RCTs, solutions are still in development. The remainder of this chapter focuses on how mixed methods can be applied in implementation science to help address these limitations. We focus our discussion on using MMR to study and help advance our understanding related to intervention effectiveness, implementation, adaptation, systems factors, culture, and partnerships.

Intervention Effectiveness: Establishing Evidence

One application of mixed methods is to determine the effectiveness of a particular intervention. Traditional RCT models call for testing of causal relationships between the intervention (independent variable) and the specified outcome (dependent variable). Researchers have typically used quantitative measures of outcome variables to facilitate measurement and testing of causal relationships. The extension of evidence to include a mix of qualitative and quantitative data has several advantages. First, qualitative methods (e.g., observations, interviews, emergent design) can facilitate identification of unintended and, in some cases, iatrogenic effects of the intervention. Second, mixed methods can facilitate elaboration of observed effects, for example, through the use of both quantitative measures and qualitative interviews. Third, mixed methods can help explain why intended effects were not achieved; for example, limitations of the measurement instruments. Fourth, the collection of qualitative data to inform development and subsequent validation of quantitative measures can help ensure cultural and contextual relevance of measures.

Intervention Implementation

In Chapter 4, we presented a mixed methods model for evaluation that addresses the multiple components of success, the CMMPE (see Figure 4.1): acceptability, social validity, integrity, implementer competence, outcomes, sustainability, and institutionalization. The model is intended not only to reflect the complexity of program evaluation but also to facilitate a comprehensive understanding of why programs do or do not work. In addition to the multiple components, we also proposed that determinations of success are dependent on multiple voices (e.g., participants, implementers, administrators; see Figure 4.1). Most important to this discussion is the potential contribution of the model to enhancing our understanding of the conditions of implementation and how these conditions contribute to program effectiveness. We described and illustrated in Chapter 4 how each component of the CMMPE can be evaluated using a mix of qualitative and quantitative methods. In this section, we extend the discussion to include the application to addressing limitations within implementation science, specifically, adapting interventions, the role of systems factors, understanding culture, and facilitating partnerships.

Intervention Adaptation

Critical questions in program adaptation concern how to adapt programs while not violating their integrity (e.g., altering surface structure without changing deep structure); how to ensure, or at least promote, cultural sensitivity; and how to accommodate adaptations by both designer and implementers (see Chapter 2 for full discussion). Intervention scientists have proposed processes for engaging in adaptation of EBIs (e.g., planned adaptation; Lee, Altschul, & Mowbray, 2008), but few have explicitly included MMR as part of the process (e.g., see Goldstein, Kemp, Leff, & Lochman, 2013). What we propose for future research is that MMR becomes a part of adaptation efforts, for example, through the application of a PCSIM process. For example, to guide designer adaptation, program developers can initiate mixed methods formative research that facilitates understanding of the culture and context and use that data to make decisions, in partnership with stakeholders, about what EBIs are relevant and how they would need to be adapted. Of course, evaluation using a comprehensive mixed methods model (e.g., CMMPE) would then inform designers and implementers about the success of the adapted program as well as guide any further implementer adaptations. Employing experimental or quasi-experimental designs with mixed methods data collection, evaluators could validate the effectiveness of the adapted intervention and confirm its acceptability, social validity, and integrity. In addition, mixed methods outcome measures would permit statistical testing of program effects, provide data to explain or elaborate on effects, and facilitate identification of unintended and/or iatrogenic effects. Furthermore, integration of mixed methods in planning and evaluating adaptations can facilitate better understanding of deep and surface structure elements and help inform future applications of the intervention.

Systems Factors

Intervention scientists have identified systemic factors as critical to informing implementation and dissemination/translation of EBIs (Fixsen, Naoom, Blase, Friedman, & Wallace, 2005; Gregory et al., 2012; Wandersman et al., 2008) and suggested models for depicting such influences. For example, Fixsen et al. (2005) proposed a multilevel model that included implementer (e.g., competence), organizational (administrative support), and macrosystemic (e.g., social, political) factors and recommended using mixed methods to guide future work in this area. Similarly, May (2013) proposed a model that included implementer capability, cultural beliefs, and actions as well as social and structural capacity of the organization. Weisz, Sandler, Durlak, and Anton (2005) advocated for the inclusion of contextual and population variables in decisions about adopting EBIs (manualized interventions). We proposed that EST (Figure 2.1; Bronfenbrenner, 1989, 1999) could help guide our understanding of the social ecology in the context of intervention research and practice. Much of the work in this area has remained at a conceptual level while acknowledging the potential role of mixed methods.

So how can mixed methods help us understand and address the role of systemic factors in implementation science? First, we propose that program development and evaluation take into account systemic factors as part of a multilevel approach to formative research, intervention design, program implementation and adaptation, and formative and summative evaluation. For example, using EST, mixed methods formative research could assess factors at individual and micro-, exo-, meso-, macro-, and chronosystem levels to gain a full understanding of the system. This research could yield information about population needs at an individual level, capabilities of potential implementers, capacity of the system to support program implementation, macrosystem factors such as policies and cultural practices, and chronosystem factors such as the history of the organization in conducting similar interventions. Combined with a model such as CMMPE, program developers could gather data at each level about acceptability and social validity from multiple stakeholders. Using a similar model for program implementation and evaluation, developers could conduct mixed methods formative and summative evaluation at multiple levels—for example, examining the impact on target population, implementers, the organization, and relevant stakeholders. Nastasi and Hitchcock (2009) illustrate the application of CMMPE to multilevel evaluation of a sexual risk prevention program, using mixed methods to evaluate program success (acceptability, social validity, outcomes, etc.) at patient, practitioner (doctor), and community levels.

Culture

Another set of factors that have been identified by implementation scientists are those related to culture (e.g., Cappella et al., 2011; Colby et al., 2013; Nastasi et al., 2004; Nastasi et al., 2010; Whaley & Davis, 2007). Critical to consideration of culture are factors related to the aspects of culture (norms, beliefs, values, etc.) of the target population, target context, and implementers and questions about how to achieve cultural grounding of programs and how to ensure that implementers are culturally competent. As we have discussed throughout this book, we routinely examine the culture of target population and context through MMR (e.g., using PCSIM) and use that information to inform development of culturally grounded (culturally relevant) programming, preferably in partnership with key stakeholders. The cultural competence of programmers (designers, implementers, evaluators) is also a critical consideration in program development and evaluation, and MMR could play an important role in ensuring such competence. For example, in addition to understanding the cultural experiences of implementers, it is critical that we assess their cultural competence for working with culturally diverse populations (particularly the target cultural group), design staff training to enhance cultural competence, and monitor and evaluate cultural competence as part of formative and summative program evaluation. We propose that mixed methods could help us do this effectively—for example, through use of interviewing, observation, rating scales, and so on. Indeed, D'Augelli (2003) has suggested that MMR provides culturally sensitive methodology. The use of MMR can thus be instrumental in helping programmers define constructs, achieve cultural grounding of programs (developing culturally relevant interventions or measures), examine cultural systemic factors (e.g., at micro-, exo-, and mesosystem levels) that might influence intervention success, and evaluate cultural competence of implementers.

Partnerships

In Chapter 2, we presented the PCSIM, a participatory approach to developing and evaluating culturally grounded interventions, which uses mixed methods. As we have discussed in Chapters 3 to 5 and illustrated in Chapter 6, participatory approaches provide a mechanism for involving stakeholders in the process of decision making about all phases of intervention development and evaluation and are critical to facilitating sustainability. Although we have discussed using MMR to capture the perspectives and facilitate involvement of partners, we have not focused much attention on the use of MMR to study the participatory process or nature of partnerships. As we noted in Chapter 7, engaging stakeholders and developing sustainable partnerships are challenging. Indeed, the participatory process might be the most challenging part of a process like PCSIM, more so than program design, implementation, adaptation, and evaluation.

We propose that future research using MMR might help us better understand the participatory process and in turn develop successful partnerships. First, mixed methods could be used to study interpersonal communication among stakeholders and between partners and to study group process as teams of stakeholders engage in collaborative decision making. Second, mixed methods formative evaluation data could help program planners identify interpersonal difficulties that are precluding effective program implementation and facilitate interventions to build better communication. Third, mixed methods evaluation of the participatory process could facilitate examination of the role of participation in program outcomes. Fourth, the study of group process could ultimately inform development of models for effective participatory approaches. One of the challenges in studying interpersonal and group processes is that, as program developers, we are typically engaged in those interactions. Although some self-reflection (e.g., self-ratings, debriefing group process) can facilitate awareness and lead to efforts to improve the process, it may not be the best way to conduct evaluation of the process. We recommend that intervention scientists and program implementers consider employing external evaluators for this purpose.

Evaluation Models

The approaches we present in this book can be further developed via two strands of work: (a) conducting additional empirical investigations using approaches such as PCSIM as part of formative and summative evaluation work and (b) examining ways in which MMR models that we describe overlap with, and can be potentially be extended, by complementary approaches to evaluation. There is little to say about the first strand; it is simply the case that more application needs to happen and such experiences are bound to lead to refinement. As to the second, we think that there may be benefit in critical examination of various evaluative approaches and theories, especially ones that highlight context specificity and participatory work where stakeholders have a role in intervention implementation. As an example, Stufflebeam's CIPP (context, input, process, and product evaluations) is a long-standing approach that encompasses formative and summative work with explicit focus on context, even though there is no explicit focus on cultural concerns, and its core values reportedly reflect a U.S. orientation (Stufflebeam, 2013). CIPP might be applied within a particular strand or there may even be ideas that can help us further refine MMR applications or a particular model such as PCSIM. If so, methodological theory (i.e., a theory around how social science methodology works) may be enhanced by comparing and contrasting synergistic and iterative MMR approaches to CIPP and clarifying how the different approaches might be used in a complementary fashion, following *a logic of mixing* whereby the strengths of one approach compensate for the weaknesses of another. Other examples of evaluation approaches that could be used in such comparative analyses include theory-driven evaluations (Chen, 1990), utilization-focused evaluation (Patton, 2008), empowerment evaluation (e.g., Fetterman, 2000; Fetterman, Kaftarian, & Wandersman, 2014), and so on. Indeed, much of MMR has its roots in evaluation work, so it seems reasonable to think that comparing and contrasting different approaches that potentially account for context and culture may yield new ideas on how we might go about doing this overall type of work.

FINAL THOUGHTS

In Chapter 1, we introduced a few questions to make the point that culture and context matter when thinking about interventions in terms of developing, applying, and evaluating them. These questions were as follows:

- What are the implications of providing mental health services to an adolescent girl who appears to be independent but hails from a culture that demands compliance and adherence to tradition?
- What if one were involved with diagnosing and treating mental health disorders but encountered a member of the Old Order Amish who was struggling with bipolar disorder?
- How should a practitioner construe clients who claim they regularly talk to God but then learns that these clients are members of a fundamentalist religious order?
- Should practitioners consider ethnic backgrounds when delivering a program designed to prevent or treat eating disorders?
- Does it make sense to use behavior rating scales normed in the United States in a country like India?
- Would you consider the cultural background of families when providing marital therapy?
- If you were trying to understand if a school environment were generally accepting of lesbian, gay, bisexual, and transgender youth, would it make sense to understand the community the school serves?
- Can a reading program designed to help Cuban Americans in Miami with word comprehension be applied to Mexican Americans in a Texas City bordering Mexico?
- How can a disaster preparedness program take advantage of familial connections that are emphasized by a marginalized group residing in a specific region?

- Would a bullying prevention program designed to be used in high socioeconomic status schools work well in schools that serve large numbers of children who live in poverty?

We went on to argue that readers can come up with examples from their own lives that quickly justify the need for approaches that can account for culture. Whether using an above example, or one of your own, it should be clear that dealing with these issues is not easy. But we hope that readers will agree that this book provides some theory, tools, and advice that not only provide the background needed to think through answers but also design interventions and evaluations that allow for competent handling of cultural factors through the use of MMR. Writing this book has been a great opportunity for the authors to reflect on issues related to application of MMR to intervention development and evaluation. Despite more than two decades of work in this area, we are continually learning from our experiences and those of others. The challenges of doing MMR in the intervention arena can be daunting, but the rewards gained from richer understanding outweigh any frustrations. We hope that readers will find this text helpful as they venture into MMR to design, implement, and evaluate interventions, and, through dissemination efforts, continue to inform the future of intervention research and practice.

Reflective Questions and Exercises

1. Consider the questions posed above (and in Chapter 1). Select one or more of the questions, and discuss how you would apply MMR to address the question(s). How would you ensure participation of key stakeholders in addressing the question(s)?

2. Identify a research article in your area of interest that describes an EBI. Critique the EBI in terms of its potential for translation to practice (i.e., implementation in practice settings). Then describe how you might apply MMR to facilitate the use of the intervention across different cultures and contexts (refer to discussion of implementation science in Chapter 2). How would you involve key stakeholders to promote acceptability, social validity, and sustainability?

References

American Psychological Association Presidential Task Force on Evidence-Based Practice. (2006). Evidence-based practice in psychology. *American Psychologist, 61*(4), 271–285. doi:10.1037/0003-066X.61.4.271

Bronfenbrenner, U. (1989). Ecological systems theory. In R. Vasta (Ed.), *Annals of child development* (Vol. 6, pp. 187–249). Greenwich, CT: JAI Press.

Bronfenbrenner, U. (1999). Environments in developmental perspective: Theoretical and operational models. In S. L. Friedman & T. D. Wachs (Eds.), *Measuring environment across the life span: Emerging methods and concepts* (pp. 3–28). Washington, DC: American Psychological Association.

Capella, E., Reinke, W. M., & Hoagwood, K. E. (2011). Advancing intervention research in school psychology: Finding the balance between process and outcome for social and behavioral interventions. *School Psychology Review, 40*(4), 455–464.

Chen, H. T. (1990). *Theory-driven evaluations.* Newbury Park, CA: Sage.

Colby, M., Hecht, M. L., Miller-Day, M., Krieger, J. L., Syvertsen, A. K., Graham, J. W., & Pettigrew, J. (2013). Adapting school-based substance use prevention curriculum through cultural grounding: A review and exemplar of adaptation processes for rural schools. *American Journal of Community Psychology, 51,* 190–205. doi:10.1007/s10464-012-9524-8.

D'Augelli, A. R. (2003). Coming out in community psychology: Personal narrative and disciplinary change. *American Journal of Community Psychology, 31,* 343–354. doi:10.1023/A:1023923123720

Fetterman, D. M. (2000). *Foundations of empowerment evaluation.* Thousand Oaks, CA: Sage.

Fetterman, D. M., Kaftarian, S. J., & Wandersman, A. H. (Eds.). (2014). *Empowerment evaluation: Knowledge and tools for self-assessment, evaluation capacity building, and accountability.* Thousand Oaks, CA: Sage.

Fixsen, D. L., Naoom, S. F., Blase, K. A., Friedman, R. M., & Wallace, F. (2005). *Implementation research: A synthesis of the literature* (FMHI Publication No. 231). Tampa: University of South Florida, Louis de la Parte Florida Mental Health Institute, The National Implementation Research Network. Retrieved from http://centerforchildwelfare.fmhi.usf.edu/kb/Implementation/Implementation%20Research%20-%20A%20Synthesis%20of%20Literature%20%20-%202005.pdf

Goldstein, N. E. S., Kemp, K. A., Leff, S. S., & Lochman, J. E. (2013). Guidelines for adapting manualized interventions to new target populations: A step-wise approach using anger management as a model. *Clinical Psychology Science and Practice, 19*(4), 385–401.

Gregory, H., Van Orden, O., Jordan, L., Portnoy, G. A., Welsh, E., Betkowski, J., . . . DiClemente, C. C. (2012). New directions in capacity building: Incorporating cultural competence into the interactive systems framework. *American Journal of Community Psychology, 50,* 321–333. doi:10.1007/s10464-012-9508-8

Jacquez, F., Vaughn, L. M., & Wagner, E. (2013). Youth as partners, participants or passive recipients: A review of children and adolescents in community-based participatory research (CBPR). *American Journal of Community Psychology, 51,* 176–189. doi:10.1007/s10464-012-9533-7

Lee, S. J., Altschul, I., & Mowbray, C. T. (2008). Using planned adaptation to implement evidence-based programs with new populations. *American Journal of Community Psychology, 41,* 290–303. doi:10.1007/s10464-008-9160-5

Lindamer, L. A., Lebowitz, B., Hough, R. L., Garcia, P., Aguirre, A., Halpain, M. C., Jeste, D. V. (2009). Establishing an implementation network: Lessons learned from community-based participatory research. *Implementation Science, 4,* 17. doi:10.1186/1748-5908-4-17

Maiter, S., Simich, L., Jacobson, N., & Wise, J. (2008). Reciprocity: An ethic for community-based participatory action research. *Action Research, 6*(3), 305–325. doi:10.1177/1476750307083720

May, C. (2013). Towards a general theory of implementation. *Implementation Science, 8,* 18. Retrieved from http://www.implementationscience.com/content/8/1/18

Nastasi, B. K., & Hitchcock, J. (2009). Challenges of evaluating multi-level interventions. *American Journal of Community Psychology, 43,* 360–376. doi:10.1007/s10464-009-9239-7

Nastasi, B. K., Hitchcock, J. H., & Brown, L. M. (2010). An inclusive framework for conceptualizing mixed methods design typologies: Moving toward fully integrated synergistic research models. In A. Tashakkori & C. Teddlie (Eds.), *Handbook of mixed methods in social and behavioral research* (2nd ed., pp. 305–338). Thousand Oaks, CA: Sage.

Nastasi, B. K., Moore, R. B., & Varjas, K. M. (2004). *School-based mental health services: Creating comprehensive and culturally specific programs.* Washington, DC: American Psychological Association.

Patton, M. Q. (2008). *Utilization focused evaluation* (4th ed.). Thousand Oaks, CA: Sage.

Stufflebeam, D. L. (2013). The CIPP evaluation model: Status, origin, development, use and theory. In M. C. Alkin (Ed.), *Evaluation roots: A wider perspective of theorists' views and influences* (2nd ed.). Thousand Oaks, CA: Sage.

Wandersman, A., Duffy, J., Flaspohler, P., Noonan, R., Lubell, K., Stillman, L., . . . Saul, J. (2008). Bridging the gap between prevention research and practice: An interactive systems framework for building capacity to disseminate and implement innovations. *American Journal of Community Psychology, 41*(3–4), 171–181. doi:10.1007/s10464-008-9174-z

Weisz, J. R., Sandler, I. N., Durlak, J. A., & Anton, B. S. (2005). Promoting and protecting youth mental health through evidence-based prevention and treatment. *American Psychologist, 60*(6), 628–648. doi:10.1037/0003-066X.60.6.628

Whaley, A. L., & Davis, K. E. (2007). Cultural competence and evidence-based practice in mental health services: A complementary perspective. *American Psychologist, 62*(6), 563–574. doi:10.1037/0003-066X.62.6.563

INDEX

Figures, tables, and notes are indicated by f, t, or n following the page number.